2/03

From Catharine Beecher to Martha Stewart

From Catharine Beecher to Martha Stewart

A CULTURAL HISTORY

OF DOMESTIC ADVICE

BY SARAH A. LEAVITT

The University of North Carolina Press

Chapel Hill and London

This volume was published with the
generous assistance of the Greensboro Women's Fund
of the University of North Carolina Press.
Founding contributors: Linda Arnold Carlisle, Sally Schindel Cone,
Anne Faircloth, Bonnie McElveen Hunter, Linda Bullard Jennings,
Janice J. Kerley (in honor of Margaret Supplee Smith),
Nancy Rouzer May, and Betty Hughes Nichols.

Library of Congress Cataloging-in-Publication Data
Leavitt, Sarah Abigail.
From Catharine Beecher to Martha Stewart: a cultural history
of domestic advice / Sarah A. Leavitt.
p. cm.
Includes bibliographical references and index.
ISBN 0-8078-2702-9 (alk. paper)—
ISBN 0-8078-5371-2 (pbk.: alk. paper)
1. Home economics—History.   I. Title.
TX15 .L43   2002   2001054202
640′.9—dc21

Cloth   06   05   04   03   02   5   4   3   2   1
Paper   06   05   04   03   02   5   4   3   2   1

For my parents

Lewis and Judy Leavitt

who furnished my first home

with books, bric-a-brac,

and love

Contents

Illustrations

Acknowledgments

Most of the domestic advisors in this book would disapprove of my own house decorating history. It's been a long time since I taped photos of movie stars to the walls, but the level of sentiment in my assortment of bric-a-brac would have made these women gasp. With apologies, therefore, for my own collections of "junk," I'd first like to thank the hundreds of domestic advisors whose books I read for being bold in their criticisms and so full of ideas.

This project was vastly improved by a research fellowship from the Winterthur Museum, Library and Garden in Winterthur, Delaware, which gave me time to read through an extensive collection of advice manuals and to be among exciting and energetic scholars. Special thanks to Shirley Wajda, and also to Pat Elliot, Margaret Welch, and Neville Thompson. Thanks to Brown University for funding much of my research with a Dissertation Fellowship. Thanks to the Interlibrary Loan staff at the Rockefeller Library at Brown University, Norlin Library at the University of Colorado, and the Boulder Public Library, and to photo and special collection archivists at Corning Incorporated, the Denver Public Library, the Nebraska State Historical Society, the Center for Southwest Research, Hagley Museum and Library, Winterthur, and the Colorado Chautauqua Association. Thank you to Sian Hunter and the editorial staff at the University of North Carolina Press for being interested in this project and for guiding it along with grace and optimism.

This book could not have happened without the constant and step-by-step support of so many important people in my life, especially during the past ten years since I started graduate school. This includes those who watched the newspapers, magazines, and television shows and sent me information about Martha Stewart, and those who endured Martha's Superbowl hors d'oeuvres, homemade crackers, and other experiments. Most importantly, thank you to my family: my parents Lewis and Judy Leavitt, my brother David Leavitt, and my grandmother Sally Walzer.

I want to take this opportunity to thank the teachers I've had over the years, especially Mr. Schaeffer, Ms. Kohler, Mr. Brumm, and the late Elizabeth Palmer at Madison West High School; Patricia Hill, George Creeger, and Michael Harris at Wesleyan University; and Robert Emlen at Brown University. A special thanks to Mari Jo Buhle, who believed I could finish the dissertation in the mountains and who made this project infinitely better with her comments. Thank you to Richard Meckel and Patrick Malone for their help with this and other projects. Many others have served as mentors and teachers in a less formal capacity: I would particularly like to thank Dione Longley and Gail Fowler Mohanty for teaching me about material culture, museums, and how to be a historian.

A special thanks is due to my incredible graduate school reading group, the Female Mutual Improvement Society (FMIS). Early members Laura Briggs and Marie Myers and most especially Sarah Purcell, Laura Prieto, Chrissy Cortina, Donna Curtin, and Jane Lancaster have read this book at various stages and have always offered good advice and encouragement. For her help with this manuscript and for many happy adventures, both scholarly and otherwise, I would like to thank Marla Miller. While at Brown, I had the great fortune of meeting people who enjoyed television, field trips, and dinner parties as well as higher education. Thanks to Susie Castellanos, Sara Errington, and Marie Myers (nobody ever had better graduate school roommates) and to Christina Abuelo, Bruce Bauer, Bill Capinski, Kim Capinski, Jay Chervenak, Matthew Coffey, Lisa Davis, Briann Greenfield, L. E. Hartmann-Ting, Dave Iaia, Colin McLaren, Laura Prieto, Sarah Purcell, Ed Rafferty, Rebecca Smith, Mark Trodden, and Grant Wilson for the general festivities during my five years in Providence.

While working on this book, I spent a lot of time not working on the book, and I am indebted to many people who shared various forms of entertainment ranging from hikes in the Rocky Mountains, to Fat Tires at Bullfrogs, to cooking extravaganzas, to board games. Though these people have not read this book, they were instrumental in its eventual completion. Thank you to my oldest and dearest friends Jessica Feierman and Ruth Friedman, and to Anita Thesen, Amy Johnson, Dana Rhode, Stephanie Morgan, Susannah Beals-Simon, Michelle Elisburg, Kim Gayle, Laura Schiavo, Beth Shakman Hurd, Marnie Reichelderfer, and to my cousins Sarah Walzer and John Barrett, and Becky and Keith Walzer-Goldfeld. Thanks to Dan and Erika Drezner, Leslie and Shaun Kennedy, Liz Skramstad, the NIST happy hour folks—especially Susie Youn, Jim Booth, Gene

Hilton, Donna Hurley and Sae Woo Nam—as well as to Jeff and Severine Hutchins, Nancy Lee Miller, Kay Oltmans, Martha Vail, and Janet McFarland, who all helped me feel at home in Colorado.

And, finally, thanks to Jay, who asked me out the week I was supposed to start working on my dissertation proposal, married me the week after I turned in the dissertation, supported me (emotionally and financially) while I revised the manuscript, and probably knows more about domestic advice manuals than I do. Thank you for the unfailing encouragement and good cheer, and for sharing my enjoyment of magnet-worthy field trips—from sod houses, to coal mines, to breweries, to the peppermint room. Most importantly, thank you for teaching me that, despite my abiding love for material culture, the best things in life are not things.

From Catharine Beecher to Martha Stewart

Introduction

The organizers of the 1996 Rhode Island Flower and Garden Show landed the perfect guest speaker for their annual luncheon. Held on a bright but chilly New England February afternoon, the event took place at the brand-new Westin Hotel and Conference Center in downtown Providence. The lunch itself, at seventy-five dollars a plate, would be gourmet fare, but it was not the reason for the large crowd. The guest speaker provided the appeal. Women from all over the region, along with a few men, gathered in the banquet hall where tables decked with early spring daffodils presented a celebratory scene. In the nearby conference hall, exhibitors presented a mind-boggling array of trees, shrubs, garden landscape projects, and exotic flowers. But for now, the lucky lunch guests turned their eyes to the stage. Enter Martha Stewart.

The topic of her lecture was the garden at her Westport, Connecticut, home. The program was to include a slide show filled with befores-and-afters, meant to excite the members of the audience with her stunning artistic sense and the beautiful projects for which she was beginning to become famous. A few minutes before the slide show was set to begin, the projector broke down, and a voice announced that the speech would be delayed. This was my chance. I approached the head table and introduced myself. I was writing a dissertation on the history of domestic-advice manuals, I explained, and I was interested to know if she thought of her work as having historical precedent. In the course of this brief encounter in the glittering ballroom of the Westin Hotel, Stewart readily conversed about the role of history in her work.

Stewart displayed a remarkable knowledge of the history of domestic advice. She cited several names of nineteenth-century advisors and noted that she had some of their works in her office, which she referred to from time to time for her magazine. Her assistant, sitting next to her, affirmed that Stewart loved to read from the old manuals and got many of her story ideas from them. Indeed, over the years *Martha Stewart Living* had featured then-and-now stories of the changes and continuities in American decorating. Stewart herself thought that the history of domestic advice and household arrangements was worthy of serious attention. She wished me luck.[1]

As a Martha Stewart aficionado myself, I felt a kinship with the women at the luncheon, even if as a graduate student the exorbitant fee had all but precluded my attendance at this feast. I was a longtime subscriber to *Martha Stewart Living*, had prepared her special-occasion hors d'oeuvres for a recent Superbowl party, and felt I had good credentials to speak to her. Though I tried to see her from an intellectual perspective, I could not help but be influenced by my (often secret) love of her work.

In fact, I had been featured in a newspaper story that morning about the upcoming visit from the domestic diva. The article, "Mad about Martha: Stewart's Rhode Island Fans Try to Live Her Way," featured several local women who called themselves Martha Stewart's biggest supporters. Linda McGowan "makes dolls, bottles vinegar and dries flowers," claimed the photo caption under an image of a smiling woman holding a teacup and surrounded by crafts of her own creation. Betsy Ose made Christmas ornaments out of old chandeliers. My role had been to comment on the historical continuity of Stewart's work in order to provide some sort of context for the domestic fervor sweeping Rhode Island. Reporter Keren Mahoney Jones noted that, for her subjects, "all this domesticity fills the free time that you have when you are not working," even though all the women featured had full-time jobs.[2] "There is a lot of chaos in the world today, chaos that we can do nothing about (or feel like there is nothing we can do about it). But we can do something about our homes."[3]

Jones had put out a call for Rhode Islanders to write to the newspaper explaining their devotion to Martha Stewart. She received dozens of responses, including some in hand-made envelopes stamped with unique designs. "I find the magazine [*Martha Stewart Living*] both informative and useful," wrote one woman. "Many of the ideas in the magazine are very practical and useful for everyday living, but some are just plain fun to look at—read—and maybe even daydream about a little." Another reader noted that "we usually dine on Corningware rather than Lenox but oh! Fantasies are wonderful."[4] These women astutely identified Stewart's writing as domestic fantasy.

The Rhode Islanders and others who share their devotion to Martha Stewart know that Stewart is a businesswoman. They understand that she has a staff of professional designers and gardeners to help her and that the ideas she brings forth usually need to be adapted according to

This Rhode Islander, "Martha Stewart's biggest fan," showed off her projects to the Providence Journal-Bulletin *in 1996. (Photo courtesy Providence Journal)*

budget and lifestyle. They harbor no illusions that their homes could conform to her television-set image of the perfect house. But they appreciate her ideas. They want to make their lives, or at least their daydreams, more delicious, more unique, more decadent, more inviting. They want to have homes and families that respect their efforts and that benefit from their supervision. After the talk and the luncheon, Martha held a book signing in another part of the hotel. Participants waited in line for several hours. Many brought homemade projects to share with Stewart, some as gifts, some simply as evidence of their devotion. Admirers from afar, these women now had the chance to share their domestic fantasies with other women and with Stewart. At the end of the twentieth century, middle-class American women recognized domestic fantasy and incorporated it into their lives. Martha Stewart had authorized them to dream.

Martha Stewart and her various projects owe a great deal to history. She and her staff continue to learn from old design books, patterns, colors, recipes, and other guidelines. They use Depression glass and old Pyrex mixing bowls, antique buckets and retro office furniture. Clearly, they have a lot of respect for the domestic advisors who came before them. However, though the staff of Martha Stewart Omnimedia may understand their debt to the past, most of Martha's fans are not familiar with the genealogy of domestic advice. Since the 1830s, many domestic advisors have paved the way for Americans, particularly middle-class American women, to understand the messages and promises of Martha Stewart's work.

Domestic advisors have always remained engaged in their culture and aware of important issues. Over the years, they helped educate women about sanitation and design, about patriotism, religion, and the family. Their domestic fantasies helped create the idealized vision of home held by so many Americans. Looking at the themes of domestic advice over time, it becomes clear that Martha Stewart has joined an ongoing discussion about domesticity that has spanned over a century. Hundreds of women in several generations have written domestic-advice manuals, regardless of the ever-changing boundaries between women and the home. The subjects discussed in domestic-advice manuals have remained remarkably consistent over time, encompassing vast changes in the role of women in American society. Domesticity, in its many different forms, transcends historical periods and continues to be meaningful to generations of American women.

Martha Stewart has achieved almost complete media saturation. She appears daily in her own television shows on both cable and network television, and monthly at the newsstands in her magazine *Martha Stewart Living*. She also appears regularly on the radio, in the newspaper, and in person at special events around the country. Her Kmart line brings her to one audience, and her lavish wedding ideas to another. Her website provides live chats, bulletin boards where visitors can share ideas, and a direct link to her catalogue, Martha by Mail. It is almost impossible to claim that she has not addressed a need in American culture for domestic advice.

But this need is not new. Indeed, her particular genre of advice has a long history, and our need to listen to her has precedent. Stewart has joined an ongoing discussion about furniture, windows, and decorating. This book, in essence a genealogy of domestic advice, locates Martha Stewart in a historical context of writing about the home that has been important to American culture for more than a century. This book investigates cultural themes in domestic advice for the century between 1850 and 1950, emphasizing the period between 1890 and 1940; it begins with some earlier works and anticipates Martha Stewart's rise to prominence in the 1990s. The themes of morality, science, Americanization, and modernism are seen from the point of view of domesticity. Later chapters explore the interest in exotic, historic cultures as expressed through household decoration and through the rise of "togetherness" in the 1950s. The emphasis on the fifty years between 1890 and 1940 demonstrates the relationships between the home and the rise of formal education and professionalization for women, as well as the dramatic influence of consumer culture in constructing expectations for the household in that period.

Furniture, curtains, and bathroom fixtures do not have inherent qualities of morality or character. Domestic-advice manuals give these items cultural significance and characteristics. Just as a cigar is never really just a cigar, a living room can never be just a living room. The sofa and the pictures on the wall, the items on the mantelpiece, and the rug on the floor, all these things combine to form a picture of the family. But who decides what that picture looks like and what it means? Domestic advisors, from their position as social commentators, have spent the better part of two centuries translating the meaning of furniture and living rooms to the American public. Their manuals and magazines, newspaper columns and trade manuals instruct Americans on how to better understand their furniture, accessories, wall treatments, fireplaces, lighting fixtures, flower boxes, and bric-a-brac.

Just like advertisements, domestic advice works as a kind of funhouse mirror, distorting reality to show a society as some people wish it could be.[5] But most of the advice was never followed. The writings of domestic advisors demonstrate cultural ideals, not cultural realities. Domestic advice cannot provide evidence about actual home decoration or what the majority of women thought about parlor sets. Instead, these rich sources illustrate the ways in which cultural ideals could be embedded in household furnishings and ornamentation. Domestic-advice manuals have always been the stuff of fantasy. Their historical value lies in uncovering the way certain women understood the connections between their homes and the larger world. At its most fundamental level, the true domestic fantasy was that women held the power to reform their society through first reforming their homes.

American domestic-advice manuals emerged in the late eighteenth and early nineteenth centuries from women's writing in cookbooks and etiquette manuals. Americans began by importing their household advice from England, but soon began to produce what they considered specifically *American* advice. In fact, many early domestic-advice manuals, such as Lydia Maria Child's *The American Frugal Housewife* (1828) and Catharine Beecher and Harriet Beecher Stowe's *The Ameri-*

can Woman's Home (1869) included the word "American" in the title to differentiate them from English works on similar subjects. American women began writing domestic advice in the 1830s and 1840s because the rise in literacy among middle-class women provided them with an audience, and because a rise in a white middle-class population provided them with a subject: the home.

The middle-class American home in the mid-nineteenth century was a crowded place. Newly available curtains, rugs, wallpapers, sofas, beds, and kitchen items filled the rooms, often to overflowing, and women turned to domestic advice in order to understand their surroundings. From mid-century on, domestic advice became more readily available. Eastern cities from Boston to Buffalo began to publish magazines such as *Home Monthly, Home Almanac,* and *Housekeeper's Annual* just to keep up with the flow of writings about the home. By the turn of the twentieth century, domestic-advice columns appeared in local newspapers, regional magazines, and full-length books. For most of the period between 1850 and 1950, the publishing centers for domestic advice remained in Boston, New York, and, to a lesser extent, in Philadelphia. But cities like Denver, Detroit, and Des Moines also published domestic-advice manuals.[6] The advice books ranged from collections of simple household tips to fictionalized tomes meant to influence and inspire. The books could be passed along from friend to friend, read aloud, or passed on to the next generation. They helped middle-class women navigate the confusing consumer world and make sense of their belongings.

Domestic advice often went hand-in-hand with education for girls and women. Catharine Beecher, a mid-to-late-nineteenth-century domestic advisor, believed in education for girls and opened her own schools where she taught her students about domesticity. As home economics became a recognized field in the early twentieth century, women found unprecedented professional employment in the field of domesticity. And, as the twentieth century progressed and women became more involved in other fields, domesticity remained an important part of American popular culture in the form of advertisements and magazines. Domestic education for women, whether formalized by Beecher or popularized by Martha Stewart, has remained a vital part of American life. Most American students take home-economics classes in public schools, learning how to care for their homes and families. Domestic advisors of the nineteenth and early twentieth centuries helped shaped the curriculum topics, such as sanitation, nutrition, and interior design, that are often still used today.

Most of the authors of this advice never became famous. However, some domestic advisors became household names in their day, including Emily Post, and others became important in their respective fields, such as Ellen Richards in home economics or Lillian Gilbreth in time-and-motion studies. Late-twentieth-century reprinting of Lydia Maria Child and Catharine Beecher's works have made these books accessible to a whole new generation, often to complement women's history reading lists at colleges and universities. Most domestic advice manuals, however, rest today in the rare book rooms of libraries and archives, their strong opinions muted by time. Some authors, including Mabel Hyde Kittredge, Fabiola Cabeza de Baca Gilbert, and Mary Northend, enjoyed important careers as home economists, teachers, and authors, and their names are recognized today by their home communities but not by the country at large. There is a building named after Sophronisba Breckinridge at her alma mater, the University of Chicago. Marion Harland appears on a women's heritage trail in her home state of Virginia. Harriet Spofford is remembered by many today as an important writer of Gothic fiction, and Emily Genauer for her 1974 Pulitzer prize. All of the writers of domestic advice, though they had widely varying careers, contributed to an important national dialogue about the home.

Why is domestic advice so compelling to American women? This book will begin to answer that question, which seems to intrigue so many cultural critics at the beginning of the twenty-first century. Martha Stewart's success is part of a legacy that has taken different forms over the decades, but that has consistently brought the promise of domesticity to thousands of American women. "So much has been written on household and domestic affairs," wrote Eunice Beecher in 1879, "that it may seem to many a worn-out topic, about which nothing more of interest can be written. But 'the household,' as we interpret it, is an inexhaustible theme."[7]

Chapter 1

GOING TO HOUSEKEEPING:

CREATING A FRUGAL & HONEST HOME

"Why," says Helen, "I have thought of the éclat of the engagement, and then the buying lots of things and having them made up in the very latest style, and the cards, the cake, the presents, and the bridesmaids. I shall have an elegant veil and a white silk, and be married in church, and have three Saratoga trunks, and a wedding trip, and—well, that's as far as I've gone. I suppose after that one boards at a hotel, or has to go to housekeeping, and I'm afraid it would be dreadfully humdrum. But no more so than flirting with one and another year after year, and seeing all the girls married off."

"For my part," said Miriam, "I have not looked at all this style and preparation that Helen describes, because I know I cannot afford it. But I have thought I should like a little home all to myself, and I would keep it as nice as I could, and I would try to help my husband on in the world, and we should have things finer only as we could really afford it. And I should want my home to be very happy, so that all who belonged in it felt that it was the best place in all the world. I should want to gather up all the good that I could everywhere, and bring it into my home, as the bee brings all its spoils to the hive."

"And I," said Hester, "want to make myself a scholar, and I shall marry a scholar, and we shall be happy in learning, and in increasing knowledge. And he shall be my helper, and I shall help him, and so together we shall climb to the top of the tree."

Vanity, love, ambition. These were the three Graces, which, incarnated in my nieces, sat on my piazza. I said to them: "Let me talk to you seriously upon the subject of a Home."

—Julia McNair Wright, The Complete Home

In Julia McNair Wright's 1879 domestic-advice manual, *The Complete Home*, she took the voice of "Aunt Sophronia" and discussed home-making with her three nieces, Helen, Miriam, and Hester. Each niece represented a certain subset of American women. Miriam, as the niece who wanted a comfortable, simple home where everyone would feel welcome, represented the ideal of most domestic advisors in the nineteenth century: the domestic fantasy.

Miriam, the ideal housewife, provides a window into the dreams of household advisors in the late nineteenth century. Her faulty cousins Hester and Helen are useful counterpoints because they help illustrate the pitfalls that domestic advisors worried about and continue to worry about in the twenty-first century. Hester is too concerned with her career and intellect and not concerned enough with her house and family. In contrast, Helen is obsessed with the frills and fanciness she imagines will accompany romance and conquest of a husband, but has not stopped to think about her home and her role in keeping that home in the future. Only Miriam, the ideal, understands the true purpose of her life as a middle-class white American woman. She knows that she can only have what she can afford, and she wants nothing more than to see her house as the embodiment of love.

How did domestic advisors such as Julia McNair Wright try to convince their readers to act and live more like Miriam than Hester or Helen? Through a long and steady campaign over more than a century, household advisors have argued that women should spend more time in their homes, conform to certain ideals, and spend less time in the wider world. They have consistently argued that women pay attention to their finances and live within their means, not trying to outclass the neighbors through a false show of wealth. Most importantly, they have made the point that a woman's virtue and worth can be found in the way she furnishes her home. Advisors saw instructions on the arrangement of the furniture and the types of wood used in the parlor not only as aesthetic concerns, but as symbols of honesty, faith, and good judgment.

Domestic advice manuals originated in the 1830s with the Victorian era and its emphasis on home and family. Throughout the nineteenth century, books, newspapers, magazines, advertisements, and other public forums strengthened the connection between women and the home. Domestic advisors, whether single, widowed, or married, tended to be white, middle-class women who had some personal experience with homemaking. They relied upon an audience of the newly literate, white middle class, a population that continued to build in America after 1800.[1] In 1840, 38 percent of white Americans of school age received some kind of formal education. By the mid-nineteenth century, most white women could read and write.[2] And women were consumers, too, making women's novels into the best sellers of the 1850s.[3] Women readers voraciously demanded constant reprints of sentimental favorites, such as *Charlotte Temple*, throughout the nineteenth century.[4] The domestic-advice manuals took advantage of this new audience.

Lydia Maria Child wrote the first domestic-advice manual for American housewives. Her *American Frugal Housewife* (1828) was already in its twelfth edition by 1832. Lydia Maria Child was a popular fiction writer who wrote poems, short stories, and the lyrics to a still-famous song called "Grandma's Thanksgiving." Born in Medford, Massachusetts, in 1802, Child was educated at Miss Swan's seminary in Watertown and worked as a schoolmistress until her marriage to David Lee Child in 1828. She edited the *Juvenile Miscellany*, a children's monthly periodical, for several years while establishing herself as a writer and an abolitionist in Boston. She became strongly identified with the antislavery cause in New England and edited *The Anti-Slavery Standard* with her husband during the 1840s. One of her more famous projects was editing the memoir of Harriet Jacobs, which later became *Incidents in the Life of a Slave Girl* (1861).

Child wrote about many different subjects. She wrote novels, including *Hobomok* (1824) and *The Quadroons* (1842). She wrote histories, about the Pequot Indians of New England and about the evils of slavery. Her domestic advice manual, which she wrote relatively early in her career, gave her some degree of notoriety, but domestic advice was only a part of her long writing career in which the emphasis was always on moral integrity.

Child's *American Frugal Housewife* was filled with admonitions about indolence, frivolity, and waste. She focused on the needs of the homemaker, but also addressed issues not directly related to the home, such as travel. Her severe attitude against spending money on useless extravagance resulted in stories that addressed themes such as a family who could not afford a vacation but took one anyway. "To make a long story short," she wrote, "the farmer and his wife concluded to go to Quebec, just to show they had a *right* to put themselves to inconvenience, if they pleased. They went; spent all their money; had a watch stolen from them in the steamboat; were dreadfully sea-sick off Point Judith; came home tired, and dusty; found the baby sick, because Sally had stood at the door with it, one chilly, damp morning, while she was feeding the chickens."[5] The story went on, concluding that the farmer and his wife would have been better off remaining at home, saving their money, and not leaving their children with strangers. *Frugal Housewife* is filled with such stories of people who squandered away their earnings instead of using every moment and every cent to further the cause of the morally pure home.

Many women in the mid-nineteenth century took up Lydia Maria Child's idea to address women's concerns through household advice. Indeed, some of the authors, including Child, Catharine Beecher, Helen Hunt Jackson, and Sarah Josepha Hale were among the most influential women writers of the nineteenth century.[6] Others also had successful writing careers, from Harriet Spofford, a popular fiction writer, to Julia McNair Wright, a Christian reformer. These women all chose the middle-class female's connection to the home as one of the most important subjects, no matter what their other interests. They wrote fiction and political treatises, travelogues and poetry. They led campaigns for women's education, for abolition, and for temperance. And they also wrote domestic advice.

Often, women used fiction and writing about domesticity as ways to deliver political messages. Helen Hunt Jackson was an outspoken critic of governmental policy toward Native Americans. She wrote scathing reports, such as "A Century of Dishonour; a Sketch of the United States Government's Dealings with Some Indian Tribes," and spent time in Colorado and California observing race relations in the West. But despite her desire to communicate her message at levels as high as the United States Congress, Jackson also believed that ordinary women could be an important audience for her ideas. Her *Bits of Talk about Home Matters* (1879) merged the theme of personal responsibility with a household-management text aimed at middle-class women.[7] Jackson also used fiction successfully; her incredibly popular novel *Ramona* (1884) openly addressed relationships between the Mexicans, Native Americans, and Anglos in California.

Fiction for women and domestic-advice manuals shared many ideals of "moral education." Sentimental novels throughout the nineteenth century, such as *Hope Leslie* (1827) by Catharine Maria Sedgwick, *The Wide, Wide World* (1851) by Susan Warner, and *The Lamplighter* (1854) by Maria Susanna Cummins, explored the lives of young girls in the context of religious growth. The heroines of these novels experienced life changes, such as losing their family and home, and turned them into life lessons. Writers of sentimental fiction explored moral integrity through broad, often epic, plot lines involving dozens of characters. The popularity of fiction for women gave domestic advisors an audience that would understand their work.

Many of the characters in sentimental novels served as symbols for religious teachings. Domestic-advice manuals would pick up on this convention, but use furniture and carpets in place of characters as symbolic teachers. In *The Lamplighter*, for example, Cummins used a character named Emily to represent religious purity for Gerty, the heroine. In one scene, Gerty repressed her natural instinct to cry out and composed herself "at the sight of Emily, who, kneeling by the sofa, with clasped hands . . . looked the very impersonation of purity and prayer." [8] Indeed, women writing about the home personified furniture with qualities such as "honesty" and "purity" just as novelists characterized people as archetypal examples of virtue.

The close connection with novels gave domestic-advice manuals a familiar literary form. This format probably helped women readers to understand the emerging genre and to know what to expect. The dozens of domestic-advice manuals published in the decades after 1830 followed a clear pattern, established to guide women readers through the house. An extensive table of contents emulated the novel's list of chapter titles. Some authors even used fictional characters. Julia McNair Wright wrote *The Complete Home* from the standpoint of musings and conversations of the fictional Aunt Sophronia, with occasional commentary from Cousin Ann and Mary. These fictional characters helped readers understand the domestic-advice manual.

Marion Harland in *Common Sense in the Household* was one of the most intimate writers. The first chapter of her 1871 volume was called "Familiar Talk":

> I wish it were in my power to bring you, the prospective owner of this volume, in person, as I do in spirit, to my side on this winter evening, when the bairnies are "folded like the flocks"; the orders for breakfast committed to the keeping of Bridget, or Gretchen, or Chloe, or the plans for the morrow definitely laid in the brain in

A VOLUME OF UNIVERSAL READY REFERENCE

FOR

American Women in American Homes,

Containing a Large Fund of Useful Information,
Facts, Hints and Suggestions
Upon the Various Topics Pertaining to Home Life,

INCLUDING

*HOME DECORATION, HOUSEHOLD MANAGEMENT, DOMESTIC
AFFAIRS, COOKERY, LADIES' FANCY WORK, MEDICAL
MATTERS, FLORICULTURE, ETIQUETTE, HOME
AMUSEMENTS, THE NURSERY, ARTISTIC
EMBROIDERY, DECORATIVE PAINT-
ING, LACE MAKING, THE TOI-
LET, THE LAUNDRY, ETC.*

With One Hundred and Eighty-Nine Illustrations.

NEW YORK:
F. M. LUPTON, PUBLISHER,
Nos. 106 AND 108 READE STREET.

1890.

Many late-nineteenth-century domestic advice manuals offered a spectacularly wide
range of information for women. This volume, for example, promised "a large fund of
useful information" about domestic subjects ranging from home decoration to floriculture.
The book, published in 1890, claimed to "include every subject in which woman is
interested, wherein information of a practical nature can be imparted through printed
instructions." (The American Domestic Cyclopaedia, title page; courtesy
The Winterthur Library, Printed Book and Periodical Collection)

that ever-busy, but most independent of women, the housekeeper who "does her own work." . . . I should not deserve to be your confidant, did I not know how often, heart-weary with discouragement . . . you would tell me what a dreary problem this "woman's work that is never done" is to your fainting soul.[9]

Harland's intimacy with her reader here emulated the sentimental novels in which authors routinely placed the reader in the position of the heroine.[10]

Marion Harland created the intimate style she used with her readers over several decades of writing. Born in Virginia in 1830, Mary Virginia Hawes Terhune (Marion Harland was a pen name) began writing stories as a teenager. Her many books included fictional stories, such as her first work *Alone* (1855), cookbooks, and even an autobiography in which she discussed her conflicted feelings about slavery. Many members of the Terhune family became influential writers. Daughters Christine Terhune Herrick and Virginia Terhune Van de Water also wrote domestic advice manuals, *First Aid to the Young Housekeeper* (1900) and *From Kitchen to Garrett* (1912). Harland's best-selling *Common Sense in the Household* was so popular that she soon revised it, commenting in the 1880 introduction that the book had to be completely reprinted. "Through much and constant use—nearly 100,000 copies having been printed from them—the stereotype plates have become so worn that the impressions are faint and sometimes illegible."[11] The popularity of Marion Harland's work in the late nineteenth century demonstrated the power that domestic-advice manuals were beginning to have in capturing an eager audience of American women.

Besides fiction, the cookbook was another popular genre of reading material for American women in the early nineteenth century. Although early cookbooks look strange to modern eyes because of their lack of particular instructions on measurements, temperatures, and cooking times, these books became quite popular in America. They included tips on how to order and cook certain cuts of meat and on how to mix up common remedies for stain removal or illness. The first cookbook printed in the new country, Amelia Simmons's *American Cookery* of 1796, proudly used recipes such as "Indian pudding" and "Johnny Cake" that would not have been included in English cookbooks of the period.[12] American domestic advisors, especially in the nineteenth century, used the cookbook as a starting-off point for their household advice because of its familiarity to middle-class American women.

Lydia Maria Child's *American Frugal Housewife* included many recipes. She provided instruction on everything from meat to pastry, including this recipe for chocolate: "Many people boil chocolate in a coffee-pot; but I think it is better to boil it in a skillet, or something open. A piece of chocolate about as big as a dollar is the usual quantity for a quart of water; but some put in more, and some less. When it boils, put in as much milk as you like and let them boil together three or four minutes. It is much richer with the milk boiled in it. Put the sugar in either before or after, as you please."[13] Child's book was in fact a combination cookbook/domestic-advice manual. As the century wore on, fewer and fewer texts would include recipes, until by the twentieth century the texts had become quite different. But for much of the nineteenth century, domestic-advice manuals retained close ties to both fictional and culinary writing traditions.

Domestic-advice manuals began to take a form in the mid-nineteenth century that would differentiate most of them from both novels and cookbooks. Catharine Beecher was an influential person in making this transition. In her opinion, domestic life was more important than any other aspect of women's existence. She, perhaps more than any other single person before or after, poured her intellectual soul into domestic writing. Beecher was born in East Hampton, New York, in 1800 into a family that would make history as one of the most influential in the nineteenth century. Her father, Lyman Beecher, was an important minister who traveled from Connecticut to Ohio spreading his religious views. Her brother Henry Ward Beecher was also a minister, and her sister Harriet Beecher Stowe was the best-selling author of *Uncle Tom's Cabin.*

Though the men in Catharine's family attracted a lot of attention in religious circles, the Beecher women made their voices heard. Several other members of her family, including her sister Isabella Beecher Hooker and sister-in-law Eunice White Beecher, also wrote domestic-advice manuals. Eunice Beecher warned her readers that the right furniture and decorative choices could "give an air of comfort and contentment to your home," whereas the wrong choices "will make you gloomy and dissatisfied every time you see" the failed décor.[14] She believed that her role as a domestic advisor was to help her readers decorate their homes "on correct principles and on sure foundations."[15]

Catharine Beecher perhaps made her strongest impact in her girls' schools, especially her Hartford (Conn.) Female Seminary. She strongly believed that administrators of girls' schools should include domestic education, educating women for their presumed profession as housewives and family caretakers. The introduction to *American Woman's Home* explained why she and her sister Harriet felt compelled to write the book: "The authors of this volume, while they sympathize with every honest effort to relieve the disabilities and sufferings of their sex, are confident that the chief cause of these evils is the fact that the honors and duties of the family state are not duly appreciated, that women are not trained for these duties as men are trained for their trades and professions, and that, as the consequence, family labor is poorly done, poorly paid, and regarded as menial and disgraceful." [16] At the Hartford Seminary, Beecher taught domestic education, using many of her own books as texts. During the course of her life, she wrote several household-advice books, including *Treatise on Domestic Economy* (1841) and *Miss Beecher's Housekeeper and Healthkeeper* (1873).

Catharine Beecher's and Marion Harland's writing careers focused extensively on the role of women in the household, but other domestic advisors had extensive interests outside of domesticity. Elizabeth Ellet, for example, wrote many books in addition to her *New Cyclopedia of Domestic Economy* of 1872. Best known as a poet, Ellet was born in Aurora, New York, and moved to South Carolina after her marriage. Her poems earned her contemporary recognition in *American Female Poets* (1853), which commented that "She is a writer of great research, of equal skill and industry." [17] She published her first volume of poetry, *Poems, Translated and Original,* in 1835 and continued to research and write about varied topics, from travelogues to histories. [18] In fact, Ellet is often described as one of the earliest women's historians because she identified and studied women for her books on women artists and women in the American Revolution.

Women writers in the nineteenth century often wrote about "women's subjects." Harriet Prescott Spofford, best known for her chilling Gothic romances such as *Sir Rohan's Ghost* (1860), focused her efforts on short stories with female subjects, including one called "Her Story," which described a woman driven to insanity by her marriage. Spofford, born in Calais, Maine, in 1835, began writing short stories to support her family. She published the stories in Boston newspapers and literary journals, including *The Atlantic Monthly.* Her domestic-advice manual *Art Decoration Applied to Furniture* appeared in 1878 after she had already begun making a name for herself in New England literary circles. Spofford became famous for her detective stories, mysteries, and science fiction, but her domestic-advice manual serves as evidence that, as a female writer, domesticity was an important subject for her to consider.

Many influential women writers in the nineteenth century had close ties to literary journals and magazines. Sarah Josepha Hale was perhaps the most important of these, as her career as editor of the immensely popular *Godey's Lady's Book* spanned four decades, between 1837 and 1877. Hale, widowed with five children in 1822, began writing and editing to support her family. She began at the *Ladies' Magazine* of Boston, which merged with *Godey's* in Philadelphia in 1837. By 1860, the circulation of *Godey's* had reached 150,000, making it one of the most widely read women's magazines in the United States in its time. *Godey's* provided information for women on subjects ranging from dress to architecture, and Hale was able to lend her support to other women writers by featuring their poetry and stories in her journal. She used her forum to praise other domestic advisors, such as Catharine Beecher for her work on training teachers.

Hale's domestic-advice manuals appeared early in her career. Her *The Good Housekeeper* of 1841 probably did not reach nearly as many people as *Godey's*, but it allowed her another way to express her ideas about the home. Hale also involved herself in political and social issues of her day. She was interested in women's issues such as female education, but also focused on patriotic causes such as fund-raising for the Bunker Hill Monument in Boston to commemorate Revolutionary War service. Today, Hale is perhaps most famous for her campaign in 1863 to establish Thanksgiving as a national holiday, but her influence among women writers in the mid-nineteenth century was probably her most significant legacy.

By the end of the century, dozens of women's magazines across the country offered versions of *Godey's Lady's Book* advice and literature. Many women's magazines included a section called "ornamentation" or "Ladies' Work Table" that printed patterns for slipcovers and workbaskets, or suggestions for creative needlework. *The Home Circle* recommended new uses for gold paint on pine bookcases—"lines or arabesque patterns"—in 1883, and *The Housekeeper's Friend*, printed in Providence, Rhode Island, in 1879, printed new designs for "napkins" and "sofa-arms." [19] All of these painstaking projects, in the words of the *Home Almanac*, "immortalized 'home' and associated with it all that is stable and good." [20]

Women wrote most of the domestic advice in the nineteenth century, but men did produce a few influential texts. Eugene Gardner wrote several advice manuals in the late nineteenth century. He often pointed out that his wife provided "aid and encouragement" for his texts and that he truly believed that women had a much better sense of house design than did men. His 1882 text pursued this point through an exploration of how a fictional Jill designed an exceptional house after her husband Jack had "proved a failure" at domestic architectural design. The preface to his revised edition noted that he got much of the inspiration for his book from a woman: "On a recent visit to the young woman whose experiences and observations are contained in this book, I was greatly pleased to find her zeal and interest in domestic architecture unabated." [21] Though Gardner wrote the book himself, he made a point of explaining in his preface and throughout the text that his ideas had come from women.

Men certainly did write about the household in the nineteenth century. English pattern-book authors and designers such as Andrew Jackson Downing advised people on the exterior of the house and on certain floor plans. Often, women's journals such as *Godey's Lady's Book* included architectural designs by men. Other men took the interior of the house as their subject. Charles Eastlake, for example, published *Hints on Household Taste* in Boston in 1874, an erudite work on the "most essential principles of good design." [22] This English domestic advisor, a fellow of the Royal Institute of British Architects, exemplified the role of male writers in early domestic advice, in that he wrote the work for professional architects and interior designers instead of ordinary women.

Women who wrote about the home (private sphere) also remained connected to and interested in the social issues of their day (public sphere). In the second half of the nineteenth century, important topics that concerned women included suffrage and the treatment of minorities. In an era greatly obsessed with women's rights, domestic advisors knew that some women would question their focus on women's "natural" relationship to the home. "There is at the present time an increasing agitation," Catharine Beecher wrote in her introduction to *American Woman's Home*, "evolving many theories . . . as to woman's rights." [23] But Beecher held strongly to her belief that the "moral power" of the home superseded all other callings for women. She did not believe that "woman's rights" outside the home would improve women's lives.

Beecher was not the only domestic advisor to openly address (and dismiss) the women's rights philosophy. In 1871, Marion Harland "whispered a word in your ear I don't care to have progressive people hear," which is, "the humble home make[s] your sphere for the present. . . . Be sure you fill it—*full*! before you seek one wider and higher." Elizabeth Ellet, commenting in 1872 on the "rights" of woman, declared that "if women from the highest to the lowest, were systematically educated to wield properly the great power [the home] they indubitably possess . . . they would have little reason to complain about power."[24] And Eunice Beecher, Catharine's sister-in-law, wrote in 1879 that if women would only view their work at home as more important, "we should hear less of the 'restricted sphere' of women; of lofty intellects, great powers and genius, dwarfed in the narrow precincts of home life, or . . . stooping to the drudgery of housekeeping. . . . If you are ambitious of leadership, you can find it here . . . in the *home* . . . you may reign a queen."[25] In another essay on the subject, Eunice wrote, "We are tired and disgusted with those women who are so greatly exercised in drawing comparisons between man and women. . . . There is no ground for any comparison."[26]

Emma Churchman Hewitt, associate editor of *Ladies' Home Journal*, addressed the "woman's issue" outright in her 1889 *Queen of Home*. Hewitt devoted an entire chapter to "occupations for women" in which she tackled the issue: "And what *is* woman's sphere?" As a working woman herself, she must have had to deal with this question on a personal level. Hewitt, born in Louisiana in 1850, was a poet and nonfiction writer who supported herself after the death of her husband with her writing and editing jobs. In *Queen of Home*, she noted that women, to be successful housekeepers, must understand "baking, washing, ironing, cooking, sewing; that is, four *trades* without the minor acts of dishwashing, sweeping, dusting, etc." She concluded that woman's sphere "is the same as that of man, *i.e.*, to do cheerfully and well the work that comes to her hand, whether it be a pen, a surgeon's knife, a dentist's drill, a pair of scissors or a broom."[27] However, given the title and subject of her 528-page *Queen of Home: Her Reign from Infancy to Age, From Attic to Cellar*, it is likely that Hewitt preferred that most women would choose their association with the home rather than with an "outside" occupation.

Domestic advisors assumed that most white, middle-class American women would be interested in their advice. They believed that there would be an audience for their books because they believed that most women truly felt a strong connection to and responsibility for their homes. Many authors' domestic fantasy was that their books would help all women see the home in the positive way that they themselves did. Even Julia Wright's fictional character Hester, who, unlike her cousins, went to college, married a scientist, and had no children, found housekeeping to be a fascinating subject. Though she herself did not want a family home, she took care of other peoples' children when necessary and taught her cousins some decorating tips, peppered with intellectual commentary.

In the nineteenth century, most domestic-advice manuals assumed a white, middle-class audience as their readership. This did not mean that advisors were unaware of significant social inequalities; in fact, many of these women devoted their careers to social reform, abolition, or other such movements. However, when it came to their fantasies of the ideal home, it is clear that most of them could only see a white woman at the helm. They understood the need for all Americans to have certain basic rights, but domesticity was reserved for their own kind.

Immigrant women often appeared as servants in manuals. Sarah Josepha Hale expressed concern in 1844 that Irish women needed much education in order to be "worthy to be the mother[s] of American citizens," and admonished her readers to "teach her needlework, and instruct her in reading and writing."[28] In the American context, many advisors believed that servants were unnecessary. The book *Practical Housekeeping*, published by a group of authors in Denver, Colorado, in 1885, noted that "the model house should not be large, nor too fine and pretentious for daily use. . . . A great house, with its necessary retinue of servants, is not in keeping with the simplicity of a republic."[29] This same manual, however, assumed that the middle-class housewife would keep at least some household help. The authors, noting that "the breakage of dishes in some houses is fearful," lamented the housewife who was "sick at heart" when her dishes broke, and "little comfort does she get from Bridget, who replies: 'La, madam, it was but a few of your dishes, and sure I could not help it.'"[30]

Some advisors even addressed the possibility of physical contamination of the house by recent immigrants. Although America experienced its highest levels of immigration at the turn of the twentieth century, advisors noted the presence of immigrants in American homes far earlier. As early as 1840, Philadelphia cookbook author Eliza Leslie noted that "servant women who have just come from Europe, not infrequently arrive with contagious diseases, produced or fostered by the heat and dirtiness of the steerage; and a clean American female is justifiable in objecting to the risk of having such a bed-fellow."[31] Elizabeth Ellet noted that "Housekeepers are mainly dependent on the Irish and German emigrants, who as a rule are utterly ignorant of household service."[32] Many advisors referred to a servant generically as "Bridget" or another stereotypically Irish or other European name to indicate, without saying so outright, that the servant was of a different social class than the mistress of the home.

Julia McNair Wright, author of *The Complete Home*, used her fictional character Aunt Sophronia to lecture her readers about proper treatment of servants. Wright, involved in many social-reform movements including temperance, wrote many books about her Christian devotion. Born in 1840, Wright connected her Christian beliefs to her beliefs about running an ideal home. When discussing servants, Aunt Sophronia reminded her nieces and other listeners that: "We forget in considering our servants our common womanhood; they are viewed by us as chattels, as animated machines to perform for us such and such offices, and, in regarding them, we forget the human tie, that God has made of one blood all the nations of the earth." However, Aunt Sophronia also believed that some fundamental differences did exist between her nieces and their servants. "The Lord gave Martha [the servant] to begin with larger hands, stronger muscles, and more simple tastes and surroundings than mine."[33]

Most domestic-advice manuals included some passages about training servants. Emma Hewitt noted: "Social problems are constantly cropping up, but the one which now agitates the country . . . [is] the 'Servant Question,' as it is now denominated."[34] Indeed, most advisors seemed interested in addressing the question. Hewitt went a bit farther than most when she noted that some servants might have aspirations: "Admitting that humanity is the same the world over—that race, climate or color makes no difference, except, perhaps, in degree— that the Lord has implanted in every human soul certain hopes and desires, ranging not so much in degree as quality, according to the surroundings and refinement of the possessor—we can but admit that in all hearts, no matter the sex, has been implanted the desire to 'some day' own a *home*."[35] Most advisors, including Hewitt, limited their discussion of servants to a dedicated chapter, in this case "Social Relations," and devoted the rest of their text to the middle-class women they perceived as their audience.

Domestic advisors in the mid-to-late nineteenth century, then, had developed a tradition of fiction and culinary writing for women into a new genre of household advice. During and after the Civil War, which disturbed households across the country, many household manuals stressed the ongoing relationship between women and their homes. These books declared that the relationship between women and their furniture, drapery, and accessories could illustrate the strength of American values in the face of troubled times. By emulating fictional ideals, such as Julia Wright's character Miriam, women could express their dedication to their new, united country.

The domestic fantasy of mid-nineteenth-century America emphasized a close relationship between women, home, and Christian ideals. Domestic advisors believed that they could illustrate religious and patriotic values, such as piety, honesty, and modesty, through furniture and decorative accessories. They wrote their texts to show readers the ways in which certain woods, certain fabrics, and certain ornaments could influence family life. Domestic advisors in the second half of the nineteenth century wrote their texts, at least in part, to teach women how to make households bring religion and patriotism to their families.

Catharine Beecher and Harriet Beecher Stowe included chapters on "A Christian Family" and "A Christian House" in their 1869 text. As daughters and sisters of Protestant ministers, they believed strongly in a Christian belief structure. Their text illustrated the connection that nineteenth-century advisors expressed between women, the home, and Protestant Christianity. "The family state, then, is the aptest earthly illustration of the heavenly kingdom, and in it woman is the chief minister," they wrote. But much of their early chapters dealt more specifically with the Christian religion. "To intelligent, reflecting, and benevolent women—whose faith rests on the character and teachings of Jesus Christ—there are great principles revealed by Him, which in the end will secure the grand result which He taught and suffered to achieve. It is hoped that in the following pages these principles will be so exhibited and illustrated as to aid in securing those rights and advantages which Christ's religion aims to provide for all, and especially for the most weak and defenseless of His children."[36] The Beech-

"In the Divine Word it is written, 'The wise woman buildeth her house,'" wrote Catharine Beecher and Harriet Beecher Stowe in 1869. This image depicts a happy home, marked with a cross, where the right values have promoted domestic bliss. Heading a chapter devoted to household organization, the drawing links mundane discussions of closets with an overarching Christian value system. (Beecher and Stowe, American Woman's Home, 23)

ers' text was filled with instructions for building kitchen cabinets, for keeping rooms well-ventilated, and for choosing the right curtain fabric. For them, these ideas came out of a deep Christian faith.

Calls for Christian homes filled many of the domestic-advice texts. Julia McNair Wright, a religious Christian herself, had Aunt Sophronia teach her nieces about the requirements of a Christian home. She discussed attendance at church and other outward signs of Christianity, but focused on the presence of religion in the home. "Be warm and enthusiastic in your Christianity if you would commend it to your families as a thing worth striving for," she suggested. "From the Christian home let 'the light of love shine over all.' Rich or poor in its appointments, it should be cheery and kindly, full of common interests and homely self-sacrifices, and mutual confidences, and good order. Nowhere else should things be more honestly what they seem. It is only by *home sentiments* that home can be made into a place whereto the hearts of children can be firmly bound."[37] Of course, given the three nieces' different dispositions, Miriam found this advice palatable, whereas Helen thought the admonition to honest home sentiments taxing. "Oh, me," she cried, "what a world of work it is to rear a family! What a burden of responsibility!"[38]

Christian doctrine informed most domestic-advice manuals. Evangelical Protestantism was an important component of middle-class life in the mid-nineteenth century.[39] Horace Bushnell, an important theologian, wrote in 1847, "The house, having a domestic Spirit, should become the church of childhood, the table and hearth a holy rite."[40] This commentary corroborated the works of other popular Christian writers, such as Henry Ward Beecher, who agreed that home life was crucial to American culture. Although church going was certainly important, the Victorian fixation on the family made the home an important space for Christian values.

Magazines often provided special instructions for household arts side by side with more overt morality tales. By interspersing inspirational Christian readings with sewing patterns, the editors suggested that both had a restorative nature for home life. The *Household Journal,* for example, began a special section in 1860: "Our lady readers will find their interest considered," the editors wrote, through a section on "brief but comprehensive essays upon subjects of interest to every family in the land." This section included household decoration along with essays on Christian living. One goal of *The Home Circle* was to make Christian literature accessible to women in the home. Advisors used the instructions on ornamentation to teach their readers how to keep their homes morally and aesthetically pure.

Domestic advisors believed that home life could have significant consequences for society. Helen Hunt Jackson's analysis led her to see the improperly decorated and managed home as "a place from which fathers fly to clubs, boys and girls to streets."[41] This vision of social arrangements put the responsibility for community health and morality on individual homes, and thereby on individual women. "When the neat home is changed for the untidy one," wrote the editors of the women's journal *The Home Circle* in 1883, "one does not wonder so much at the attractive power of the saloon."[42]

The advisors' warnings about imminent doom pointed to a salvation through proper attention to the home, whereby the family, and thus the whole nation, would prosper. The home was simply a way to address larger societal concerns in a way that women could understand and perhaps even respond to. Domestic advisors translated Christian values into household terms. Most important was the directive to have only what you could afford and to refrain from what would much later be called "keeping up with the Joneses." Often beginning with an explanation of Christian values, like the Beechers, advisors then went on to be more specific about how to express those values (such as honesty) in the home.

Advisors tried to keep their readers on a steady moral course as they made recommendations for decorating the complicated nineteenth-century home. There was much at stake. Households filled to overflowing with ornaments, and furniture ran the risk of succumbing to an indulgent, showy status. Upholstery, rugs, curtains, paints, and wallpapers needed special direction. As Harriet Spofford wrote in 1878, "The art of furnishing . . . [shapes] the family with the gentle manners that make life easier and pleasanter to all."[43]

The room-by-room survey of the ideal home began with the entrance hall, which "should be furnished with an umbrella and hat stand, and chairs or hall seats," according to Elizabeth Ellet.[44] These directions for hallway furnishings helped to encourage certain types of behavior associated with "proper" culture. The furniture could speak for the family, declaring that this family believed it was important to keep dry in the rain, to obey the formality of wearing a hat, to leave a calling card, and to provide guests with a place to sit while they waited to be shown into the parlor.[45] A family could use furniture to express their values, which would be evident from the moment a visitor walked in the door. Ellet continued, "If there is a closet for hanging up hats, cloaks &c., it should be near the door. Door scrapers should always be placed near the entrance."[46] This information broadcast the need for visitors to be welcomed and clean before they entered the home.

Dining rooms, despite their obvious function, often provided complications. Laura Holloway Langford was an author and poet who wrote books about the First Ladies' lives in the White House, and even one book on the "Buddhist diet." In her 1883 domestic-advice manual

Nineteenth-century hall furnishings provided a place for visitors to hang their hats and outerwear, to rest their umbrellas, and to fix themselves up in the mirror before being seen by their hosts. This example illustrates a simple variety with slight architectural embellishments. Hall furniture might also include more shelves for small items such as gloves, boot brushes, or calling cards. (Varney, Our Homes and Their Adornments, *287; courtesy The Winterthur Library, Printed Book and Periodical Collection)*

The Hearthstone; or, Life at Home, a Household Manual, she outlined her rules for the "well-organized home."[47] She believed the dining room to be one of the most important rooms in the house:

> The dining-room is the tell-tale apartment of the house; whatever it is, so is the parlor, the up-stairs rooms or the kitchen. Cracked dishes, soiled covers, dingy carpets — these bespeak one kind of housekeeper, as neat napkins, clean chairs, and tidy ornaments another. The dining-room ought to be the pleasantest place in the house; it is the meeting room where the family are expected to be always present at stated times, and where the events of the day are talked over while the pleasant business of eating is being discussed.[48]

Langford insisted there was no need for a clock in the dining room: "Americans do not require to be reminded of time at the table — they spend less at it than any other civilized people." She believed that families should use the dining room only for "eating, talking and reading [the newspaper]."

Langford recommended a sparse dining room. She commented that, "A bronze ornament for the mantel, and a couple . . . of vases, will be sufficient in the way of small articles of a strictly ornamental kind." She accepted a "water-colored fruit piece" as the only picture on the wall, did not recommend "figured paper" for the walls, and insisted on "plain frames" for any pictures. The walls of various rooms demanded attention, and invited decisions about whether to cover them in paper, paint, or decorate with pictures or mirrors. Laura Langford was especially particular in her discussion of the dining-room walls, which she thought should not have elaborate designs; rather "striped paper . . . and panel paper is more suited to such rooms."[49] In contrast to the rest of the home, the sparseness of the room reflected a masculine ideal. Although the woman of the house should arrange the room, she did not sit at the head of the table.

Domestic advisors often saw the dining room as the only "masculine" room in a house. "The husband that has all as he wishes in the dining-room will be tolerably sure that . . . the wife shall have all she wants in the drawing room," wrote Harriet Spofford in 1878.[50] This trade-off would allow women to make the rest of the house more feminine by ceding this one room. Certainly, in smaller, middle-class homes with no designated room such as a library or billiard room for men to retire to after dinner, the dining room took on the significance of these rooms as a masculine space alongside the more feminine parlor.

Despite commentary on other rooms of the house, by far the main focus of mid-century advisors' moral crusade was the parlor. The room, relatively new and certainly popular in this era, occupied much space in mid-nineteenth-century manuals. Although the parlor tends to be seen as symbolic of the Victorian era, it was a contested and controversial space to contemporary observers. The parlor is an example of the way in which advisors thought of rooms having moral values. Clarence Cook, one of the few men who wrote about the middle-class home in the nineteenth century, commented that "I use the word 'Living-Room' instead of 'Parlor,' because I am not intending to have anything to say about parlors . . . [since] none but rich people can afford to have a room in their house set apart for the pleasures of idleness."[51] The parlor, then, worked as a way to get at those ideas of "vanity, extravagance and idleness" that Lydia Maria Child had brought forth early in the century.

The parlor, in its original sense, entered the floor plans of American homes in the mid-eighteenth century. Many wealthy homes included a "front," or "best" parlor, filled with fold-top card tables, drop-leaf breakfast, or Pembroke tables, pier tables between the windows, and many chairs. Families often placed their furniture against the wall, and moved it to the center of the room only when needed for entertaining. Mirrors, curtains, and paintings ringed the walls. The seven-piece, upholstered parlor suite became a mainstay of the parlor by the 1860s and included a sofa, an armchair, an armless "lady's chair," and four smaller chairs. Bright color often filled the room, on carpets and wallpaper, curtains, and upholstery. The parlor was a sign of wealth, of gentility, of the ability to include an extra room in the house just for entertaining.[52]

The "best" parlor was more than a place for furniture; it included a set of rituals as well. Rules governed the serving of tea and the style of conversation.[53] Women and men had different roles to play, and the furniture helped to dictate where they would sit and how they would interact. Filled with rich brocades, thick carpeting, and mahogany furniture, the parlor was more than a room. It was a barometer of the station of the family. Certain woods, such as mahogany, cherry, walnut, and rosewood, came to indicate wealth. Later in the nineteenth century, new processes of veneering would enable the middle class to emulate these woods, but the best parlors of the upper class had only

This parlor depicts the show room that so many domestic advisors tried to avoid.
Godey's Lady's Book *provided illustrations of fancy parlors, fancy clothing, and other*
temptations in the late nineteenth century. This parlor included a decorated ceiling,
matching parlor furniture, carpeting, heavy drapes, and a portiere, the doorway curtain.
Domestic advisors would be familiar with parlors designed like this one, down to the clock
and figurine on the mantelpiece and the plant stand between the windows.
(Godey's Lady's Book *[January 1885]: 11)*

the real thing. Horsehair fabric, prickly but fashionable, covered the
sets of chairs.

Middle-class families began to include parlors in their homes, making parlor furniture an excellent example of the new abundance in mid-
nineteenth-century America. The room, by definition, was extraneous to the daily survival needs of the family and existed only because
the family could afford a room for show. It represented a major cultural shift from the period of the early republic. In the Victorian era,
the era of the parlor, middle-class families actuated the marketplace.
Their needs produced an industry of furniture manufacturers, as well
as manufacturers of pianos and organs and picture frames. Domestic
advisors who wrote about the parlor struggled to bring this emblem
of abundance into their definition of frugal character.

The parlor would come to represent the culture of the Victorian
era. This room became a symbol of the way in which people used
· furniture to demonstrate their place in the world. The middle class
populated the parlor with photographs, portraits, and prints. They
demonstrated their knowledge of culture with piano music and with
bookshelves filled to overflowing. Knowledge of letters and of the arts

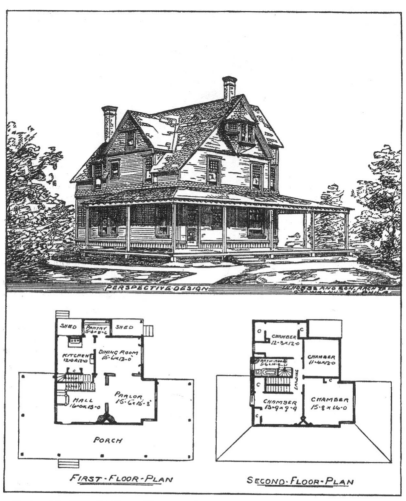

Designed by Philadelphia architects, this house was available for sale in the suburbs in the 1880s and included "a parlor having sliding doors." Parlors appeared in the floor plans of most middle-class homes of the late nineteenth century. The parlor, larger than other rooms in the home, would be on the first floor and provide a formal place for entertaining. Godey's Lady's Book *presented floor plans and house elevations, making the design of the home as important as the fashion and short stories the magazine featured. (*Godey's Lady's Book *[November 1884]: 534)*

virtually dripped from the walls and the shelves. The pride people felt in their parlors was often demonstrated by the plethora of photographs of families and couples in these busy rooms.[54] However, the admiration of the general public for the formerly elite parlor was not shared by the domestic advisors of the period.

Domestic advisors disagreed violently with the general public on the subject of parlors. Although many suggestions given by domestic-advice writers were followed, such as suggestions on room arrangements and craft ideas, the parlor was one subject that stayed in the realm of fantasy. No matter how hard they tried, and they did try, domestic advisors' fantasy of the simplified, livable living room never replaced the appeal of the show parlor for most American families. Readers of domestic advice may have trusted that, in theory, they could give up the parlor in favor of a more honorable value system, but they continued to decorate their homes in familiar, comfortable ways, and that included the fancy parlor well into the nineteenth and the turn of the twentieth century.

Parlors varied in degree of luxury and appeared across the country in vastly different settings. Middle-class families in large cities such as Philadelphia, Chicago, and Denver had access to richly upholstered chairs, gilded mirrors, carpets, and wallpapers and curtains of good quality. They hung paintings on the walls and arranged knick knacks, such as vases and clocks, on their mantels. But the Victorian parlor was not only the bastion of the rich and urban. Frontier families, homesteading in Nebraska in the late nineteenth century, followed the same rules, installing different wallpapers, less fancy center-table lamps, and cheaper fabric for the curtains, perhaps, but the meanings of the rooms were the same. When domestic advisors criticized the parlors of the Victorian era, they looked not only to the middle-class residents of eastern cities, but also to the West. Many Americans brought their parlor and all of its attributes with them.

In the waning decades of the nineteenth century, many advisors looked at the best parlor and criticized the values that seeped out of the mahogany and horsehair. The parlor did not encourage family togetherness or love, but false opulence. "Who does not glance back," wrote Lida Clarkson in 1887, "almost with a shudder, at the old-fashioned times of stiff, uninviting rooms with cold, dead walls [and] horse-hair furniture?" [55]

"The parlor should be the rallying point in daily family life," wrote Susan Anna Brown in her 1881 *Home Topics*. She criticized the use of the parlor as a "best" room and advocated a "room in which centers the soul and throbs the heart of home life." This recommendation addressed the use of the room as a space where the family's values would be formed. Susan Brown wrote several books about the home in the nineteenth century, each expressing her frugal values. Her 1883 *Mrs.*

*Families across the country decorated their parlors with matching sets of furniture,
curtains, display cabinets, and bric-a-brac. This interior photograph of a parlor in
Denver, Colorado, is an example of fancy parlors that Americans continued to decorate
well after domestic advisors recommended more simple arrangements. Hundreds of
photographs just like this one demonstrate the predominance of this type of parlor
in American homes. (Photograph by Harry M. Rhoads; courtesy
Denver Public Library, Western History Collection)*

Gilpin's Frugalities would help women by introducing "remnants and
200 ways of using them." Her thoughts about the middle-class parlor
expressed this theme, urging women to carefully consider furnishing
parlors only "within—truly within—our means."[56]

Brown wrote about the parlor as if it could personify the home.
About the room where it was impossible "to have a good time," she lamented: "They were dark and dismal; they were full of ugly furniture,
badly arranged." In a properly arranged room, "it did you good simply
to sit there,"[57] because the furniture created a positive "heart" for the
home. She described the perfect parlor set-up: "Leave space for the new
volume and the magazine upon the table, and for the bright evening
lamp; space upon the floor for the children's toys, and for themselves
to frolic; and let not even the honest dog or the gentle cat be banished lest they break or mar some frail piece of fancy work. So shall

*Even in a sod house in Nebraska, the ideal of the parlor held strong. The Hoaglands
translated parlor conventions such as pictures on the walls, patterned wallpaper, curtains,
and a table with a white cloth and lamp to their frontier home. Too cluttered to appeal to
domestic advisors, this late-nineteenth-century image reveals the widespread
appeal of the parlor. (Courtesy Nebraska State Historical Society)*

we be kept from the worry and care of too many treasures, and find
time for reading, for study, for play with the little ones, and perhaps
for practicing at times the almost lost art of plain sewing." [58] The compendium *Household Conveniences, Being the Experience of Many Practical
Authors* of 1884 also indicated that "carpets and furniture may be of the
latest styles and costly, and yet the rooms fail to be home-like." [59] These
manuals pointed out that stylish furniture would not create the home
atmosphere without attention to its honest construction and loving
organization.

To combat the negative effects of the parlor, domestic advisors
spoke out against what they called the "show-room." Because they
wrote texts for those who did not have homes with two parlors, a
library, a drawing room, a nursery, and several bed chambers, they
found the parlor all the more insincere as a separate room. When in-
venting their image of the moral home, advisors thought that each
room should have a purpose that related to the creation and suste-

nance of the Christian family. The parlor, dedicated to entertaining, card playing, and showing off silver tea sets, did not fit into the picture of the moral home. This room, above all others, represented the idle gentility that the advisors cautioned against. The show room, to the domestic advisors of the mid-nineteenth century, was impractical and ostentatious and did not come from the "right" set of values. As author Agnes Bailey Ormsbee wrote of the parlor in 1892, "It is least used by the family, and in too many households [it] is a closed and awful place."[60]

Show rooms provided a good tool for American advisors to champion democratic values. The anti-show-room philosophy held steady in American domestic-advice manuals throughout the nineteenth century. "I would strongly recommend [to every young woman], if she wish to spare herself and her family much discomfort, to avoid having show-rooms,"[61] wrote Frances Harriet Whipple in 1838. In the 1870s, Elizabeth Ellet issued a "warning to beware of showy, veneered, vamped up furniture,"[62] and in 1883 Laura Langford Holloway advised women to "do without your show drawing-room altogether."[63] The domestic advisors made a clear distinction between the kind of family life that would ensue with a show room (bad), and without one (good). These ideas remained consistent throughout an entire century.

Specific elements of parlor decoration came under attack as early as Lydia Maria Child's 1828 *Frugal Housewife*. She recommended many things to avoid, such as "Brussels carpets, alabaster vases, mahogany chairs and marble tables," and suggested instead "Kidderminster carpets and tasteful vases of her own making."[64] The Brussels carpet, often cited as the villain in these texts because it was an example of an expensive purchase, first appeared in Belgium in the eighteenth century. The carpets were produced on special Brussels looms with Jacquard attachments in Philadelphia in the 1820s, but it was many decades before power looms made the carpets widely available to middle-class households. The Brussels carpet was often invoked as the primary symbol of middle class' aspirations to the upper class. English Kidderminster carpets, on the other hand, could be produced widely in the United States by the 1830s and were cheap and accessible to the middle class.[65]

The sins of extravagance and vanity played prominent roles in Lydia Maria Child's picture of moral corruption. "There is nothing in which the extravagance of the present day strikes me so forcibly," she lamented, "as the manner in which our young people of moderate fortune furnish their houses." She believed that by furnishing the home with woods and fabrics that they could not afford, a young couple's "foolish vanity" would make them "less happy, and no more respectable."[66]

Harriet Beecher Stowe set up several fictional scenarios in which show rooms proved to be the end of the happy family state. The fancy parlor stood as a direct antithesis to her rules for "Christian Living." In her 1869 essay "The Ravages of a Carpet," Stowe told the tale of a life-loving family who spent most of its time in the sitting room until the purchase of a fancy Brussels carpet. This purchase eventually led to removal of all birds and plants from the room (lest they shed on the carpet), the shutting of the blinds (to prevent sun spotting), and new furniture (to match the caliber of the carpet). Eventually the room was closed off and unused.[67] Stowe's collection of stories entitled *House and Home Papers* was an anthology of such occasions, with essay after essay detailing the lives of families who became oppressed by their fancy households in which nobody was comfortable. Stowe attacked the furniture and the rugs as a direct cause of family dysfunction.

"The cheerfulness and attractiveness of your rooms," wrote Eunice Beecher, "depend more largely upon the style and color of your carpets than upon the furniture." Carpets, indeed, provided an important subject for the advice manuals. Floor coverings demanded constant attention because they varied widely in price, style, and color. Eunice Beecher proclaimed that the most important judgments to make concerned "fast and durable colors," because the sun would fade all but the strongest dyes, she recommended specific colors: "Bright, clear scarlets and dark, rich greens usually wear well."[68] Expensive carpets enforced strict rules about food and plants in the room. Most advisors, then, did not endorse the fancy, expensive carpets with evanescent colors and instead wrote about the values inherent in choosing the practical floor coverings.

Advisors considered decisions about the placement of pictures on the walls quite weighty. Laura Langford recommended some pictures, but cautioned "Do not hang one above another," because that made dusting more difficult.[69] Elizabeth Ellet thought the moral influence of pictures made them indispensable to the home. She commented that pictures add to a room "an air of completeness, and a home look. . . . The subjects must be such as we can truly sympathize with, something to awaken our admiration, reverence, or love."[70] Ellet thought pictures on the wall could teach values and inspire families. Catharine

Beecher believed in "the educating influence of these works of art," making even the walls a site for learning.[71]

Some advisors provided specific instructions on acceptable wall art. Emma Churchman Hewitt, for example, though she admitted pictures could be expensive, encouraged their use, but only under certain circumstances. "Let me beg of you not to spend money on oil paintings or chromos. The best pictures for your purpose will be always black and white, such as the Adolph Braun autotypes and photographs, or Goupil's photogravures, in which a new process produces results as soft and rich as the etcher's point and acid. With these black and white pictures, one or two water-colors will give beauty to your walls, but even here you must know enough to be sure you are getting good work."[72] Hewitt went on to recommend some individual works, such as "Miss Fidelia Bridgyrs [sic] foreground sketches." Fidelia Bridges was a painter, best known for her watercolors of flowers, birds, and blossoms. Hewitt's recommendation indicated her preference for natural, simple, botanical scenes.[73]

Emma Hewitt's picture recommendations included comments on the use of certain frames. Believing always in honesty over fakery, she cautioned against lacquer. "Your pictures will look much better in plain cherry," she noted, "or oak band, than in the cheap lacquered frame."[74] Catharine Beecher and Harriet Beecher Stowe suggested that readers make their own picture frames. After recommending certain "chromos," or color reproduction prints of famous works of art, by Albert Bierstadt and Eastman Johnson, the Beecher sisters noted that "these chromos, being all varnished, can wait for frames until you can afford them." Or, to demonstrate creativity, women could "Make for yourself pretty rustic frames in various modes." They suggested such humble materials as acorns, mosses, or ocean shells.[75]

When people made their own frames and furnishings, they could determine the types of wood they used. Domestic advisors called into question the "honesty" of the wood used in mass-produced furniture. Factories produced tables and chairs made from cheap wood, but veneered or stained to look as if the wood was more expensive. Advisors believed that such imitations diluted the moral power of the furniture and cheapened (quite literally) the effect of the home. Ella Rodman Church, a writer for such literary publications as *Appleton's* and the *Ladies Repository*, wrote in her *How to Furnish a Home* in 1881, "A pine table is a proper thing, but a pine table that pretends to be black walnut is an abomination." She believed that the "sincerity" of the furniture expressed itself through the lack of "veneered woods, ornaments glued on, or substances that, being one thing, pretend to be something else." If a housewife could not afford expensive furniture, advisors warned her to be happy with what she could afford, making her parlor "chaste and modest." [76]

Eunice Beecher agreed that poverty was no excuse for dishonest furniture: "If you cannot afford the most costly furniture, there is no reason why you should not endeavor to secure articles of neat and attractive shape and color." [77] She went on to describe the way in which taste was more important than cost in choosing a pattern for a carpet. "A coarse, ungainly scroll," she wrote, "will cost as much as a neat and tasteful pattern . . . with graceful vines and flowers, true to nature." [78] The distinction Beecher made here was between a pattern that imitated nothing and a pattern that imitated the natural beauty of a living plant. Readers would find therein a room decoration that would leave the family feeling "happy and cheerful," in "nature" rather than in artificial and dishonest renderings of abstract scrolls.

Ascribing character traits to furniture served to demonstrate that the home could embody values. "Let no piece of furniture be bought that is not solid and of honest strength and durability," wrote Agnes Bailey Ormsbee in 1892.[79] She suggested various types of chairs and tables, and wallpaper and draperies, but concluded, "whatever . . . [is] chosen, let them be thoroughly good of their kind." [80] Honesty was an important value both in a patriotic (think of George Washington) and Christian context in the nineteenth century. By relating honesty to furniture, domestic advisors managed to convey their message that household goods could transmit values. Emma Churchman Hewitt cautioned that if a reader could not afford a "well made" parlor suite, she "best eschew 'suites' altogether, and furnish [the] house with odd pieces." She warned readers not to give up the search for the proper kind of furniture. "Chairs can be found in sensible plain forms, and this is just what you must hunt for till you find it."

Advisors overwhelmingly recommended ignoring fashion in favor of honest furniture. It was much more admirable, in their estimation, to have well-made, inexpensive furniture than shoddy imitations of more fashionable wares. Elizabeth Ellet's discussion of bedroom furniture noted that "mahogany, maple-wood and oak" would be the "best and prettiest" choices for wood, but if these were not available, the reader was to look for "very serviceable, well-polished, stained wood imitations of all these three." The unacceptable solution was to find "very common and trumpery imitations . . . generally badly put together." Even though these common chairs might look like the fashionable wood varieties, they "do no service," and Ellet dismissed them as so much "rubbish." [81]

In Julia McNair Wright's *The Complete Home*, Aunt Sophronia often lectured her nieces about how to spend their money in the home. She strongly believed that beautiful homes often were the cheapest. Indeed, "the least handsome parlor that I ever saw was a very expensive one—not a book or engraving to be seen. Staring, ill-painted family portraits, which had cost a good price, deformed the walls." Instead, she insisted that:

> True beauty does not belong to things showy and insubstantial. Some people get cheap, showy furniture and carpets, thinking that as it is cheap they can afford more of it; while the truth is that the more of it the worse it looks, and that a few good things are far better than a good many poor ones. When we must get cheap things because we have but little money, then let them be very plain; for nothing is uglier than cheap gilding . . . if the things are showy and cheap, the money has gone for paint and gilding, which will soon tarnish and crack off, the wood will warp, the glue prove treacherous, and our possessions will be a wreck.[82]

Advisors often commented on specific types of places to buy furniture so that the pieces would represent the right values. Because they considered furniture to be so important a symbol of the family morality, advisors spent a great deal of time reminding their readers "to have only what she can afford to have!"[83] This important dictum meant that the integrity of the housewife was in question in the purchase of a specific item in the display of that item in the home. Advisors, then, reminded their readers only to shop at certain stores. Elizabeth Ellet recommended "avoidance of all cheap, showy furnishing establishments." This caution served to encourage women to avoid the new furniture warehouses and to stick to "good, old-established houses of business."[84] As Emma Whitcomb Babcock wrote in 1884, "There is a higher vision even in carpet buying."[85]

The care with which rooms must be furnished, papered, ornamented, and carpeted, occupied the pages of many advice manuals. Designed for first-time home arrangers, these books provided an important introduction to the special relationship American culture had forged between women and their homes, as well as to the importance of this subject for the national well-being. In dispensing all of the different rules and recommendations about furniture, walls, and floors, the domestic advisors took on the role of benevolent teachers dictating household arrangements and formations. Navigating through the practical lessons that, they believed, led to moral purity, the domestic advisors invented their version of the fantasy home. Domestic advice was a form of writing by women in the nineteenth century that allowed for women themselves to be in control of a collective, female moral destiny. They contributed to a national dialogue about character and its importance to their vision of society. Though the advice was not always followed, it gave white, middle-class women a common vocabulary and a place to begin their own journeys with home (and moral) improvement.

Aunt Sophronia, who advised her nieces Helen, Miriam, and Hester on the proper way to run a household throughout Julia McNair Wright's *The Complete Home* of 1878, believed strongly in the message of frugal living. "I tried to impress upon my nieces from the time when they set up housekeeping for themselves that saying of Cicero: Economy is in itself a great revenue." Throughout the book, Sophronia insisted that saving money and having only what you could afford in your household were virtues to be admired. Following the line of advice from Lydia Maria Child's 1828 book through advice in the 1870s demonstrates a clear progression of similar requests. Aunt Sophronia's nieces, like Wright's American women readers, had different reactions to the strictures. Helen commented that "the 'work hard' and the 'economize' would be equally difficult to me, for I hate both." After listening to Aunt Sophronia's lecture, however, Miriam, the symbol of the frugal and honest homemaker, concluded "I eschew extravagance with all my heart from this time forth." [86]

Chapter 2

THE RISE OF THE DOMIOLOGIST:

SCIENCE IN THE HOME

*It may be assuming too much to claim that the true standard of beauty
in house-furnishings conforms strictly to that required for the best sanitary
conditions, but, surely, it is not extreme to declare emphatically that the
conventional standard is far from being one either of beauty or of health.
Pure air and sunshine, two essentials of healthful living, cannot be
obtained in full measure in the modern elaborately furnished house. And a
common and growing mistake is this of using our houses chiefly as a means
of displaying the objects which our tastes and our wealth permit us to
procure, while we disregard the far more important claims of good health.*

But how can furnishings injure health?
  a) By preventing free access of light and air.
  *b) By laying unnecessary work on the shoulders of the busy housewife,
so that the proper care of her home becomes a burden to her.*
  *c) By forming catch-alls for dust. Dust is composed of many widely
different things: particles of carbon (soot), of granite, sand, or other mineral
matter; pollen of flowers, bits of plant stems, bark, leaves; manure, small
pieces of hair, dried skin, shreds of clothing, and microscopic forms of
life such as bacteria and molds—these are some of the almost infinite
possibilities of dust. The housekeeper's concern is centered on the
microscopic forms of life in dust. Some of these germs can attack the
human body, causing disease.*
—*Ellen Richards and Marion Talbot*, Home Sanitation

Ellen Richards and Marion Talbot included these warnings in their early-twentieth-century, domestic-advice manual *Home Sanitation*.[1] The advice represents a shift, at the turn of the century, toward domestic advice with an emphasis on health and sanitation: science had entered the home.

Richards and Talbot, in fact, recommended much the same things as their predecessors in the nineteenth century. They encouraged women to rid their houses of unnecessary ornament, textile, and upholstery. They believed, just like nineteenth-century writers, that women should stay away from "elaborately furnished" houses. That their motives were driven more by science than by Christian doctrine was the only difference.

What had happened in the decades between Julia McNair Wright's nieces who learned about homemaking from their Aunt Sophronia and the more methodical and often less personal style of Richards and Talbot? How did the same kinds of domestic advice take on new meanings about health and sanitation? Catharine Beecher, Julia Wright, and their colleagues had certainly noticed and discussed sanitation in the home. They believed in the importance of clean rooms and fresh air. But they did not have, or feel the need to apply, a scientific vocabulary to describe their ideas. The dust and decay of textiles and heavy upholstery took on new significance as Americans began to learn about germs and disease.

Advisors used the word "science" to bring a secular authority to their texts and to their vision of the ideal home. The middle-class women who read and wrote domestic-advice manuals at the turn of the century began to turn to scientifically based ways to understand their homes. Americans began to believe that science could solve every problem and cure every disease, and many saw the laboratory as a place of hope for the future. Domestic advisors appropriated the belief in science as salvation and turned it into a domestic fantasy for the new century. They educated middle-class women about how science could make their homes safer and cleaner, and how, therefore, their homes could become better assets to the larger society. Their advice turned every home into a small laboratory, where women could control the experiments.

Science influenced domestic fantasy. Women began to think about the ways in which their houses could conform to new ideals and new standards of cleanliness.[2] Could visitors see the dirt? Was the kitchen a laboratory or an old-fashioned disaster? Domestic advisors encouraged women to worry about disease as a way to encourage their conformity to the new regulations. This version of domestic fantasy demanded that women be educated, and it gave them power based on that education. Science added new responsibility to the care of the home, but also gave women new authority to protect their families from danger.

In turn-of-the-century America, science was everywhere. Scientists began quantifying human nature, providing statistics on brain sizes and on sexual activity.[3] New technology astounded Americans, as gears, steel, and factory lines filled the popular imagination with images of science at work. Erector sets became popular in the 1910s, encouraging children (especially boys) to learn about how buildings were made and how scientific principles were used to build cities.[4] Universities began offering classes in new fields of social sciences, such as psychology and sociology. The idea that anything could be rationally discussed, analyzed, and experimented on caught the attention of many women who brought that scientific attitude to the discussion of home management.

Helen Campbell wrote in 1881 that, "we are but on the threshold of the new science."[5] Campbell, who died in 1918, would not live to see many of the changes that the "new science" made in the field of household management. However, her late-nineteenth-century domestic-advice manuals, *The Easiest Way in Housekeeping and Cooking* (1881), and *Household Economics* (1896) introduced many ideas that she believed would be important in the new century. Campbell's work represents a transition from the Christian teachings of the mid-nineteenth century advisors to the educated, scientific advisors who would emerge in the twentieth century.

Campbell noted that she could read both "poverty and luxury" and "intelligence" through furniture. To illustrate the way in which furniture selection reflected upon its owner, Campbell stated: "In its intimate relation to human life, furniture forms a direct expression of the class, age, sex and condition of servitude of its user." According to her manual, most housekeepers at the turn of the century displayed little intelligence when furnishing their homes. This problem, wrote Campbell in 1896, "will be remedied when the household economist has voice in the choice . . . of the home and its furniture."[6] Campbell decided that the problems she saw in the home could only be solved by domestic scientists.

Campbell had a varied career of writing and advocacy. She taught home economics at various schools, including the University of Wisconsin and Kansas State Agricultural College. In New York in the 1880s, she wrote a column, "Prisoners of Poverty," for the New York *Tribune* based on her experiences with the urban poor in that city. Her 1891 *Darkness and Daylight: Or, Lights and Shadows of New York Life, a Woman's Narrative of Mission and Rescue Work in Tough Places, with Personal Experiences among the Poor in Regions of Poverty and Vice* used interviews and observations to paint a bleak picture of the poor in New York.[7] Helen Campbell participated actively in Women's Club work in New York and befriended many of the most influential women of her time. She dedicated *Household Economics* to Fanny Baker Ames, a charity organizer, suffragist, and teacher, and to Charlotte P. Stetson, (later Charlotte Perkins Gilman), a writer and social reformer. At the 1893 World's Columbian Exposition in Chicago, Campbell took the stage after Vassar College history professor Lucy Salmon.[8] Discussing the industrial condition of women and children, Campbell was in the company of women who had devoted their lives to studying and improving the condition of American women.

Campbell treated the household as a space for rational, scientific improvement. In *The Easiest Way*, she discussed household ventilation, drainage, and the chemistry of food. Her *Household Economics* suggested the idea that women could no longer be expected to run their households without the help of trained specialists:

> More and more, we see, the trend is toward scientific handling of all that makes up civilized living. The single housekeeper is at a steadily increasing disadvantage. We are being pushed—often against our wishes and protesting wildly as we go—but still pushed, toward that combination which alone can lighten burdens, lessen expenses, and make possible for the majority the good things known now only to the minority. This business of living is a science, nor can any one woman master all its countless details. The time has come for the work of the specialist, and the end of the smattering of knowledge which thus far has been the allowance of most women.[9]

Campbell mirrored many nineteenth century advisors in her belief that housework could be "lovely and noble."[10] However, she also thought that housework for women needed to be reexamined and that women needed specialized training, even a university education, in order to understand all the parts that made up the proper home. "It is time," she wrote, "that this business of cooking and cleaning for humanity should be transferred to the hands of experts."[11]

Campbell knew that her wish was beginning to come true. American secondary schools and universities began offering coursework in domestic science in the mid-nineteenth century. The foundation for these programs was the Morrill Land Grant Act of 1862. This government program provided land for state universities that agreed to begin a program to train students for practical fields. According to the act, universities would get money for "the endowment, support, and maintenance of at least one college where the leading object shall be, without excluding other scientific and classical studies and including military tactics, to teach such branches of learning as are related to agriculture and the mechanic arts, in such manner as the legislatures of the States may respectively prescribe, in order to promote the liberal and practical education of the industrial classes on the several pursuits and professions in life."[12] Land-grant schools promoted subjects such as agriculture and engineering. The State College of Iowa at Ames was the first to offer a course in "domestic economy" in 1871, and home economics soon became one of the basic offerings of land-grant schools.[13] The federal government hoped that these subjects would, after the Civil War, help Americans rebuild with a population of trained professionals.

Land-grant schools soon opened in every state. Faced with segregation in the South, African Americans began to found their own teacher training schools, and in 1890 a second Morrill Act expanded the land-grant program to include these historically black institutions. These "1890 Institutions," including Tennessee State, Florida A&M, and Prairie View A&M (in Texas), were located in the seventeen southeastern states where the original land-grant school had denied access to "colored students." A century later, in 1994, the Equity in Educational Land-Grant Status Act authorized land-grant status to twenty-nine colleges for Native Americans. Today, each state plus the District of Columbia, Guam, Puerto Rico, and the Virgin Islands has a land-grant university dedicated to "practical education."

The trend for home-economics education spread across the country in the nineteenth century. By 1892, fourteen universities offered courses in sanitary science, household administration, domestic science, or home economics. The University of Chicago founded its influential Household Administration program in 1904, led by faculty members Sophonisba Breckinridge and Marion Talbot. Many other colleges and new universities followed, and by 1905 most land-grant colleges had Home Economics departments. Ellen Richards, a founder of the movement, outlined its tenets: "Home Economics stands for: Ideal home life of today unhampered by tradition of the past; The resources of modern science to improve home life; Freedom of the home from the dominance of things and their due subordination to ideals; That simplicity in material surroundings that will free the spirit for the more important and permanent interests of home and society."[14] Home-economics leaders took familiar ideas, such as simplicity and freedom from extravagance, quantified them, taught them to students across the country, and made them important on a national scale.

Home economics became a standard subject in middle and secondary schools, as well as in colleges and universities. In the first few decades of the twentieth century, advocates lobbied for saturation of the country's public schools, focusing on the middle-school grades. Bringing home economics to the public schools would bring the field to a much wider range of people. Helped by federal legislation promoting vocational education, the second decade of the twentieth century saw the implementation of a home economics curriculum in schools across the country. By 1938, the United States Office of Education found that 76 percent of seventh- and eighth-grade girls attended home-economics classes.[15]

The professionalization of home economics provided job opportunities for many women. To make sure the field was respected as an academic endeavor, home economists began a yearly meeting at Lake Placid, New York, in 1899, named their professional organization the American Home Economics Association (AHEA), and began publishing a journal.[16] These tactics helped bring the field respect among other social scientists, and it gave their articles, books, and newsletters an academic authority.

Many home economists had ties to culinary schools. Food science was an early branch of the field, and the study of nutrition helped launch specialists in other home-related fields. Because women had a traditional connection to food preparation, the kitchen was a logical place to begin the professionalization of all the home arts. Fannie Merritt Farmer, in the dedication to her famed 1896 *Boston Cooking School Cookbook*, still in print over a century later, praised the president of the cooking school for "her helpful encouragement and untiring efforts in promoting the work of scientific cookery, which means the elevation of the human race."[17] The Boston Cooking School trained many women in nutrition and basic food preparation and provided jobs for many home economists as teachers.

Maria Parloa was an early teacher at the Boston Cooking School. Her household advice manuals, *Parloa's Young Housekeeper* and *Home Economics: A Guide to Household Management*, both published in the 1890s, probably reached a wider audience because of her connection to the first Boston Cooking School cookbook and because of her contributions to magazines such as *Good Housekeeping*. Most of her published works were cookbooks, including *Appledore Cookbook* (1872), *Camp Cookery* (1878), *Miss Parloa's New Cook Book* (1880), and *Miss Parloa's Kitchen Companion* (1887). She taught her readers how to use the new labor-saving cooking devices, how to measure temperatures, and how to can fruit. Her texts made use of the new technologies, and she also offered helpful kitchen solutions:

> How to arrange the covers of the saucepans is always a problem. There is nothing to hang them by, and one rarely has shelf-room enough for them. I have found that a long rack, such as is placed under the meat when roasting in the oven, is an excellent contrivance for holding these covers. Place it in one corner of the shelf, and slip the edges of the covers between the bars, arranging the covers according to size, the largest at one end, and the smallest at the other. This little convenience economizes both space and time, for a cover can be found or replaced without a moment's delay.[18]

Friendly and accessible, the home economists attempted to bring rational thinking and practical solutions to the kitchen.

Parloa, born in 1843, was part of the beginning of the home-economics revolution. She enjoyed small fame in late-nineteenth-century Boston, even being written up in *Good Housekeeping* magazine, which many of her articles on home management. The *Good Housekeeping* "Notable Nothings" column of February 1890 provided an intimate look at Parloa: "Picture to yourselves a woman a little above the ordinary height, and just stout enough to look comfortable, a plump, rosy face, frank, friendly hazel eyes, and dark hair a little sprinkled with gray, rolled back smoothly from a broad forehead. She always seems happy and jolly." Her own home, claimed the article, "is what every home ought to be. An expression of herself. It is in a lovely location, near Franklin Park, and it abounds in light and sunshine."[19]

In the second half of the nineteenth century, when Maria Parloa was teaching cooking in Boston, it was still unusual for women to be considered authorities in science-based subjects. Parloa gave lectures all over New England, beginning in New London, Connecticut, in 1876. She gave cooking lessons at Chautauqua summer schools and other adult-education centers all over the country. Parloa enjoyed success both as a writer and a lecturer, in part because her field was dominated by women, both as teachers and students. Women achieved success in home economics, and they continued to widen the definition of the field to include sanitation, sewing, and other subjects, as well as food preparation.

Ellen Swallow Richards, one of the founders of home economics, put her efforts into creating a place for women in the sciences. Richards, born in Massachusetts in 1842, graduated from Vassar College and began her scientific career at the Massachusetts Institute of Technology (MIT) where she became the first woman student to graduate in 1871. She soon began teaching at MIT, eventually being appointed instructor of sanitary chemistry. Richards established a Woman's Laboratory at MIT in 1876, welcoming other women into the newly emerging field of domestic science.[20] During her long career, Richards worked on several major projects, including a water-sanitation study that led to new standards for sewage treatment in Massachusetts. She also worked for a fire-insurance company, studying household ventilation, and wrote more than a dozen books. Later in her life, she joined with others to form the organization that would become the American Association for University Women, an important resource for the growing numbers of women in colleges across the country.[21]

Ellen Richards and other women scientists in the late nineteenth century realized that the subjects they studied could have practical applications in the household. Richards's technical papers and books, such as *Notes on Industrial Water Analysis: A Survey Course for Engineers* (1908), had a direct connection to her books about the home, such as *Home Sanitation: A Manual for Housekeepers* (1911). While her study of water was meant for a specific, educated audience, *Home Sanitation* had a wider appeal for ordinary women. She believed that women scientists could achieve important things in the lab, but she also thought they had a special responsibility to watch over and protect their homes from dangers caused by poor ventilation or sanitation. The first female graduate of MIT, the founder of home economics, and the inspiration for countless women scientists, Richards shared her ideas about home furnishings with women across the country.

Richards was an important role model for aspiring home economists at the turn of the century. Sophonisba Breckinridge and Marion Talbot, both important domestic advisors, followed her into home economics and created their own places in the field. Sophonisba Preston Breckinridge was born in Lexington, Kentucky, in 1866, and returned home after college to become the first woman to be admitted to the Kentucky bar. Legal practice was not to keep her interest for long, however, and she soon moved on to get her Ph.D. in political science at the University of Chicago, where she also graduated from law school. Despite these advanced degrees, her interest turned to home economics, and she spent eight years teaching at the University of Chicago in the Household Administration department.[22]

Political activities consumed much of Breckinridge's career in Chicago. She became involved in social-welfare programs, edited a journal called *Social Science Review*, and helped organize various civic groups. She joined the Women's Peace Party, the National American Woman Suffrage Association, and the Children's Bureau. She also worked with Chicago's Immigrants' Protective League, the National Association for the Advancement of Colored People, and Hull House, an important settlement house in Chicago. Participation in so many social causes still left Sophonisba Breckinridge time to write, and she authored more than twelve books, including a household-advice manual that she co-wrote with Marion Talbot.

Marion Talbot was closely involved in the early-twentieth-century professionalization of home economics. She studied with Ellen Richards in Boston and taught at Richards's school of housekeeping, which opened in 1897. Richards had hoped the school would teach immigrants to be good housekeepers, but soon gave up on that idea and began to concentrate on teaching educated women the scientific principles of household management. The short-lived school had two purposes: to teach women the basics of home economics and to provide opportunities for women as teachers. Talbot used the experience to launch her own career in teaching; she soon left Boston to become the first dean of women at the University of Chicago.

Talbot believed that higher education for women could solve the problems of contemporary home life. In *The Modern Household* (1912), coauthored with Sophonisba Breckinridge, she wrote: "We hope that the statements and suggestions in the following pages, supplemented with the questions, will lead housewives, either separately or in study classes, and students of social conditions in college and elsewhere, to find ways by which the household of moderate income and with children may realize its possibilities as an organized group of human beings."[23] Talbot believed that by reading her books and by studying together, women could begin to solve some of the problems in home life. She specifically cited "the increasing frequency of divorce, the lowered birth rate, the multiplication of hotels and tenements, the increase of public places of amusement, and the desertion of families, either temporarily or permanently, by husbands and fathers."[24] These worries were similar to the concerns of the nineteenth-century domestic advisors. However, whereas Child and Beecher addressed these problems in terms of their Christian beliefs, Talbot and her colleagues believed in the power of higher education and science.

Women such as Richards, Breckinridge, and Talbot had public careers and wrote many books. However, many lesser-known home economists around the country also published household-advice manuals. These texts appeared throughout the 1910s and 1920s, with increasing numbers in the 1930s. For example, Mary Lockwood Matthews, dean of Home Economics at Purdue University in Indiana, published *The House and its Care* in 1926. Matthews offered her book "for use in the senior high school and the junior college, or by the homemaker who desires practical information on these matters."[25] Maude Richman Clavert and Leila Bunce Smith published their *Advanced Course in Home Making* in 1939 with a forward by Boletha Frojen, supervisor of home-economics education, State of Florida, and insular supervisor of home-economics education for Puerto Rico.[26] These are only a few of the dozens, perhaps hundreds, of available home-economics texts in the early twentieth century.

Home-economics textbooks had a standardized form. Mary Lockwood Matthews's book of 1926, for example, included basic information about certain types of furniture. "A dressing table is designed for a woman's use," she explained. "It is a low table with drawers beneath, supporting a mirror or series of mirrors before which the woman sits on a stool or low-backed chair designed to match the dressing table. The mirror should be rectangular or square in shape."[27] Matthews went on to describe the kinds of articles that could be placed on a dressing table. She then led her readers on a room-by-room tour of the house, outlining rules of display and arrangement. "When the dining room table is not in use," she insisted, "all dishes and table linen should be removed and a doily should be placed at the center, on which may be set a bowl of flowers or some attractive piece of silver or china."[28] Most home-economics texts of the 1920s and 1930s gave similar advice. Their domestic fantasy was the well-ordered home, arranged according to certain principles of organization.

Home economists from all over the country had access to articles written by their colleagues for national journals and newsletters. Indeed, most state universities with Home Economics departments published their own bulletins and newsletters. These included more localized information and personalized advice. Margaret M. Justin and Lucille Osborn Rust, dean and professor of home economics at Kansas State University, made use of these sources. In their introduction to *Home Living* (1935), they recommended that their readers "gradually build up a personal collection of Home Economics bulletins from the State College, State University, United States Department of Agriculture, and good articles from the household magazines" and that this library would "help you solve your problems of home living."[29]

In 1935, the New York State College of Home Economics published its tenth annual report. Flora Rose, the director of the college, noted that most homemakers "are not always conscious . . . that a soiled rug, an inconvenient kitchen, a tired-out worker, or a splintery floor may be responsible directly or indirectly for increased poverty or ill health."[30] Through home bureaus in thirty-six counties in New York state, Rose and others believed that women could learn firsthand how to clean up their rugs, fix up their kitchens, and exchange the splintered, old-fashioned wooden floor for linoleum. The New York college's annual report, like those from most states with significant rural populations, betrayed a strong belief in the power of home economics to solve most every social problem. The 1935 report pointed out that home-economics teachings had helped rural New Yorkers get through the Depression. They agreed that "home Economics should be of great service in the progress of civilization."[31]

Domestic advisors tried to make home economics accessible and even fun. Ethel Peyser's 1922 household manual *Cheating the Junk Pile: The Purchase and Maintenance of Household Equipments* appeared first in serial form in the women's magazine *House and Garden*. Her book educated women in the languages of electricity and "vacuum cleanerese." She coined the word "domiologist" to mean "home scientist." Peyser compared the work of domiologists to the health profession when she said they practiced "hospital efficiency" in the home. She quite self-consciously used words like "scientist" and "hospital" to relate her domestic texts to the ideals of home economics.[32] However, Peyser, whose other books covered the history of music and opera, was not a home economist, and she claimed her "book is in no way intended to be a book on household efficiency, in the usual sense of the world—it is no religio-culinaris, no domestic Baedecker."[33] Instead, her text brought home economics out of the academy and tried to make it friendly.

Many advisors agreed with Peyser that the ideas of home science should be accessible to all women, even if they did not study home economics formally. Most home economists, indeed, believed that women should learn about all the branches of industry and life that affected the home. As Peyser noted in 1922, "Neither the employment of women in war-work nor the radical challenges of the ultra-feminist has altered the fundamental fact that the home is women's realm."[34] In the early twentieth century, home economists and other household advisors began to broaden that realm through civic and community efforts and by speaking to women as corporate sponsors. Their efforts continued through the rest of the twentieth century, and even today.

"The household, in its evolution of related industries, is the parent of the state," wrote Helen Campbell in her *Household Economics* of 1896.[35] She believed that women who understood the workings of their homes would be better prepared to understand the laws that affected their homes, such as gas and electric regulations and food sanitation. She argued that women should learn about several "industries, all growing out of household life and needs."[36] To Campbell, home economics was "the link between the physical economics of the individual and the social economics of the state."[37]

Domestic advisors understood that the home could be a way for women to participate in national debates and policy making. They felt that women, considered to have expertise in only limited areas, needed to focus on the home in order to be heard in the larger public arena. In 1912, Marion Talbot and Sophonisba Breckinridge described how women's influence over the household should include influence over various government groups and industries.

> The housekeeper shall be present either in her own person or in the person of her agent where the food of her family is prepared. She must inspect the farm from which her milk is brought to the city, the

dairy in which it is prepared, the trains on which it is transported, the centers from which it is distributed. She must take part in the decision as to the standard required, the method of enforcement devised, the rate at which that standard shall be raised. . . . When she sees how her presence is needed in all the places which have been named, she "will arise and go" to the polling booths, to the city hall, to the factory, to the school . . . to all the places where those who prepare and serve her food and make her clothing work and live. . . . All of this will grow out of her realization that a woman's presence is demanded throughout the range of interests which constitute her home.[38]

Domestic scientists believed that women should understand the business and technological aspects of their work, always keeping the focus on the household. Once women understood this, they needed to use that knowledge beyond the home. The home formed only one piece of a larger puzzle in which active connections, made with the help of the new sciences, became essential. Women, as household managers, could play increasingly important roles in this new social order.

Talbot and Breckinridge called for political participation by women. "She will appropriate the ballot as a domestic necessity," they wrote in 1912, eight years before national suffrage for women.[39] However, they couched their prosuffrage position in domestic terms, believing that women needed the ballot because of their natural interest and responsibility for home life. The history of home economics is complicated because its proponents believed both in the strong connection between women and the home and in the participation of women in new industries and political groups. The presence of women in civic-leadership roles, such as Sophonisba Breckinridge in Chicago, and in corporate leadership roles, such as the home economists of Corning Glass Works and Armour Foods, brought women new career opportunities. But the home, now a place of science and technology, remained women's sphere.

Kitchen efficiency became the focus of many women's clubs around the country. The popular magazine *The Modern Priscilla* founded the Priscilla Club of Domestic Science for Everyday Housekeepers. Writing about the club in 1915, director Henrietta Grauel claimed that "women are growing more sensible each day in the selection of their working tools and the management of their workrooms."[40] Experiment stations blossomed in the 1920s and remained popular for several decades. These stations brought the ideas of domestic advisors more authority because the public could view their experiments and understand their results.

Christine Frederick ran a model kitchen called the Applecroft Experiment Station at her home on Long Island in the 1920s. Frederick, born in 1883, graduated from Northwestern University in 1906. She opened her experiment station after marrying, having children, and considering the problems of homemakers firsthand. During the 1920s, Frederick toured the United States and Europe, giving lectures about home efficiency and management. As consulting household editor for the *Ladies' Home Journal* for nine years, Frederick answered up to a thousand letters weekly from women asking questions about "devices and appliances with which to make possible this 'new housekeeping.'"[41] She used her "experiment station" to demonstrate which new appliances could be useful for housewives and which would not end up saving women time in the kitchen.

Frederick tested many different kinds of kitchen and home products at Applecroft. One of these, a pulley-operated cellar icebox, eliminated the need for women to keep walking up and down stairs.[42] Others included labor-saving devices and new kitchen arrangements. "Housekeepers will be surprised," she wrote, "how fascinating it is to make over their own into 'Efficiency Kitchens,' and how easily and with but a few changes they can convert them into modern step-saving and sanitary 'home workshops.'"[43] This essay, a promotional piece for "Vollrath ware" kitchen accessories, made efficiency seem easy and sensible. Frederick used Applecroft as a way to teach herself and other women how to operate efficient kitchens through experimentation and testing. She published diagrams of efficient kitchens and encouraged women to change their own households to conform with her ideas.

Christine Frederick's emphasis on efficiency was part of a larger movement for scientific management that became popular in the United States in the 1920s and 1930s. Lillian and Frank Gilbreth, along with Frederick Taylor, led the movement for scientific management in the United States. Taylorism, as efficiency was colloquially known, concentrated on making the factory workplace more efficient. Taylor's *Principles of Scientific Management* of 1911 had been used to organize management hierarchies. By seeking to understand the different personal reasons for various work-related actions, they hoped to crystalize to the most basic elements of each particular movement. The Gilbreths employed specialized photography systems to record

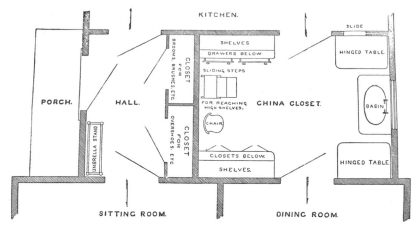

Maria Parloa's Kitchen Companion *of 1887 included a chapter on "an Ideal Kitchen" in which she discussed the need for a separate room to store dishes and dry foods. The room, almost as large as the kitchen itself, was filled with such modern conveniences as a copper basin for washing, and it included thoughtful additions like a chair to stand on to reach the high shelves. Parloa noted that "in case there be two or more servants in the household, the door from the closet to the kitchen need not be opened at all while a meal is served" since there was an opening to pass plates between the storage room and the kitchen. (Parloa,* Miss Parloa's Kitchen Companion, *26; courtesy* The Winterthur Library, Printed Book and Periodical Collection)

every action and to cut down each task to its fewest possible movements. Lillian Gilbreth, Christine Frederick, and others transferred the techniques of scientific management to the home.

Lillian Gilbreth is best known as the mother of the *Cheaper by the Dozen* children. Her large family was the subject of many news articles and stories, and her son and daughter wrote a best-selling book about the antics of the dozen Gilbreth children growing up with the scientific-management movement in their home. Gilbreth published an account of her marriage titled *The Quest for the One Best Way* in 1925 and followed that with *The Homemaker and Her Job* in 1927. Both books illustrated her belief that women could work to improve themselves by learning the most efficient way to do home cleaning and cooking. Not a home economist by trade, Gilbreth held two doctoral degrees, including one in psychology from Brown University. Her careful work with home efficiency earned her speaking engagements across the country, and it continues to influence the way kitchens are built in modern homes.

"Home Taylorists" usually concentrated on the kitchen as a good

[*The Rise of the Domiologist*]

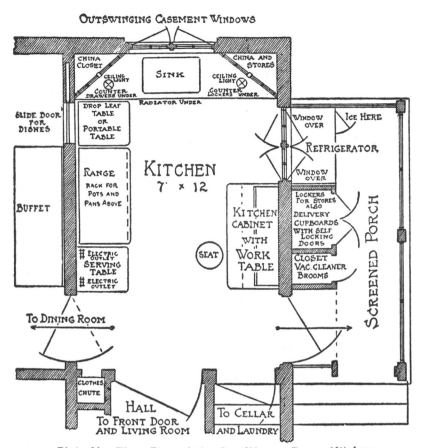

OUTSWINGING CASEMENT WINDOWS

CHINA CLOSET

CHINA AND STORES

SINK

CEILING LIGHT

CEILING LIGHT

COUNTER DRAWERS UNDER

COUNTER LOCKERS UNDER

SLIDE DOOR FOR DISHES

DROP LEAF TABLE OR PORTABLE TABLE

RADIATOR UNDER

WINDOW OVER

ICE HERE

REFRIGERATOR

BUFFET

RANGE

RACK FOR POTS AND PANS ABOVE

KITCHEN
7' × 12

WINDOW OVER

LOCKERS FOR STORES ALSO

DELIVERY CUPBOARDS WITH SELF LOCKING DOORS

SCREENED PORCH

KITCHEN CABINET
WITH
WORK TABLE

SEAT

CLOSET VAC. CLEANER BROOMS

ELECTRIC OUTLET
SERVING TABLE
ELECTRIC OUTLET

TO DINING ROOM

CLOTHES CHUTE

HALL
TO FRONT DOOR AND LIVING ROOM

TO CELLAR
AND LAUNDRY

Plate 61.—Floor Plan of the One Woman-Power Kitchen

Ross Crane, Chicago architect and decorator, included a diagram of the "one woman power kitchen" in his 1933 text. The phrase, used as early as 1925 by the editors of the Modern Priscilla, *demonstrated the modern understanding that middle-class women would be doing their own kitchen work. The power kitchen, more efficient than the nineteenth-century model, included an area for china and a convenient drop-leaf table. However, the slidethrough in this example went directly to the dining room. The kitchen also included windows and extra light fixtures to make the room more cheerful.* (Crane, Ross Crane Book of Home Furnishing and Decoration, 24; *courtesy* The Winterthur Library, Printed Book and Periodical Collection)

site to improve home efficiency. Gilbreth's search for the "one best way" in the kitchen began with charts and graphs outlining every possible physical movement. For a study of dish washing, Gilbreth "cross sectioned the sink, walls, and floor, as we were anxious to see what motions the worker made with her feet." She photographed the movements of several different dishwashers, then lined up the film negatives to observe which worker had the most efficient ideas. "We can then select all the shortest and best elements and combine them in a new chart into the One Best Way,"[44] she explained. With the chart placed within easy sight of the sink, the worker could refer to it periodically.

Lillian Gilbreth designed at least five demonstration kitchens. Her "continuous" kitchen, a series of linear workspaces, emulated the efficient factory. One of her basic demands was for appropriate heights for kitchen counters and workspaces. Suggested as early as 1888 by Sallie Joy White, who wrote that "the height of the working-table" was the cause of "the constant strain on the muscles across the small of the back,"[45] the appropriate height for kitchen counters still had not taken hold in all kitchens in the 1920s. Fitting every woman to her own kitchen would be impossible, but the notion that kitchen-counter heights should be appropriately high to reduce strain on necks and backs was indeed an important concern. Gilbreth's ideas were tested by other home economists who published photographs of "test kitchen" women in white laboratory coats demonstrating the back strain induced by incorrect counter heights.[46]

Gilbreth received wide acclaim for her work. Her "wide practical knowledge," wrote Greta Gray in an essay titled "The Kitchen" in 1931, "leads her to insist that every kitchen should be individually arranged to suit the height . . . of the woman destined to be its mistress."[47] Gray used a statement issued by Hildegarde Kneeland of the United States Bureau of Home Economics about Gilbreth's kitchen, outlining the "five major requirements": "Separate working surfaces, Arrangement of large equipment, Compact working area, Convenient heights from the floor, Grouping of small equipment around the working center."[48] Home economist Elizabeth Burris-Meyer commented that "the modern domestic-science kitchen, with all its machinery, is really a laboratory . . . and as such should not be cluttered up with the knickknacks of the old wood-burning stove days." Burris-Meyer admitted that the old type of kitchen held a certain "charm," but she was unwavering in her support for Gilbreth and the efficiency kitchen. "The quaintness of the old kitchen cannot be introduced into the modern one without making both seem out of place," she wrote.[49] She saw the new kitchen as progress and recommended that her readers not look back. The *Modern Priscilla Home Furnishing Book* in 1925 dubbed the new, "comfortable, convenient, efficient" modern kitchen a "One Woman Power Kitchen."[50]

Corporate test kitchens provided home economists with unique opportunities to communicate with other women about domestic-science matters. Many companies with home-related products, such as food, paint, dishware, and linoleum, used domestic advisors to reach out to the public and recommend their goods. Kraft foods, Sears and Roebuck, and Piggly-Wiggly food stores all hired home economists in the early twentieth century.[51] This relationship gave the corporations credibility with female consumers and helped boost sales. Popular etiquette and household-advice writer Emily Post was featured as a home expert on the *Cellophane Radio Show* sponsored by DuPont in the early 1930s. The company hoped her expertise would convince housewives of the significance of the new moisture-proof film. The advisors appeared in advertisements and brochures, dispensing advice and recommending the company's products. These successful partnerships continued through the twentieth century, and many companies still use home economists to communicate with their female consumers.[52]

In 1917, Armour and Company, manufacturers of "choice food products," hired Jean Prescott Adams as a domestic science director. She wrote a booklet titled *The Business of Being a Housewife* for them, which was coedited by the director of the Good Housekeeping Institute.[53] The collaboration with domestic advisors was important to the credibility of Armour Foods. In turn, Adams's connection to the business world gave her a wider audience for her ideas. Echoing the words of Marion Talbot, she wrote that "questions of pure foods and Government Meat Inspection are of great importance" to the housewife, because "the responsibility for the health and well-being of the family is hers." As the Armour trade manual stated, "The distribution and spending of the family income is largely in the hands of the housewife." Advisors trained in domestic science declared that the housewife had a responsibility to educate herself about the various companies and industries that brought food and other products into her home. Adams claimed that "in this connection the Armour Department of Domestic Science . . . is a most active aid."[54]

Jean Adams used the platform of the Armour booklet to develop some ideas about kitchen decoration. Under the watchful eye of the Good Housekeeping Institute, she recommended placing the kitchen equipment "at the proper height," and she included ideas about church suppers and auto parties. So as not to bore women with too many rules about meat inspection, she also wrote about paint color in the home. "When buffs and light soft browns and yellows are used on the wall and woodwork," she claimed, veering away from a discussion of bullion cubes, "the restful light relieves eyestrain."[55] Tempering her expectations of community involvement with recommendations for paint color was a way for domestic scientists to reach their readers.

Test kitchens allowed corporations to discover how their products could best be used by the public. Perhaps the most famous and long-lasting test kitchen was the "Good Housekeeping Experiment Station," set up in 1900, which later became the "Good Housekeeping Institute."[56] The Good Housekeeping Institute, then as now, tested products and services in test kitchens and, if the product passed the test, awarded the "Good Housekeeping Seal of Approval." The seal demonstrated to consumers that the product had survived the rigorous testing and could be trusted by the American public. Good Housekeeping modeled behavior and products in the household setting.

One of the most successful corporate-domestic scientist relationships was between Corning Glass Works and home economist Lucy Maltby. Maltby, who had an undergraduate degree in home economics from Cornell University and a master of arts degree in the subject from Iowa State College, had worked as a home-economics teacher. She approached Corning in 1929 with the notion that their product line of Pyrex glass would be greatly helped by the insights of women consumer experts and home economists. That same year, she was hired to build a Home Economics Department at Corning, a company she worked with for close to four decades.[57] Maltby helped Corning reach out to female consumers and produce successful lines of cookware.

A basic tenet of scientific-domestic fantasy was that home-economics education would benefit home life. However, it was also thought that home-economics education, and specifically women's knowledge about the home, could benefit the larger world. Lucy Maltby thought that she and other educated women understood Pyrex dishes on a level that neither the chemists nor the corporate executives at Corning (men, all) could ever hope to match. Maltby and others helped Corning move its glassworks department into consumer products in the 1920s by convincing them that heat-resistant glass would sell. The new glass was unbreakable and allowed easy cleaning. Food smells would not stick to the glassware, easing concerns about germs and grime. Corning began to market Pyrex to middle-class women by emphasizing its housekeeper-friendly characteristics.[58] Readers of domestic advice would understand the ways that the new products could fit into their fantasies of the scientific home. Home economists helped

Home economists tested every new product at Corning Incorporated. This image from 1946 depicts several home economists in their white laboratory coats at the main plant's test kitchen. Corning believed that home economists could help them manufacture products that would sell to female consumers. Photographs such as this one, often appearing in newsletters and in other publications, helped convince consumers that Corning's products could be trusted in the kitchen. (Courtesy Corning Incorporated Department of Archives and Records Management, Corning, N.Y.)

build bridges between the academic world, the political world, the corporate world, and middle-class women.

In 1905, a young woman named Frederica Shanks took a course in household arts at Roxbury High School in Boston, Massachusetts. Her class notes provide a wonderful example of the way in which domestic science entered the lives of the generation of American women who came of age in the first few decades of the twentieth century.[59] Frederica studied many topics in her class, including planning and building the house, furnishings and decorating, lighting, heating, plumbing, water supply and disposal of waste, cleaning, laundry work, and study of foods.[60] She read *Home Economics* by Maria Parloa, studied the works of Ellen Richards and Lillie Hamilton French, and also read Eugene Gardner, author of *The House That Jill Built*. Her notes included information on house construction and sanitary concerns, as well as on ornamentation and decorating. Shanks's notebook indicates that girls and women in school did indeed read the works of domestic advisors and that they learned and thought about scientific issues in the home.

Frederica took notes from her readings and class discussions. She pasted photographs and drawings from various texts into her notebook, perhaps to fulfil an assignment or because she particularly liked certain arrangements. The pages of her notebook show that she covered some subjects in detail, such as the benefits of certain materials. "Linoleum is expensive and endurable," she wrote in her section on floor coverings. "It is cork pressed into a fine powder and mixed with a kind of linseed oil. It is then pressed on to a piece of burlap and then painted." She also wrote about different types of carpets, citing the good and bad aspects of each. She studied the rules of gradation of color, learning the rule that the lighter color should go on the ceiling, and she studied the history of certain rooms including the living room, which descended from the European common hall. "The living-room means a room where the particular individual taste is collected," she noted. "In this room are a large table, chairs. . . . A fire-place and others [*sic*] things representing comfort and rest."[61]

What did students such as Frederica Shanks learn about the scientific aspects of domestic advice? Though home economics curricula did include the traditional sewing, cooking, and cleaning, in fact, students and general readers of domestic advice also learned about technical aspects of drainage, plumbing, and ventilation. Shanks also learned practical hints for day-to-day operation of the kitchen. She noted that "water can be polluted by a leakage in the pipes or cesspools" and learned three ways to purify the water (boiling, distilling, and filtering). The teacher made sure the students knew that there was reason to worry given that at "about the middle of last century there was an epidemic of cholera and all the deseases [*sic*] were traced back to a well at Broad St."[62] Home-economics teachers believed that housewives needed to take responsibility for making sure their families drank clean water. At the turn of the twentieth century, girls in school learned the steps necessary to make that happen.

Shanks's notebook indicates that she probably saw a diagram similar to the one presented by Harriette Plunkett in her *Women, Plumbers, and Doctors: or, Household Sanitation* of 1885. Plunkett was the editor of the "sanitary department" at the New York *Independent,* and Helen Campbell noted in her 1896 *Household Economics* that Plunkett's book "is one of the best sanitary hand-books in existence."[63] Ellen Richards

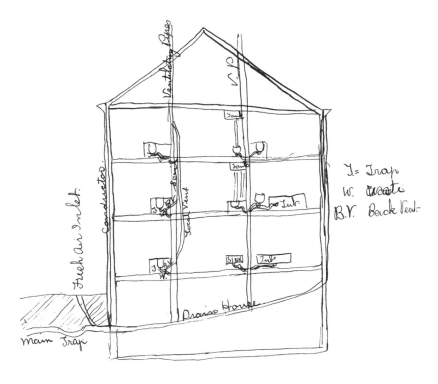

In Frederica Shanks's home economics course, she probably saw a plumbing diagram similar to the one featured in Harriette Plunkett's book. Shanks's drawing of house plumbing and drainage is quite similar and indicates that books on home sanitation found their way into high-school classrooms at the turn of the century. Teaching girls about vents, traps, and pipes widened their knowledge from home decorating to the inner workings of the household. (Courtesy The Winterthur Library, Joseph Downs Collection of Manuscripts and Printed Ephemera, no. 85 × 62)

and Marion Talbot included this same drawing in their 1911 edition of *Home Sanitation*. This diagram, "a plan of the system of pipes," and others like it, helped train American women about the basics of household plumbing.

The diagram represented a cross section of a typical house. It included pipes, such as the rainwater pipe and the overflow pipe, and the placement of sinks, laundry tubs, and bathtubs. Referring to the

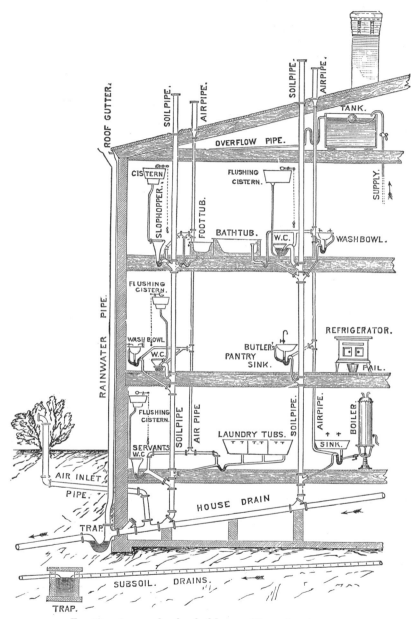

Fig. 17.—A properly plumbed house—Woman's sphere.

plan, Talbot and Richards noted: "The *soil pipe* conveys the contents of water-closets and urinals to the house-drain. It may also receive the contents of waste-pipes. The *waste-pipes* carry other refuse fluids, as of tubs, sinks, washbowls, etc., only. These pipes may discharge either directly into the house-drain, or into the soil-pipe. The *house-drain* is the pipe which receives the contents of the soil and waste pipes, and conveys them outside the house. It is nearly horizontal, with an inclination of at least one in fifty, while the soil-pipe should be vertical."[64] When these home economists and their colleagues wrote that women's sphere included all of the city services that affected the home, they meant it. They wrote their textbooks to instruct high-school students like Frederica Shanks, as well as older American women, about the scientific properties of their homes.

Lessons on home construction often led to discussion about ventilation and fresh air. Marion Talbot and Ellen Richards warned their readers to let air in through the windows: "[Windows] are for the purpose of admitting light, and sometimes air," they wrote. "This purpose cannot be accomplished where, as is not uncommon, they are barricaded with two sets of blinds, two sets of shades, and lace curtains or heavy draperies. If their owners would take away half these barriers and leave the others raised and open, the good cheer and vigorous life which stream in with the sunshine would speedily convert regret at the loss into rejoicing at the greater gain."[65] Home economists joined with other health officials and the general public in the late-nineteenth and early-twentieth-century belief that fresh air was the key to good health. Their role as household advisors meant they translated this belief into concrete instructions for the home.

The hunt for pure air dominated domestic-advice manuals for much of the late nineteenth and early twentieth centuries. Even the Beecher sisters wrote about ventilation: "The most successful mode of ventilating a house is by creating a current of warm air in a flue."[66] Their chap-

Harriette Plunkett, seeking to show that "if women and plumbers do their whole sanitary duty, there will be comparatively little occasion for the services of the doctors," published a detailed analysis of home sanitation in 1885. Her diagram, in a chapter on sewerage and plumbing, demonstrated the ways that water should flow through the house, providing several outlets for waste and appropriate drainage. The sketch, captioned "Woman's Sphere," was reprinted in several books including Ellen Richards and Marion Talbot's Home Sanitation *of 1887. (Plunkett,* Women, Plumbers, and Doctors, *112; courtesy The Winterthur Library, Printed Book and Periodical Collection)*

ter on "scientific domestic ventilation" included drawings of ventilating tubes, such as those employed in mines, and it explained various methods used by chemistry laboratories and other places with poor ventilation. The Beechers understood clearly that only "a few of the more intelligent and wealthy" had employed recent advances in household ventilation.[67] The chapter concluded with the hope that "any intelligent woman who has read this work" could guarantee proper ventilation in her own home.

To domestic advisors, scientific ventilation meant that fresh air would come into the household, unrestricted by heavy window textiles. They pushed their readers to lose the heavy curtains, heavy rugs, and heavy bedclothes of the nineteenth century. For them, fresh air epitomized good health, and they would be the harbingers of fresh air into the home. All the scientific language, such as diagrams of pipes and the use of words such as "ventilation" instead of just "air," expressed the same basic idea. One of the most fundamental goals of scientific-domestic fantasy was to make "fresh air" into a positive attribute, one that American women would yearn to bring to their own households.

As the twentieth century progressed, Americans transferred the belief in fresh air into other parts of their lives. President Theodore Roosevelt began to establish national parks across the country to encourage Americans to enjoy the great outdoors. With the increased use of automobiles, outdoor camping and hiking became more accessible to many Americans. Fresh air was an important theme in American culture in the first few decades of the twentieth century, and domestic advisors picked up on this idea. When Virginia Terhune Van de Water, nineteenth-century household advisor Marion Harland's daughter, suggested household exercise in 1912, she recommended that women "take the exercise with the window open" for added benefit.[68]

All over the country, health officials opened fresh-air schools. In these special schools, students afflicted with tuberculosis wrapped themselves in many layers and huddled by the stove with the windows wide open to let in the invigorating air. Because tuberculosis afflicted the lungs, exposure to clean air could prolong the life of the patient by removing some of the contaminants. Desperate for a cure, families embraced the ideas of the fresh-air movement and endured cold temperatures in the hopes that the air would restore their health. City officials even began to incorporate the fresh-air theory into many civic build-

[*The Rise of the Domiologist*]

ing projects, providing outdoor waiting rooms at train stations, for example. Though relatively short-lived as a national trend, the fresh-air movement did make its way into countless domestic-advice manuals.

Domestic advisors expanded the doctrine of fresh air beyond its use as treatment for tuberculosis patients. Maria Parloa cautioned that bedrooms carried the most risk for the family. "The beds should be thoroughly aired every morning," she warned in a *Good Housekeeping* article titled "Stuffy Homes: How to Avoid Having Them" and "the sheets, blankets, pillows and mattresses so disposed that there shall be a current of air about them; and if possible they should be exposed to the sunshine."[69] The advice was often simple: Open the windows. "A great volume of pure air sweeping through the house," wrote Parloa in *Household Economics*, "will in ten minutes remove the impure air more effectually than airing for an hour or more with windows only partly opened."[70]

Advisors worried that bedrooms contained stagnant, impure air. They recommended that children spend their days outside, or at least out of the bedroom, so as to get fresh air and sunshine. Domestic advisor Agnes Bailey Ormsbee wrote about children's rooms in 1892: "A room with the windows opening to the south is the best for the nursery. While this cannot always be commanded, one with a northern outlook is to be avoided. Such a room is cheerless, cold, and unhealthful. A chamber is also better than a ground-floor room, as it is less likely to be damp, and the floor will be much warmer. Great care should be taken with the ventilation of this room, where children are to spend so many hours, and it should not also be used for a sleeping-room when such use is avoidable."[71] Ormsbee and other advisors worried about the health hazards of the average household. For women reading these texts who had no other access to ideas about what caused disease, these suggestions could be valuable.

Advisors often used fresh flowers to demonstrate the importance of light and air in the home. Because cut flowers lived or died depending on the conditions of the household, they could be used as thermometers to rate the air quality. "The first essential test for a cheerful room is sunshine," began Susan Anna Brown in 1881. "Flowers cannot blossom in [a dark room,] neither will people. Nobody knows how many men and women have been killed by dark rooms."[72] Lillie Hamilton French eloquently described the sensation of entering a home "filled with growing plants," which would assure visitors that the house was properly warmed and ventilated. "On entering a room where flowers flourish . . . you recognize instinctively the existence of heat. You realize that unless it were warm the flowers would droop."[73] Flowers brought life and health into the home and could be used to convince visitors that the homemaker practiced those scientific principles that allowed life to flourish.

At the turn of the twentieth century, domestic advisors stepped up their attack on dirt and disease.[74] Ideas about where germs could hide in the house began to scare advisors into ever more frenzied cleanliness. "Many draperies are not to be desired," wrote Agnes Bailey Ormsbee in 1892; "they catch and hold dust and infection most successfully."[75] Including infection as one of the dangers of thick textiles indicated that advisors paid attention to national debates about health. In 1918, Lucia Millet Baxter linked curtains and disease when she lamented that "it is deplorable that so many houses are kept dark by draperies and blinds." She urged her readers to walk through the city and notice how many houses continued to block all light with unnecessarily thick blinds. "Who knows what demons of disease may be lurking in the dark corners within?" she asked.[76]

Most home economists and other domestic advisors joined together in their call for the removal of textiles from the home. The thick brocades of the nineteenth century attracted insects and dust, and the layers of textiles on all the windows negated the good qualities that windows could bring to a home. However, this demand proved difficult for most American women. Fabric in the home had long been a marker of social class, and middle-class homes in the nineteenth century used their textiles as symbols of moderate wealth. Just as in their attempts to eradicate the parlor from the domestic vocabulary, advisors worked against a strong tide. While households became more reserved and unadorned as the twentieth century progressed, textile removal was a battle that the advisors won slowly. They did their best to make simplified homes seem appealing, and they pressed on with their admonition that textiles and stuffy houses bred disease. "Woolen stuffs absorb dust and odors," wrote Maria Parloa in 1910. "They should not be used if they cannot be subjected to frequent dusting and airing."[77]

Scientists proved that disease-causing germs could be present even when invisible to the naked eye. Advocates of the "germ theory" of disease identified microorganisms as the cause of disease and proposed that these germs could spread from a single source. In the 1890s, public-health officials began to identify dust as a new danger given that it could serve as a hiding place for tuberculosis germs. The germ theory, established by European scientists Louis Pasteur and Robert Koch in the 1870s and 1880s, took several decades to make an impact on ordinary Americans. But in the decades after the turn of the century, domestic advisors did their best to help spread the information to American women.[78]

As the decades progressed and scientists learned more about how germs spread contagious disease, the cleanliness instructions took on more urgency. Mary Krout, an advisor who wrote *Platters and Pipkins* in 1910, warned her readers to pay attention to the new theories: "There are still some doughty souls who have not been intimidated by the hue and cry after microbes. They still cling desperately to their carpets fastened down with tacks. But the change to rugs and polished floors which I appear to have emphasized with perhaps tiresome iteration, *is* an incalculable improvement, and it is an object to which the truly public-spirited may devote their energies with profit to the country at large in order that the fashion may be universally adopted and remain."[79] Against the odds, advisors tried to inform their readers about the real dangers lurking in their curtains and other textiles. Though most Americans kept their carpets and curtains well into the twentieth century, the domestic-advice manuals and home magazines continued their campaign.

"The use of upholstered furniture or of heavy woolen draperies . . . should be reduced to the lowest possible point," wrote Ellen Richards and Marion Talbot in 1911.[80] They continued their attack on domestic textiles: "Carpets entirely covering the floor cannot be kept thoroughly clean, and are, moreover, a constant temptation to the economical housewife to exclude the sun. Mattings and loosely woven carpets allow dust to sift through them to the floor beneath, whence it cannot be removed. Hard polished or painted floors, with rugs, are preferable to carpets or mattings. And the amount of care required by bare floors is little more than that demanded by carpets which, to be thoroughly cleaned, must be taken up at each annual or semi-annual housecleaning."[81] These demands featured the strong desire of home scientists to redesign the middle-class household. In this domestic fantasy, women would approach the decoration of their parlors armed with effective suggestions for scientific housekeeping.

Wicker and other unupholstered furniture enjoyed popularity with home economists concerned about dust. Wicker furniture first became popular during the late Victorian era in the 1870s and 1880s. Brought to American markets by Cyrus Wakefield, who, the story goes, found

"Willow furniture is another class which is very popular and which has a distinct use in many modern homes," wrote Amy Rolfe in her 1917 domestic-advice manual. She illustrated her discussion with this photograph depicting a "sun parlor" filled with wicker furnishings. Rockers, armchairs, and couches all made use of the durable and easily cleaned material. (Rolfe, Interior Decoration for the Small Home, *104)*

extra rattan lying around on a Boston wharf and suddenly realized its potential for furniture, wicker came into fashion because of its ornamental qualities. Soon, Wakefield, whose rattan company merged with Heywood Brothers' furniture company in 1897, manufactured wicker furniture for porches, baby carriages, and invalid chairs. Its elaborate curves and curlycues appealed to many women and men in the nineteenth century. But it also had twentieth-century appeal. Wicker furniture woven from rattan, cane, bamboo, and willow was easy to clean and did not attract dust as much as fabric-covered furniture. Often used for outdoor spaces such as porches, wicker encouraged people to sit outside, in the fresh air. Advisors thought of wicker as natural, clean, and a promoter of outdoor living. They often included the material in their discussions of "camp" furniture in summer settings.

Walking a line between fashion and science, advisors found ways to appeal to their readers. They tried to find examples of items that women might want in their homes and to explain which ones could be safely included in the hygienic, sanitary household of the twentieth century. Wicker furniture in the nineteenth century represented elaborate design in a relatively cheap product. Twentieth-century advisors, seeing the popularity of the furniture, seized on wicker (and its materials, rattan, cane, and willow) as a perfect substitute for over-upholstered furniture. Willow, wrote the editors of the *Modern Priscilla Home Furnishing Book* in 1925, "is good-looking, comfortable, inexpensive, and most of all not at all hurt by moisture; you can, in fact, turn the hose on it and give it a good scrubbing when it is soiled." [82]

Rooms where food was prepared and served provided special sanitary concerns. Because the dining room was full of both food and furniture, advisors took special precautions. In the nineteenth century, many advisors had recommended that the dining room be decorated with a man's taste in mind. This continued into the twentieth century, and modern advisors used science and disease as further excuses to rid the room of excess textiles and feminine touches. "Do not have couches with cushions or stuffed chairs in this room," wrote Mabel Hyde Kitt-redge. "The room in which we eat must be sanitary, and furniture that collects dust is never really free from the possibility of germs." [83] Advisors used words like "germs" freely, scaring their readers into changing the ways they decorated their homes. "So much of the health and comfort of the family depends on the kitchen," wrote Maria Parloa, "that the most careful thought must be given to its furnishing." [84] *House and Garden* noted in 1919, "A sanitary kitchen means less work. . . . A sanitary kitchen is more pleasant to work in; its white walls radiate an atmosphere of cheer." [85]

Luckily for twentieth-century advisors, the field of household science helped bring about a consumer revolution of sanitary home products. Whereas Catharine Beecher had recommended oilcloth for kitchen floors in the 1860s, advisors of the 1920s began to recommend new materials, such as linoleum. [86] Because of its sanitary qualities, linoleum became a popular item in domestic manuals. "Linoleum is the best yet for hall floors," wrote Lois Palmer in 1928. The material could "retain its good appearance and [was] easy to care for." [87] A decorative, easily cleaned, and widely available floor covering, linoleum played to the advisors' favorite theme of sanitation. As *The Modern Priscilla Home Furnishing Book* declared in 1925, "Linoleums are comfortable, economical and sanitary, and they come in many patterns and colors." [88]

In the 1920s and 1930s, readers could learn about linoleum from many domestic-advice sources. Blanche Halbert, home economist from the University of Chicago, featured a chapter titled "Wall and Floor Finishes and Coverings." "Linoleum is made of linseed oil and

Agnes Foster Wright, in her 1924 text for Armstrong Cork, provided examples of how linoleum could be used throughout the home. This image featured a "spotless kitchen, with its shiny, waxed and polished linoleum floor." The room, shown with a whistling teapot ready to provide a comforting snack for the folks in the friendly breakfast nook, demonstrated that modern technology and kitchen sanitation could coexist with homey charm. The booklet was filled with images of linoleum in almost every room in the house, demonstrating the usefulness of the sanitary material. (Wright, Floors, Furniture and Color, *40; courtesy The Winterthur Library, Printed Book and Periodical Collection)*

ground cork. It is mixed to a plastic mass and applied to a burlap backing." She praised linoleum for its "qualities of sanitation, low maintenance cost, and durability." But linoleum was not only recommended for its practicality. The Armstrong Cork Company hired successful decorator Agnes Foster Wright to produce a trade manual in 1924 called *Floors, Furniture and Color*. Wright, a former president of the Interior Decorator's League of New York, suggested different patterns for each room in the house. The booklet noted that, "while linoleum is not a new product, its present day recognition as a modern floor material . . . is due in large part to the recent developments in floor design."[89]

The consumer goods available due to the rise in sanitary housekeeping did not stop with linoleum. In the first few decades of the twentieth century, advertising aimed at women promised sanitary qualities in everything from white porcelain toilets to countertops.[90]

Home economist Christine Frederick noted in 1929 that many women did not fully understand the science behind the theories, but that they purchased sanitary products in any case. "I know many college educated women who are still very hazy as to what the germ theory is," she wrote in *Selling Mrs. Consumer,* "but you may be sure that in their daily family work they meticulously act upon the assumption that germs must be outwitted. The mounting sales of antiseptics and germicides surely prove this."[91]

Companies such as Corning and DuPont saw many uses for their new inventions beyond the laboratory. Helped along by home economists, they began to develop products specifically for the home and for women. DuPont's celluloid plastic and colorful laquers found their way into kitchen products. Originally intended only for decorative purposes, DuPont also marketed cellophane for food storage once it was made moisture-resistant.[92] All of these products, like Corning's Pyrex glass, appealed to the consumer who had read about the sanitary concerns of domestic advisors. The new plastics and glasses could be heated, cooled, cleaned, and cared for with relative ease.

By the 1920s, sanitation was as synonymous with the future as dust and disease were with the past. In 1925, the forward-looking *Modern Priscilla Home Furnishing Book* exclaimed that, "dingy mid-Victorian interiors went with the frail and fainting feminine type that was also the mode of the period. . . . Dyspepsia and other ills flourished in the depressing darkened rooms of the Gothic revival. Modern days have taught us the value, mental and physical, of plenty of air and sunlight."[93] Linking disease directly to the nineteenth-century home, advisors created a connection between the modern, scientific twentieth century and good health. In so doing, they expanded women's roles from managing their own homes to making connections between individual homes and the wider social context of the communities in which they existed.

In turn-of-the-century America, women brought science into the home. Home economists and other domestic advisors wrote countless textbooks filled with the domestic fantasies of correct drainage, pure air, and sanitary surfaces. "The object of this manual," wrote Ellen Richards and Marion Talbot in the introductory chapter to *Home Sanitation,* "is to arouse the interest of housekeepers in the sanitary conditions of their homes." Though the book was filled with the dire consequences of misuse of textiles, furniture, and pipes, they noted: "In thus pointing out the sources of danger, and the ideal standards of sanitation in the perfectly healthful house, the compilers do not intend unnecessarily to alarm or discourage the householder. It is their aim to urge the intelligent oversight of these matters, and to indicate the points requiring investigation, the methods of examination, and the practical remedies."[94] Richards, Talbot, and the other home economists believed that their books would inspire middle-class American women to strengthen their houses, and through them, their communities and the entire country, with scientific knowledge.

Chapter 3

AMERICANIZATION, MODEL HOMES,

AND LACE CURTAINS

One of the two girls who were told to set the table was a little Russian Jewess. Her fingers were all thumbs and she didn't know what dishes the different things required. The other girl was a brisk little American who corrected the other's mistakes.

"The table looks crowded to me," said the Jewish girl to the American girl.

"It looks alright to me," the American girl answered.

"No wonder she thinks there is too much on the table," the teacher whispered. "Sophie's people practically never sit down to a meal, they are just on the edge of destitution and eat whenever and wherever they can get the food." For Sophie, the simple school lunch established a standard of luxury. To establish home standards is the most important work the public school can do, and these standards can be most directly and most unconsciously established through the study of housekeeping.
—Martha Bensley Bruere, Increasing Home Efficiency

In 1912, Martha Bensley Bruere set out to demonstrate the national importance of household education. She told this story in her book *Household Efficiency* to show that middle-class professionals could reach out to immigrant girls and women and teach them how to be Americans. Referring to a woman who believed that the home was a haven in which to hide from the world, she wrote: "She seems to think that her function is to preserve the home as a sort of shrine, a thing apart, an end in itself. She does not see it as part of the great factory for the production of citizens, nor understand that her job is exactly the same as that of any other factory manager."[1]

In the early twentieth century, faced with record numbers of immigrants from foreign countries, Americans struggled with national identity. For many, the foreign-born represented trouble, difference, and ignorance. Home economists, social workers, and other household advisors often agreed with those opinions, but also believed that through study of the household and its various functions, immigrants could be transformed into responsible Americans. Martha Bruere and her colleagues would write books, prepare "model homes," and teach classes in order to make immigrants (and even minorities) into their idea of good Americans.

"Too often," wrote social worker Florence Nesbit in 1918, "the sum total" of an immigrant woman's household knowledge "is the traditions . . . inherited from her ancestors." Nesbit considered this to be a problem, because "such training . . . [was] often in a foreign country where conditions were entirely different."[2] She believed in the power of domestic advice to Americanize immigrant women. Through household education, she and other advisors could reach those women and girls whose mothers had only old-world experience to guide them. In *Household Management*, Nesbit wrote that the immigrant woman's "need of the latest discoveries . . . is urgent."[3]

Science and Americanization both appeared as major themes in the writings of domestic advisors in the early twentieth century. The authors of these books believed that by changing behaviors in the home, they could change society. Each of these groups of women wanted to see the end of Victorian textiles and ornaments, but they had different reasons. The scientific advisors provided evidence of germs and disease as their rationale for ridding the house of textiles and carpets. The advisors who tried to Americanize the home saw old-world or old-fashioned ideas as "germs" and tried to persuade their readers to simplify their homes and rid themselves of those trappings of immigrant and working-class culture. For them, home improvement would not only influence the spread of disease, but could literally change the social class of their readers.

Many domestic advisors continued to limit their audience to middle-class American women. However, for the first time in this period, some advisors wrote for tenement dwellers and immigrants. They also wrote texts for those social workers who lived and worked with these populations. They wrote manuals because they believed that the arrangement of the furniture, the fabric in the curtains, and the items on the mantle were of national significance. With the attitude that crowded, unsanitary homes represented the enemy, domestic advisors battled the lingering reminders of Victorian and old-world excess. These women wrote about the home as if it had the power to influence one's national values.

At the turn of the century, many Americans worried about growing urban populations. Domestic advice became part of a larger reform movement. Between 1900 and 1920, fourteen million people immigrated to the United States, and many more people counted themselves as first-generation Americans.[4] Cities filled with foreign-language speakers, people with many different customs. Many immigrant women looked toward domestic advice to learn the ways of their new country, and many domestic advisors set their sights particularly on immigrant women.[5]

Though immigrant women made important subjects, most domestic-advice texts left out black women. For most domestic advisors, black women existed only as servants. Lillie Hamilton French lamented the ineptitude of her mother's "colored maid-servants" who wanted "the fun of gossiping daily at the town pump" instead of learning to use labor-saving devices.[6] In 1913, *Good Housekeeping* included a letter to the editor concerning the inability of black servants in the South to change with the times. "We employ colored help altogether in this part of the south," wrote a woman from Alabama; "most housekeepers consider this class of labor unsatisfactory and stupid in the use of labor-saving household devices."[7] In order to conform to the new American ideal, the advisors and many of their readers thought that white women needed to embrace new techniques. Their criticism of black servants was in general based in prejudice and racism, but in particular it shows that advisors used a stereotype of black women as a warning to their white audience.

Middle-class Americans often thought that they had a responsibility to help the immigrants, and women led many of the reform movements. In the early twentieth century, settlement houses and other child and family welfare programs developed in several large cities. Reformers organized groups to remove children from the streets and to improve housing conditions.[8] They organized groups to agitate for protective labor laws and provided job-training classes. By 1900, the General Federation of Women's Clubs boasted 150,000 members, and twenty years later they had close to a million.[9] Many of these clubs had social-action agendas. These women believed that a uniquely female capacity for benevolence required them to act on behalf of the less fortunate.

The settlement-house movement, in particular, gave middle-class women important opportunities and careers at the turn of the century. Women set up settlement houses in many American cities to educate, protect, and influence immigrants. The settlement-house staff offered courses in English, playgrounds for the children, and job training. By 1910, at the height of the settlement movement, over four hundred settlements catered to the needs of the urban working class.[10] The settlement house enjoyed a strong following by middle-class women because they believed that the home was the place to solve society's problems. By reforming immigrants' homes, they believed they could reform their lives.

Most settlement workers did not hold the master's degree in social work, but the profession grew.[11] Although men filled many of the top positions in professional social work, by 1910 female college graduates turned to social work more than to any other career aside from teaching.[12] The 1920s and 1930s were important decades for the professionalization of the field. By 1940 there were forty-one schools in the Association of Professional Schools of Social Work. Settlement houses themselves became part of professional organizations, including the National Federation of Settlements and the National Settlement House League. Jane Addams's Hull House in Chicago, Lillian Wald's Henry Street Settlement in New York City, and many others gave jobs to hundreds of women in the early twentieth century and reached out to large populations of immigrant families, especially women and girls.

Social workers who lived and worked in settlement houses often wrote domestic-advice texts. Martha Bensley Bruere was one such person. Women "must follow the spinning wheel into the world," she wrote in 1912, to "take up her share of the duties of citizenship."[13] Bruere had a strong belief that the role of every woman was to help her society. Born in 1879, Bruere grew up during the decades of intense immigration and worked as a social worker through the Depression years. She witnessed poverty firsthand and filed reports to the government during the 1930s about housing and work conditions in industrial cities such as Buffalo and Rochester, New York.[14] She wrote about the usefulness of various relief programs, complimenting those that gave the people independence and criticizing others, noting that people she talked to "didn't like to have the sweaters that were given out by the home relief all so alike that anyone who saw you would know you were on relief."[15]

Bruere trained, like many other social workers and home economists of the period, at Vassar College and at the University of Chicago.[16] She worked at Hull House while in Chicago and wrote extensively on household issues in the first few decades of the twentieth century. Her articles appeared in *Outlook, Harpers, Collier's, Success,* and *The Women's Home Companion,* and she served for several years as editor of *Good Housekeeping.* Bruere also wrote lighthearted books and articles, including *Laughing Their Way: Women's Humor in America,* published near the end of her life in 1945. Demonstrating her diverse interests, she also wrote a few texts about America's forests, one for the U.S. Department of Agriculture.[17]

Social workers who wrote domestic-advice manuals often used their experiences in their writings. Florence Nesbit, a social caseworker for the mothers' pension department of the Chicago Juvenile Court, visited the homes of the urban poor. Nesbit considered these women to be naturally inept at proper housekeeping, and her goal was to help them. "Women who need cooking classes and food demonstrations the most—namely, those who have the least money," she wrote in 1918, "are the very ones who remain outside such present-day activities, unless approached understandingly one by one. When thus sought out, they are eager to learn and eager to apply their new knowledge."[18] Nesbit's book, written in part for other social workers, outlined the ways in which professional women could help the less fortunate. "It is in general true," she wrote, "that the lower the income the greater need has the homemaker for the fullest training and most complete knowledge of all the arts and sciences included in home economics."[19]

Nesbit embraced patriotism along with her domestic advice. The forward to her wartime *Household Management*, published during World War I in 1918, included a note from the editor. "The civilized countries of a world at war are looking to America to show her highest generalship. . . . The task is one in which the humblest householder . . . may add permanently to the health and morale of her own people."[20] Domestic advisors saw the home, traditionally a place of shelter and protection, as a place to preserve American faith. For these women, the arrangement of furniture and the cleaning of walls could be patriotic issues. They came to the profession of household advisor because they believed, as Mabel Hyde Kittredge wrote in her *The Home and its Management* of 1918, "The home is really the most important factor in the nation's life."[21]

Kittredge worked overseas during World War I, and she compared her service during the war to her efforts in household management at home. Tucked into the front cover of her *The Home and Its Management* of 1918 was a note from the publisher, the Century Company of New York, proclaiming the importance of this new book to American women. "President Wilson has called upon every woman to practice strict economy and thus put herself in the ranks of those who served their country," noted the publisher, making the purchase of this manual into a patriotic duty. Kittredge's text, since it included advice on "inexpensive furnishing [and] practical marketing,"[22] among other things, could serve as a model for American women trying to conserve while their nation was at war.

Mabel Hyde Kittredge was one of the most influential household advisors in the early twentieth century. She devoted her life to helping people and concentrated many of her efforts on ensuring better food and homes for the underprivileged.[23] Born in 1867, Kittredge grew up in New York City, where she lived most of her life. She is credited with founding the hot-lunch program for the New York public schools, serving the first school lunch herself in 1901. She continued to work with the school-lunch program for two decades and finally succeeded in getting financial aid from the Board of Education to fund the program in 1920. Kittredge served in Belgium during World War I, working for Herbert Hoover and the Belgium Relief Committee. Before and after her war work, Kittredge wrote extensively about the home and housekeeping.

Bertha Smith, writing for the Craftsman *in 1905, raved about Mabel Hyde Kittredge's work with model tenements. Her article included photographs of the New York project that featured social workers teaching immigrants how to arrange their homes. This image depicts the ideal living room and shows simple white curtains, unupholstered chairs, and sparse decorations. Smith and others who valued plainness over clutter understood that some people had to live in small spaces but insisted that simplicity could be achieved in most cases. (Smith, "The Gospel of Simplicity," 81; courtesy The Winterthur Library, Printed Book and Periodical Collection)*

More than even school lunches or wartime service, the household was Kittredge's main focus. She wrote extensively about the home in various settings, from houses with servants to tenement flats. "Every housekeeper responsible for home work, whether she does it herself or directs others to do it, should understand her fire—making it, feeding it and cleaning the stove," she asserted. "This work can be very dull or can be really interesting. If a woman thinks of homemaking as a profession, and is determined to play her part in the family partnership with the greatest efficiency, she will look upon the kitchen stove as her most valuable tool." [24] Kittredge believed, above all, in strict education for women about the workings of their households. She set up sites called "Practical Housekeeping Centers" in which she and other trained domestic scientists taught visitors how to prepare food, clean rooms, and decorate their homes.

Kittredge's Practical Housekeeping Center was one of many such places in cities such as New York. Lillian Wald's famous Henry Street Settlement, for example, included a tenement apartment rented by home economists and set up as an ideal home fitted with appropriate furniture. "Intelligence and taste were exercised in equipping it inexpensively," Wald wrote in 1915, and "classes were formed to teach housekeeping in its every detail. . . . [The girls] all were eager . . . to establish better organized and more intelligently conducted" homes.[25]

The idea to set up a "model house" as an example for American women began as early as the 1890s and lasted well into the twentieth century. Katharine Bement Davis opened what was perhaps one of the earliest examples at the World's Columbian Exposition in 1893, beginning a practice of household-demonstration centers at expositions and fairs that would last for many decades. Davis had a busy career as a health-care advocate, prison reformer, and social worker. As a new graduate of Vassar College in 1892, she was appointed as the director of the New York State Workingman's Model Home at the World's Columbian Exposition. The project led her to devote her career to reform the working class. After earning her Ph.D. at the University of Chicago in 1900, she went on to become the superintendent of the Reformatory for Women in Bedford Hills, New York. An influential voice in turn-of-the-century reform, she began with the belief that a proper home was an important first step for a working or immigrant family.

Davis furnished the house with furniture, kitchen utensils, and even a model family of Irish descent.[26] The house demonstrated how a family could arrange and decorate a house on a budget of $500 per month. She served the family actual meals based upon a nutritional diet of her creation. The house, built on a twenty-five-foot lot, included a living room, kitchen, and bath on the first floor, with three bedrooms on the second floor. Davis and her committee used paint on the floors and the walls for sanitary purposes and purchased appropriate furnishings. She spent three dollars on bric-a-brac and even bought a sewing chair and a clock to encourage industriousness and timeliness in the home. Her model house was a popular feature of the fair, and visitors bought copies of the plans in pamphlet form, which went through two printings during the life of the exhibit.

As demonstrated by Davis's successful model-house exhibit, domestic advisors had large roles to play at fairs. Throughout the first half of the twentieth century, home economists and other domestic workers continued to set up exhibits and to serve nutritious meals at the state buildings. Fairs were an ideal place to reach large groups of people and deliver messages, whether about wallpaper or grains. Visitors to America's world fairs and expositions included large numbers of immigrants and the working class, providing an ideal opportunity for educating these groups. Ava Milam Clark, dean of home economics at Oregon State, led her students in a tearoom project at the Panama-Pacific International Exposition in 1915. They prepared the tea, organized the exhibit, and served the visitors. From coast to coast, home economists created a space for ideas about Americanization and home management at fairs.[27]

Fairs, though an ideal setting, tended to be temporary, and advisors looked for more permanent ways to address their audience. Mabel Hyde Kittredge set up a trailerlike building to look like a home where tenement women could observe a model household. "The Housekeeping Centers, where the lessons are given," she described in her book, "are tenement flats, just such dwellings as the people occupy who take advantage of the instruction. The furnishings and management of the model flats are in themselves a practical lesson in economy, and an illustration of the sanitation and beauty which lie within the reach of the laborer's income."[28] Urban girls and women visited the centers and watched "correct" housekeeping practice in progress. These centers allowed domestic scientists to reach out to those women who perhaps could not afford their books or could not read them in English.

Kittredge's centers also offered homekeeping classes. Hands-on learning enabled girls and women to practice the new techniques at the "model flat." Kittredge published extensive rules for the courses, including the formation of classes "from the [same] immediate neighborhood," (perhaps to ensure ethnic homogeneity) and the "course card bearing [the student's] name" that would be "punched by the teacher as [each task] is satisfactorily performed."[29] The rules laid out in this book were quite specific. "A Dinner Class consists only of children who have satisfactorily passed the first and second courses," she wrote. "The pupils in the class meet once a week. . . . They arrive about 5 o'clock, make out the menu for dinner (being allowed so many cents for each person) according to their knowledge of food values. They do the marketing as well as the preparation of the meal. . . . 'Cleaning up' must be done well."[30] She felt strongly that immigrant women must learn how to be American within the confines of a strictly defined and controlled curriculum.

Mabel Kittredge's model flat attracted attention from national publications. Gustave Stickley's journal *Craftsman* welcomed articles from

Sample of First Course Card

. . . .

The holder of this card has

1 Made a fire.
2 Washed dishes.
3 Washed dish towels.
4 Cleaned sink.
5 Prepared soda and cleansed pipes.
6 Scrubbed floor.
7 Scrubbed table or tubs.
8 Cleaned kitchen.
9 Washed and aired food tins.
10 Washed windows.
11 Made bed.
12 Fought bedbugs.
13 Cleaned toilet.
14 Dusted bedroom.
15 Cleaned drawers.
16 Scrubbed woodwork.
17 Dusted down walls.
18 Boiled out cleaning cloths.

Mabel Hyde Kittredge prepared detailed instructions for courses taught by the Association of Practical Housekeeping Centers in New York City. Her classes "of six or more girls . . . usually from the immediate neighborhood" provided a basic education in housekeeping. This course card, when completed, would indicate that the holder had learned all the rudimentary level steps to homemaking and had demonstrated proficiency in such tasks as fighting bedbugs and scrubbing the floor. (Kittredge, Housekeeping Notes, *16; courtesy The Winterthur Library, Printed Book and Periodical Collection)*

Teaching immigrant girls about "proper" cleaning techniques was an important component of the model-tenement movement. Social workers such as Mabel Hyde Kittredge taught girls how to polish, scrub, and otherwise make the apartment spotless. By starting the students young, Kittredge and others tried to influence the following generation. Bertha Smith included this photograph of girls attacking dust in the model tenement in her 1905 article, "The Gospel of Simplicity." (Smith, "The Gospel of Simplicity," 91; courtesy The Winterthur Library, Printed Book and Periodical Collection)

all different kinds of advocates of simple design. Bertha H. Smith's "The Gospel of Simplicity as Applied to Tenement Homes," appeared in the *Craftsman* in 1905. The article discussed Mabel Hyde Kittredge's model flat and praised its use of "economy of money and space."[31] Smith applauded the model flat for bringing "a semblance of order . . . out of the chaos of crowded conditions."[32] She quoted Kittredge's explanation of her project: "Many have asked me why . . . the Model Flat? This is my answer: The foreigners who come to this country want to adopt our civilization. They want to do things as we do them. But they have no way of knowing what to choose and what not to choose. They have not been educated to choose between that which is in good taste and the tawdry. . . . The responsibility is greater with the foreigner who wants to be taught and is in danger of learning the worst of our ways for lack of better example."[33] Kittredge truly believed that her model

This bedroom was part of the model cottage built by domestic-science teacher Theodosia Ammons for the Colorado Chautauqua summer school in 1899. The features and furnishings in the home, which included a wraparound porch, were specially designed to provide a model for healthy living. Visitors to the summer retreat and women who took Ammons's courses either at Chautauqua or at the state agricultural college used the cottage as a textbook. Ammons hoped they would learn about the benefits of open-air living, easily cleaned furniture and simple decoration. (Courtesy Colorado Chautauqua Association)

flat, filled with women and children taking classes and observing her techniques, could help immigrants become better Americans.

Housekeeping centers existed all over the country in the early twentieth century. Many creative variations conformed to regional differences and needs. In Boulder, Colorado, home to the Texas-Colorado Chautauqua summer school, domestic scientist Theodosia Ammons planned a "Model Cottage" in 1899 to demonstrate the correct way to live properly in an outdoor setting. Ammons was a domestic-science professor at Colorado's land-grant school, then called Colorado Agricultural College. A member of one of Colorado's influential pioneer families — her brother Elias Ammons served as Governor from 1913 to 1915 — Theodosia came to Colorado from North Carolina in the 1870s and grew up in Denver. She built and furnished her own model home, which she named "Gwenthean Cottage," after herself and her two sisters (Gwendolin and Anne) who each spent time there with their families. She held classes and lectures there every summer, and members of her family continued to live in the house for several generations.

Ammons, as the principal of the Chautauqua School of Domestic Economy, taught classes in addition to setting up her model home. The Chautauqua summer school, mainly attended by teachers, provided a way for domestic scientists to reach a large audience of women. Ammon's cottage was so successful that she lectured on the subject of summer cottages at a home economics conference in Lake Placid.[34] The model cottage gave her a setting for exactly the same kinds of hands-on learning that Kittredge and others had embraced at the Practical Housekeeping Centers in New York City. Gwenthean Cottage became a gathering place for the young women who studied at the Chautauqua summer school — hundreds of women each summer in the first few decades of the twentieth century. Women who came to the Chautauqua included members of the Woman's Christian Temperance Union from as far away as Chicago.

Ammons set up her cottage with metal beds and furnished the wraparound porch with wicker chairs and tables. The porch built on the current teachings about fresh air, and Ammons probably intended it as an outdoor living room. The porch could be enclosed by canvas curtains that rolled down from the roof to provide a sleeping area, and it also included room for outdoor eating. She featured wooden floors with area rugs for easy cleaning. Many of her furnishings remain in the cottage today.[35]

Model homes helped advisors discern which objects and furniture could serve a worthwhile function. Harriet Gillespie, who operated a "home experiment station" in New Jersey in the early twentieth century, wrote about her "year's housekeeping" in a 1913 issue of *Good Housekeeping*. Quantitative research had proved to her that labor-saving devices "do away with the necessity for drudgery in the home." Her experiments, under the auspices of the New Jersey Federation of

Women's Clubs, provided scientific proof of the benefits of machines in the home. She ended the article by suggesting that her readers study her experiments "and then translate these principles into their homes. In that way each woman can start herself toward an appreciation of the value of domestic engineering."[36]

All of these model houses, tenement apartments, and vacation homes provided resources for women in the first half of the twentieth century. Though they were rarely, if ever, indications of what was actually going on in people's houses, these model houses provided tangible evidence of the domestic fantasies of dozens, if not hundreds, of home economists and social workers around the country. These formally educated women believed that their ideas about home efficiency and Americanization would penetrate homes across the country, reaching the citizenry and new immigrants. In the cases where they believed their ideas could not be accessed by a certain group of people, they took to the road and brought their ideas directly to their constituents.

Home-extension programs brought domestic advice into homes across the country in the early twentieth century. In 1914 the U.S. Congress passed the Smith-Lever act, which created matching funding from the federal government to states and counties that would hire home- and farm-demonstration agents.[37] The law created, in effect, a federal separate-spheres policy, giving men information about farm equipment and women information about household technology. After World War I, President Warren Harding's "Return to Normalcy" program included the creation of the Bureau of Home Economics, committed to funding home managers across the country. This solidified the government's position that women's role on the farm was inside the farmhouse.

Home-extension agents brought the rules of science and sanitation to rural locations. And they brought Americanization with them, directly from the college campuses of state universities to remote towns, farms, and ranches across the nation. As home economists and social workers knew, home improvement involved far more than simple rules about cleaning and cooking. In this country, decorating and furnishing the home could mark a woman's class status and her acceptance of American values. Home-extension agents, trained to believe in the "one best way" for furnishings and household efficiency, spread out across the country. They offered a combination of practical information about vegetable canning and more subjective household advice.[38]

Cornell University, the home of many domestic-science programs, sponsored a series of "rural manuals" in the early twentieth century. The editor of the series claimed it contained information "primarily for rural conditions." While many of the volumes included information meant for men, in 1919 the editor was "glad to add a book in his series on the work and welfare of women." The book included lessons on decorating with "good furniture . . . sincerely built from honest material."[39] The advisors at Cornell felt that rural women needed a book that would address their unique concerns.

Black women and girls attended segregated home-extension clubs. In South Carolina, several African American agents lobbied actively for new black recruits when the federal Capper-Ketcham act of 1932 provided money for each state to hire new agents. With more black agents, more black women and girls had access to household advice in South Carolina and in other heavily segregated states. Genevieve Wheeler worked as a home-extension agent in black communities in Georgia and Florida in the 1930s and 1940s. Many years later, she reminisced about her experience: "Families were anxious to learn more. . . . It was a wonderful experience. . . . We made furniture out of baskets and orange crates. We taught Red Cross nursing courses. We helped families learn how to plant gardens so they might feed themselves."[40]

Fabiola Cabeza de Baca Gilbert of New Mexico was an influential home-extension agent. Born near Las Vegas, New Mexico, in 1894, Gilbert graduated from New Mexico Normal School in 1921 and got another degree in home economics at New Mexico State University in 1927.[41] A writer and teacher, she spent her career influencing both the way that Hispanic New Mexicans viewed mainstream American culture and the way that Americans all over the country viewed New Mexico. Her cookbooks, *Historic Cookery* (1931) and The *Good Life: New Mexican Traditions and Food* (1949) introduced New Mexican foodways to the country at large. Written for a broad audience, the books described ingredients and methods for nonnative New Mexican cooks. *Historic Cookery* was probably the first cookbook of New Mexican foods to be published, and it helped begin a nationwide fascination with chiles and pine nuts.

In *We Fed Them Cactus* (1954), Gilbert told the story of the late-

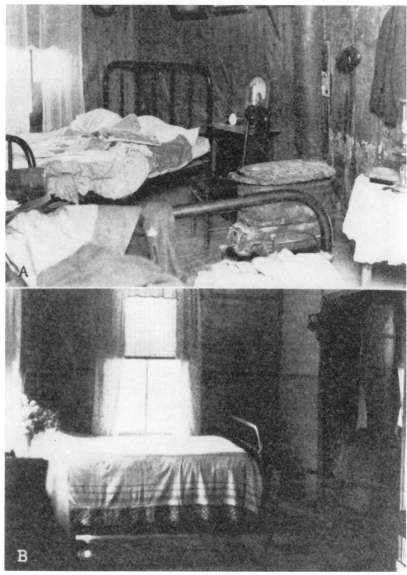

These photographs depict the before-and-after state of a bedroom in Pulaski County, Arkansas. The Better Homes campaign, supported by domestic advisors such as Hazel Shultz, tried to demonstrate that households could be improved by renewed dedication to cleanliness and order. Distressed by clutter and disorganization, Shultz used this image to demonstrate the positive effects of household organization on family morale and well-being. (Shultz, Making Homes, *fig. 34; courtesy The Winterthur Library, Printed Book and Periodical Collection)*

nineteenth-century world of her ancestors, describing life on the sheep ranch based on oral histories she collected and on other research. This book expressed her life's work in the meeting place of change and cultural continuity. She began the book by noting her family's long history in the region: "This is the story of the struggle of New Mexican Hispanos for existence on the Llano, the Staked Plains. Through four generations, our family has made a living from this land—from cattle and sheep, and lately by selling curios, soda pop, gasoline and food to tourists traveling over U.S. Highway 66."[42] Her book evoked a sense of the past with its practical understanding of the ways that modern life had both positive and negative repercussions for her family. Her career expressed her belief that the traditions of New Mexican women could remain strong while they also learned from the benefits of American home-economics teachings.

Fabiola Cabeza de Baca Gilbert served as the home-demonstration agent for Santa Fe County between 1929 and 1940. She also taught at normal schools in Santa Rosa and El Rito, New Mexico, and wrote a weekly column on the home in a Spanish newspaper. As part of her work for the Agricultural Extension Service, she visited numerous households, emphasizing the importance of both government-style canning and native handicrafts. She believed that native diets could be enhanced by rather than superceded by modern methods such as canning. She wrote extensively for home-economics journals and for various other organizations interested in the diet and nutrition of New Mexican women. Gilbert also spent some time in Mexico as a representative of the United Nations, helping to train extension agents and setting up household-demonstration centers among the Tarascan Indians.[43] Throughout her career, she worked both for the U.S. government and for Hispanic women, whose ideas about housekeeping and nutrition often differed. She managed to negotiate a way for Spanish-speaking New Mexican women to welcome her and her American ideals into their homes.

Household visits by home-extension workers complemented the lessons young girls learned in public schools. "Every girl in Chicago can now learn housekeeping in the public schools," raved Martha Bruere in 1912.[44] Some school curricula focused specifically on particular ethnic groups. In 1926, board-of-education employee Emeline Whitcomb surveyed the Amelia Street School in Los Angeles and found that the training "develops worth-while Americans."[45] Pearl Ellis's 1929 book *Americanization through Homemaking*, published in

Home economist Fabiola Cabeza de Baca Gilbert had a long and distinguished career in New Mexico. She taught home economics to Hispanic girls and women across the state and taught Anglo women about native New Mexican cooking through her newspaper columns and cookbooks. In addition to her work as a home-extension agent traveling all over the state, she taught home economics at a rural school in New Mexico. Her class at El Rito Normal School posed for a photograph with their teacher (top row, left) in the 1920s. (Courtesy Center for Southwest Research, General Library, University of New Mexico, negative no. 000-603-0014)

Los Angeles, documented techniques used by the Bureau of Education at predominately Hispanic schools there. In these schools, both boys and girls learned about American culture by studying the government system and English. Girls, however, had a special relationship to Americanization. The school separated the girls for special instruction, including arts and crafts and "home interior arrangement."[46]

Some ethnic groups embraced Americanization on their own terms and with their own publications. Jewish-immigrant women in New York had, by the 1920s, access to household advice in Yiddish.[47] Yiddish household manuals and magazine articles expressed many of the same ideas as their English-language counterparts. In 1913, the Yiddish newspaper *Di Froyen-Velt* claimed that one of its goals was to teach Jewish women "how to behave at home and to raise children; to deal with issues having to do with the kitchen."[48] The newspaper included dress patterns and home crafts, along with stories and advice. Other magazine articles and advertisements explained how to cook with American ingredients. They urged women to join in the trend for design reform, instead of persisting in old-fashioned decorating techniques in the home. They provided pictures to explain to readers how to style their hair and their houses in appropriate ways. These books served to Americanize Jewish women through their bodies, their choice of foods, and the objects in their homes.[49]

Many advisors demonstrated their interest in ethnic cultures by featuring foreign recipes in their texts. Advisors may have thought that by showing some interest in ethnic cultures, they could convince their readers to relegate those old-world customs to special occasions and otherwise embrace American foods and ideas. They often made the foods seem particularly exotic.[50] Lucia Millet Baxter included a section on "foreign cooking" in her *Housekeeper's Handy Book* of 1918, with recipes such as "Frijoles," "Bacalau a la Peruana," and "Swedish Meatballs." She also criticized the tendencies of other cultures to prioritize meat in their diet, linking the "stimulating character" of the "carnivorous, or meat-craving, appetite" to alcoholism.[51] Domestic advisors who included ethnic foods in their texts may have helped ethnic foods seem more familiar, but most remained wary of including any ethnic foods and techniques into the American diet.

While most domestic advisors ignored any evidence of ethnicity they found in the homes of immigrants, some did write about the foreign arts that graced tenement homes. Lillian Barton Wilson wrote a piece for the magazine *The Modern Priscilla* about Hungarian sewing in the homes of immigrant women. She praised the "very characteristic and interesting embroideries [and] the painting of pottery in bright primary colors."[52] Her article followed one by Hilda Richmond in the magazine, who claimed that often "the mistress of the shabby house works with might and main to make it so attractive."[53] These women saw what others missed.

Florence Nesbit was conflicted about the middle-class messages she handed out to the immigrant population. She wrote that "customs and habits differ widely in different countries," and she seemed disturbed that social workers "reduce these standards to sameness." As the social workers passed through neighborhoods, she worried, they trained immigrant women to simplify their households according to an inappropriate standard. "The Italian or Polish woman gives up making the crocheted lace with which she so lavishly decorates her bed coverlets, chairs, mantelpiece, etc. . . . Without it her rooms lack a certain native charm." In her volume, written for social workers in Chicago, she cautioned that, "Americanization is too often a ruthless destroyer of beauty and charm."[54] Her household-advice manual was unique in that it stepped back far enough to realize the significance that a phrase like "simplicity" held for immigrant women.

A regular column in the journal *Practical Home Economics* followed home-extension agents and educators to some of their more challenging locales. In August 1935, Altha Tedrow described her experiences with the Pipestone Indian School in Pipestone, Minnesota. Tedrow began her article by noting: "Home Economics courses in the Indian schools are based upon the needs of the Indian home and upon the need for appropriate standards of living. Of course, this information and training must be simple and practical enough to be translated into the girl's experiences either in her parent's home, or in her own, for Indian girls marry early." Though she had a patronizing attitude toward the girls whose lives she believed she could improve, she did echo Florence Nesbit's worry about Americanization. "Of course," she wrote, "it could not be an Indian house without Indian handcraft here and there, particularly the Indian pipe of the famous pipestone quarried a half-mile from the school."[55]

Understanding that her students "have little with which to improve their homes" provided the basis for the recommendations. Tedrow taught the girls in her class how to attack problems such as "How can I make Furniture from Boxes." The room included: "A chest made from a strong box; a baby bed of two cardboard boxes . . . a clothes closet fashioned from 8 orange boxes, a broomstick, an old sheet and a print curtain . . . a dressing table made from 2 orange boxes and a flat apple box with print curtains and oilcloth cover with a stool that was once a cranberry box."[56] Tedrow's description of decorating with boxes shows the depth of the home economist's ingenuity.

Anthropologist and explorer Louise Brigham wrote domestic advice for those who could not afford regular furniture. Her unusual career led her to a business of creating furniture out of boxes. Her anthropology-research travels had led her to remote parts of Norway, seven hundred miles north of the Arctic Circle, and to Egypt, China, the Philippines, and Bermuda, and all the while, she experimented with the boxes that had carried the necessary equipment to the camp. She produced furniture for display at the Child Welfare Exhibit in New York, where she thanked Jacob Riis for alerting her to the problems of the poor. At the Panama-Pacific International Exhibition in San Francisco in 1915, she demonstrated her craft at a "box furniture making school." Brigham was an unusual domestic advisor, but she believed in the "latent possibilities of a box," and she used her knowledge in an attempt to help others who "care for simplicity and thrift, utility and beauty" but who could not afford the real thing.[57]

Brigham could build furnishings for an entire home with boxes. Her boxes could be transformed into dressing tables and nursery furniture, as well as into the more ordinary chairs, desks, beds, and tables. "To make a footstool: Requirements: Body: 1 Roach Food Box. . . . Construction: Make the legs 6½ inches long and round off the corners of one end of each leg, otherwise the constant moving about of the stool will have a tendency to split off the sharp corners. Remove the cover. Turn the box upside down and train a leg on each corner and clinch the nails on the inside. Invert the box, set it upon the legs, and place the false top on it." Her clear message was that families could be resourceful "where limitations of space have to be considered," creating a home out of whatever was available to them.[58]

Mabel Kittredge demonstrated how women could use a slim budget to produce an American home. She suggested yellow paint (for brightening), shelves for china in the dining room, shelves for books in the living room, and a specific regimen of shelves in the kitchen. She tried to use building materials that immigrant women might have at their disposal, suggesting that "a good receptacle for soiled clothes is a pickle barrel, price fifty cents. Holes should be bored in the sides to admit air, and a barrel top purchased. . . . This is kept in the kitchen and serves also as a seat."[59]

"It is desired to have pictures in the bedroom," wrote Kittredge. Realizing that frames might be too expensive, she suggested that women "paste the prints on the painted walls and . . . wash over them with liquid shellac. Pictures and wall may then be washed at the same time."[60] Kittredge knew her readers would be concerned with the cost of household improvements, so she included the prices for "white liquid shellac (one half pint for twenty-five cents)." This suggestion was one of Kittredge's many attempts to clean up immigrant homes. She knew that immigrant homes often had newspaper clippings and magazine pictures nailed to the walls, and her recommendations always tried to alleviate the clutter.

In her 1911 manual *Housekeeping Notes*, Kittredge specifically addressed apartments with a limited number of rooms. "In a four-room flat for five persons," she wrote, "a good arrangement is a kitchen, a living and dining room, and two bedrooms. In a three-room flat, used for five persons, one room will serve as kitchen and dining room; there will be also a bedroom, and the third room may be used as a living-room, which, with a couch, can be converted into a bedroom."[61] Most social workers recommended as little furniture as possible to help the problem of crowded quarters. Mabel Kittredge noted that "it must not be cluttered with unnecessary furnishings, for the occupations of the family will need all the room possible."[62] Advisors such as Kittredge who spent a lot of time in tenement flats understood the special needs of these apartments. Convinced that simple decorating was better in all cases, they tailored the rules to fit each example.

Domestic advisors brought their ideas about privacy to crowded tenement apartments. They believed that crowded conditions would breed crime. "As to the small flats and apartments that are going up on every side," wrote Lillie Hamilton French in 1903, "I never escape a pang of sympathy and regret when I think of their tenants." She believed that "family life in its better sense cannot exist" in the tenements she visited. "There is moral danger, as well as discomfort, in cramped quarters."[63] Hazel Shultz, head of the department of Home Economics at the laboratory schools of the University of Chicago, believed that, "too many persons per room means disturbed rest. . . . Many authorities believe that bad housing conditions are a direct cause of crime."[64] Shultz felt that her training as a social scientist could help her teach women how to alter their living surroundings to conform to an American ideal. "When social workers find four and five members of a family sleeping in the same bedroom," she wrote in 1931, "they try to plan some way to provide more space and privacy."[65] These advisors thought that their teachings could make the tenements safer places to live.

Domestic advisors wrote extensively about the value of refinement in American homes. Mabel Hyde Kittredge connected certain kinds of decorating with negative results. "Remember that the people in the house are judged more or less by the house," she cautioned. "If the furniture is tawdry, the ornaments sham, the pictures cheap and with showy frames, every one is sure to think that there is something a little vulgar in the minds of the people living in that house." Kittredge believed that the American values she respected would only be available to immigrant and other populations through a certain type of decorating. "Refinement," she concluded, "is expressed by simplicity."[66] She wrote books and taught classes in model homes to teach women precisely that lesson.

Lace curtains became a favorite symbol of the cluttered working-class home. Whereas lace curtains had once been a prized possession for Americans, the twentieth-century factories brought the cost down and gave them new meaning. Paintings of elite New Englanders had featured lace curtains to symbolize wealth in the early-republic period, but that image began to fade during the nineteenth century.[67] By the twentieth century, lace curtains were widely available and varied greatly in price between the cheaper Nottingham lace and the more expensive Brussels and Swiss laces.[68] The lace curtain was newly available to a more general public, appearing in the Montgomery Ward catalogue in 1895.[69] As a bearer of middle-class goods across the country and across class lines, catalogues such as Montgomery Ward and Sears Roebuck changed the way Americans furnished and decorated their homes by making the same goods available to people in every region of the country.[70]

The criticism of "cheap imitations," fiery well before 1900, took on new force at the turn of the century. Advisors had long recommended against decorating a parlor or living room with "cheap lace in imitation of those who can well afford the real thing," as Emma Whitcomb Babcock expressed the sentiment in 1884.[71] As part of their Americanization campaign in the early twentieth century, advisors increased the attack. Mabel Hyde Kittredge, in 1905, compared the lace curtain to other vulgarities: "The showy lace curtain, the big hat, the riotous upholsteries, the exaggerated styles of dress make the loudest bid for their [immigrants'] attention; and in their anxiety to be like us we find them adopting our barbarities instead of our better things."[72] The lace curtain, deemed cheap and tawdry, became more than a window treatment. Advisors used it as an example to decry the use of inferior household accessories in pursuit of the American dream.

By the 1930s, Americans used the term "lace curtain" as an adjective to describe "copying middle-class attributes; aspiring to middle-class standing."[73] The derogatory comment referred specifically to people who could never reach American middle-class respectability. In 1934, the author James T. Farrell officially linked the phrase to an immigrant group—the Irish—in his Studs Lonigan trilogy. In a scene from *Young Manhood*, the young Irish Catholic protagonist took his girlfriend to a hotel dance and felt instantly "determined to become a part of it." After looking around, however, he decided that the glamour of the event was "artificial." "They were trying to put on the dog," he said to himself, "show that they were lace-curtain Irish, and lived in steam heat."[74]

In this scene Lonigan recognized something that domestic reformers had been noticing for several decades already. Home decoration could define who was an American. The term "lace-curtain Irish" would have meant nothing without decades of American household advice written by and for women. To domestic advisors, and to increasing numbers of Americans who encountered and learned from them, lace curtains represented the past, the unsanitary, stuffy, frilly nineteenth century. The modern twentieth century, the age of efficiency kitchens and sparse furnishings, would welcome only those women who embraced the new ideals about American decoration.

The process of Americanization, when applied to immigrants and the working class, may seem distant from the homes of the middle class. Surely most readers of domestic advice did not decorate with orange boxes. However, advisors believed in the possibilities of Americanization and perfect housekeeping. Trained as home-extension visitors and social workers, they visited the homes of Jewish immigrants in Chicago, Hispanic ranchers in New Mexico, and the crowded tenements of New York City. They exhibited their ideas for all to see at fairs, in special trailers, and at a summer school in the foothills of the Rocky Mountains. These women believed that by showcasing the perfect kitchen, tent, or tenement, they could make an American out of just about anybody, even a "Russian Jewess" who did not know how to set a proper table. Social reformers believed that respectable American homes could—and must—come from humble circumstances.

MODERNISM: NO JUNK!

IS THE CRY OF THE NEW INTERIOR

Among the educational exhibits at the recent Mechanics' fair in Boston was one attempt at instruction which gave interesting evidence of the general tendency of public taste in house furnishings. Side by side were two spaces representing typical living rooms. One was a multi-colored aggregation of bric-a-brac, furniture and pictures, with a gorgeously bedraped "cozy corner" as its crowning touch. The other, in subdued green, was simply furnished—comfortable chairs, a well-filled bookcase and a few good pictures. Between the rooms was a sign: "These rooms were furnished for the same price. Which would you rather live in? Which would you rather have to keep clean?" The comments of the crowd which stopped to gaze . . . are significant of the sort of house furnishing which prevails. Notes taken by an interested bystander run something like this:

A mother and daughter, disposing of the plain room with a hasty and uninterested sweep of the eye, come to a full stop before the other. "Now, ma, there's a cozy corner like what I want for our sitting room. Can't we fix one?"

"It is lovely isn't it! I should think we could. They do make a room look so artistic. There's that portiere we got and never used—" And they do not move until they have a detailed mental picture of the conglomeration.

Two girls: "O Marie, there are those Sylvia heads! I want them for our parlor! Aren't they adorable?"

"Sweet! Doesn't it make a room cozy to have a lot of pictures? That room looks so bare!"
—Elizabeth Mainwaring, "The Two Rooms"

In 1902, an exhibit at the Mechanics' Fair in Boston presented the public with two examples of "typical living rooms." Set up to demonstrate the difference between old-fashioned, Victorian and new, "modern," design, the rooms illustrated a striking disagreement in household decoration. The first room represented the past, whereas the second room foreshadowed the modern era, which would, many domestic advisors hoped, change the way Americans thought about their homes.

Domestic advisors, including those who organized the Mechanics' Fair exhibit, tried to urge American women to let go of the past. The exhibitors asked leading questions to which the obvious best answer was the modern room. With its uncluttered lines and minimal use of upholstery, this room was a model for the way that advisors pictured the dawning of the twentieth century and the modern era. To domestic advisors in the early twentieth century, the term "modern" was a code word for "simple" and "uncluttered," for "taste" and "good character." The sentiment had been the same since the late nineteenth century, but gradually took on the vocabulary of modernism.

Many domestic advisors urged women to give up their attachment to Victorian decorating. Elizabeth Mainwaring, who wrote the article for *Good Housekeeping* quoted above, noticed a gendered difference in responses to the Mechanics' Fair exhibit. She documented the overwhelming disgust female visitors felt for the modern room. "Yes, simplicity's all well for some folks," said one woman, "but if I had to live in that room, it would make me gloomy. I should feel as if I was walking over my own grave!" Male visitors had a different response to the exhibit. One male visitor praised the second room to his friend, pleased that there were "no vases to get smashed if I jerk my elbow. My wife has vases all over the house. Brings one home from every bargain sale. What earthly use are they, anyway?" His friend answered disdainfully, "they *are* good to drop burnt matches in." Men had a "modern" response to the Victorian room, criticizing the cozy corner for "always coming down on my head" and preferring the room with little furniture and less clutter.[1]

Mainwaring's article for *Good Housekeeping* showed that she, like many other women, disagreed with the female visitors to the fair. Although the female public at the turn of the century may have clung to Victorian decoration, domestic advisors certainly did not. Mainwaring investigated the "interesting evidence of the general tendency of pub-

Turkish cozy corners, popular in the United States in the late nineteenth and early twentieth centuries, featured fabric and cushions set up in the middle of otherwise unassuming parlors. This photograph, taken in Denver, Colorado, shows a corner draped with tapestries set up over a large mattress and several pillows. This type of arrangement was singularly unpopular with contemporary domestic advisors, who decried the excess textiles and dusty drapes. (Courtesy Denver Public Library Western History Collection, X-25993)

lic taste in house furnishing." When she found that women tended to like the old-fashioned room and men the modern space, she labeled that evidence "not encouraging."[2]

Domestic advisors found a way to take up a banner of modernity of their own. As Mainwaring showed, from the first years of the twentieth century, observers have identified Victorian decoration as feminine and modern simplicity as masculine.[3] Domestic advice, however, complicates this familiar picture.[4] Many women writers, instead of being excluded from the tenets of the modern era, in fact embraced modern ideas. While certainly some women advocated and sustained the ornamentation of the nineteenth century, others spent many decades trying to influence their readers with pleas for morality, science, and Americanization. Female domestic advisors appropriated the modern agenda in design for their own purposes in American homes. To them, the language of modernism was simply an echo of what domestic advisors had been saying since the mid-nineteenth century. Through

In contrast to the Turkish cozy corner, this sparsely decorated living room featured clean lines and simple decorations. Virginia Terhune Van de Water featured this image, taken from the Arts and Crafts design school, in her 1912 manual. Living rooms like this one provided calm alternatives to the cluttered parlors of the nineteenth century. Domestic advisors, through books and displays, tried to convince American women that this type of room was the better alternative for the modern era. (Van de Water, From Kitchen to Garrett, pl. facing 70; courtesy The Winterthur Library, Printed Book and Periodical Collection)

books and articles, advocates of a modernist domestic fantasy tried to convince American women that the clean, simple lines could have meaning for them.

The word "modern" defined a strict set of decorating rules for twentieth-century domestic advisors. The Mechanics Fair of 1902 helped mark the beginning of the emphasis on modern design, and the word showed remarkable staying power. Modern design tended to be simple and unadorned. Living rooms and bedrooms kept upholstery to a minimum, and advisors recommended limiting most types of ornamentation. The Turkish cozy corner, long a mainstay of Victorian parlors, slowly began to lose favor. This fad involved draping cloths from the ceiling and piling up pillows within a kind of tent, representing the decadent leisure associated with Turkish harems. The cozy corner represented a world of decorating problems for the modern age. Domestic advisors recommended eradicating anything even resembling a cozy corner and limiting the decorations to clean lines, sanitary surfaces, and new materials.

The modern era in design and home decorating was concurrent with the movements for scientific and American homes. Advisors who wrote for magazines such as *Good Housekeeping* about modern design echoed their counterparts writing in home-economics and social-work journals. During the first few decades of the twentieth century, household advice remained remarkably static, always emphasizing the "value of elimination." Almost as if they worked together in a conspiracy to simplify, simplify, simplify, the writers of domestic-advice manuals took on the language of modernism and recommended sweeping changes in American homes.

Domestic advisors helped create an atmosphere of longing and an appetite for goods and ideas that most people could not access in the early twentieth century. Domestic fantasy introduced middle-class women to the possibilities that awaited them and to a new angle of the platform advocating the elimination of Victorian decoration. In the modernist fantasy, women moved through a simplified world, unencumbered by heavy clothing or heavy dusting. The women depicted in the manuals moved freely through their homes, not restricted to or barred from certain rooms. They sat on chairs made of new plastics and metals, and dreamed of new appliances. Although the early twentieth century was certainly a time of hardship and uncertainty for many, it was also a period of intense creativity, innovation, and change for American homes.

Advisors used the language of modernism comfortably. Because they wrote for an audience not familiar with design movements, they often took on the role of educators. The *Modern Priscilla* magazine published a manual in 1925, the combined work of twenty-nine authors. Their *Modern Priscilla Home Furnishing Book* opened with the assurance that all of its readers could learn how to be modern.

Now then, is there any hope for those of us who were cheated out of those cradle lessons in discrimination; whose childhood's home associations were of the Early Pullman period of American home decoration; when the cozy corner held its sway and chenille curtains, crocheted tidies, beaded portieres, ubiquitous grill-work, plush upholstery and embroidered piano drapes formed dust catchers all over the house; when massive, ugly battle-axe black walnut furniture was our heart's desire, and inflammatory color schemes in wall and floor coverings helped to make us a nation of color illiterates?

Yes. Any one may acquire good taste. It is the result of education and not a matter of feeling.[5]

The authors of the *Modern Priscilla* book claimed that modern design embodied rational principles and could therefore be quantified, studied, and learned. These same ideas guided the principal leaders of the home-economics movement. All of these women tried to bring a sense of control into household design.

Modern Priscilla hired many women as editors and writers. Their 1925 text included advisors such as Amelia Leavitt Hill, Gladys Becket Jones, Mary Harrod Northend, and Mary Quinn, who each wrote full-length volumes on their own.[6] These women, some of whom had credentials in home economics or civic reform, made careers out of writing for women's magazines. Others wrote articles on the side. Gladys Jones, for example, was president of an organization called the Garland School of Homemaking; she also assisted in the Home Economics Department of Boston University. Mary Northend was a writer and photographer who specialized in Colonial Americana. Many of the design experts remained anonymous, worked as part of large editorial staffs, or only surfaced in brief articles in the various women's magazines of the period. *Modern Priscilla* joined other women's magazines of the early twentieth century in providing a vehicle for women to share their ideas about decorating and housekeeping.

Women's magazines flourished in the early twentieth century. Often referred to as the "Big Six," *Women's Home Companion, Good Housekeeping, Ladies' Home Journal, McCall's, Pictorial Review,* and *The Delineator* dominated the market. Later in the century, the power shifted to the "Seven Sisters," *Good Housekeeping, Family Circle, Woman's Day, Redbook, McCall's, Ladies' Home Journal,* and *Better Homes and Gardens;* however, smaller magazines and journals with local readerships also did well. These magazines often published articles on civic corruption and political issues, giving women an education in important topics of their times. Women's magazines always provided readers with ample articles, pictures, and short stories about the home, food, and decoration. Beginning in the early twentieth century, magazines with large staffs often published book-length treatments featuring their most popular advice.

Those women who worked for magazines made careers out of writing about the home. The authors of the *Modern Priscilla* book-length work also wrote many shorter articles for newspapers and magazines. Interior decorator Elsie de Wolfe, along with home economists and social activists Martha Bruere, Helen Campbell, and Maria Parloa, all wrote for *Good Housekeeping.* Many of these women achieved a small renown during their careers. In most cases, when the contributors to magazines published their own texts, they noted in the introduction that readers might have seen their work already in magazines. This gave the authors credibility. Dorothy Tuke Priestman, for example, published her *Home Decoration* in 1909 with the announcement that "Portions of this book have already appeared under the nom de plume of Dorothy Tuke" in various periodicals.[7] Priestman and many other modernist advisors did not achieve the same notoriety as those women who busied themselves with civic projects and professorships. But their contributions, though small, form a large and significant body of work when considered together.

Perhaps the most famous domestic advisor of the first few decades of the twentieth century was etiquette maven Emily Post. Post, born in 1873, lived in New York most of her life and socialized in upper-class circles. Post wrote novels, short stories, and a travel book. She worked for several women's magazines and also served as a traveling correspondent for *Collier's* national weekly. In 1922, at the age of fifty-one and a divorced mother of two, she wrote her first *Blue Book of Social Usage.* This 700-page work became an immediate best-seller, and she revised it nine times in her lifetime.[8] Post also wrote books about etiquette for particular situations, including for debutantes and for brides.

Though most famous for her etiquette advice, Post also wrote a book of household advice. *The Personality of a House: The Blue Book of Home Design and Decoration* first appeared in 1930. Filled with information about rooms and arrangements, Post introduced many modern ideas. Written "frankly, and from an essentially unprofessional point of view,"[9] the book agreed with most modern advice about removing Victorian excess from the American home.

* Another unpleasing room—not vulgar, but frumpy—is one that is turned into a museum of sentiment. In such a room the owner will eliminate nothing that any member of her family ever fancied. All the table-tops and twice as many cabinets as the room should hold are packed solidly with treasures that range from Sevres, Royal

Worcester and cameo vases to dozens of picture-frames, baby's rattles and small china dogs and kittens associated with the users of the rattles. Or perhaps mistaken ideas of house beautification induce the preservation of Rogers groups, embroidered plush hassocks, or conch shells. Perhaps the owner of one such room believes that a miniature Alpine hat with a feather labeled "Gruss aus Innsbruck!" is an embellishing ornament.[10]

Post, simply the most famous of all the modern-age advisors, wrote eloquently about the campaign to rid America's homes of useless ornament. It was a long struggle.

Female domestic advisors encountered a dilemma in translating the machine age for their audience. They had to appeal specifically to women while disparaging a movement (Victorian design) that many women had found emotionally and aesthetically satisfying. Victorianism, and the female taste that went along with it, was rejected by many influential male modernists. The movement, especially in Europe, was dominated by an elite group of male artists. They wanted to influence the "average person" with their designs for airplanes and pencil sharpeners, but often expressed open disgust for the aesthetic sensibility of the middle-class public. The machine age was a critique of the specifically *feminine* nature of nineteenth-century design. One of the major complaints of the modernist artists and architects was against the "feminine display" they found in the middle-class home. Despite their difficult position, domestic advisors joined the elite architects and designers in rejecting the Victorian sensibility in design.

The discussion of the modern movement was laden with value judgments. As Lucy Ann Throop wrote in her *Furnishing the House of Good Taste* in 1912, "The fussy house is, luckily, a thing of the past, or fast getting to be so, but we should all help the good cause of true simplicity."[11] By 1912, the "fussy house" was in fact still extant in America, but domestic advisors continued to advocate its eradication. "The simplicity and clear, defined lines" of modern design, wrote Dorothy Todd in 1929, "are as characteristic of the twentieth century as the over decorated and over furnished muddle . . . is of the late nineteenth century." Modern advisors attacked the "muddle" with a new ideal of the "simple" and the "practical." In household arrangement, they demanded "order and repose."

Many modern design texts opened with a lesson on the important concepts of modernism. Le Corbusier (Charles Edouard Jeanneret), one of the most famous French architects of the modern movement, wrote with obvious distaste about the "bourgeois king" with his "bric-a-brac mind," and advisors studied his work and repeated it for their readers. When Corbusier lamented the "windows hung with lace curtains" and "walls papered with damask," both trademarks of the middle-class Victorian parlor, domestic advisors of the period largely agreed.[12]

In her *Home Furnishing* of 1935, Anna Hong Rutt introduced her readers to Le Corbusier's concept of the home as the "machine in which we live."[13] Rutt, a professor of art at Northwestern University, wrote her book "as a textbook for classes in home furnishing, as a practical book for homemakers, and as a book for general information for interior decorators."[14] As an art professor, Rutt believed that certain principles guided the furnishing of a home. She used Corbusier as a place to begin her discussion of modern design, stating that the modern "effect is achieved by stripping off all non-essentials in designs for furnishings and houses."[15]

The *Better Homes Manual* of 1931, a compilation volume, included an essay explaining Le Corbusier's theories. "The rational perfection and precise determination of machine products . . . create in them a quality which gives them a style."[16] The author, C. R. Richards of *Good Furniture and Decorating* magazine, went on: "Le Corbusier says: 'Modern art, which is machine made, needs no decoration—can have no decoration.' He says that the rational perfection and precise determination of machine products made solely for functional ends create in them a quality which gives them a style. I doubt that this is the final word." In the essay, "Modernism in Furniture," Richards paved the way for female domestic advisors to create their own space in modernism, which would admit some nonrational decoration while staying within the basic guidelines of Corbusier's ideas.

In America, modernism took its cue from European art movements. The influential *Exposition Internationale Arts Décoratifs et Industriels Modernes* took place in Paris in 1925 and helped define a new age of design. The ideal of the machine as a pure design also developed in Europe under the auspices of various avant-garde design schools such as the Dutch de Stijl and the German Bauhaus school. The Bauhaus school, active in Germany between 1919 and 1933, did include some women in the textile department, but for the most part they did not play a large role. Because of political troubles and wars in Europe, many of the more famous industrial designers, such as Paul Frankl, came to do much of their important work in the United States. The American movement was also helped along with important exhibitions at the Museum of Modern Art in New York, The *International Exhibition of Modern Architecture* of 1932 and *Machine Art* in 1934. The terms "art moderne" and "art deco" derived from the French exposition.

Advisors adopted the language of modernism. In an interesting twist on the term art moderne, home economist Anna Cooley described a text as "home economics moderne" for its "new" approach in her introduction to Evelyn M. Herrington's *Homemaking: An Integrated Teaching Program* (1935). This demonstrates the infiltration of the usage of the French "moderne" in American parlance at the time, at least among academics. Evelyn Herrington was head of the Department of Home Economics at Scarsdale High School in New York, and Cooley was professor of household arts education at Columbia University. Their text, which included a note from Marion S. Van Liew, chief of the Home Economics Education Bureau at the University of the State of New York, demonstrated links between public and private institutions as well as between secondary and college-level educators. Home economists and arts educators welcomed modernism into their texts.

Modern design covered a broad spectrum of forms, finding its way into flower vases as well as cars.[17] Industrial designer Raymond Loewy developed a theory of the all-encompassing aesthetic. Through a series of pictorial charts, he demonstrated the similarity between the evolution of the telephone and women's bathing suits from 1878 to 1930. Loewy believed that every form could be made better through the principles of modern design. The industrial designers of the 1920s and 1930s worked with plastics, metals, bridges, and kitchen sinks. Although many career industrial designers probably considered the machine age more applicable to cars than to furniture, domestic advisors helped bring the movement into the home.

Meanwhile, female art collectors introduced the ideas to an intellectual crowd. Museums became an important tool for showcasing the controversial art-moderne designs in the United States. Although the curators of these exhibits tended to be influential and well-connected men, the location of the exhibits marked an important moment for women in the history of American museums. Lillie Bliss, Abbie Aldrich Rockefeller, and Mrs. Cornelius J. Sullivan, all influential New Yorkers, founded the Museum of Modern Art (MOMA) in New York in 1929.

Gertrude Vanderbilt Whitney and Juliana Force opened the Whitney Museum of American Art a year later. Certainly, these were well-connected women, yet it was not only their money that led them to open these particular museums. While the men in their families, especially John D. Rockefeller Jr., collected traditional, centuries-old art that was already respected, the women carved a place for themselves in the "new" genres of American art and modern art. They found their own voice in these different movements that were not widely esteemed.

MOMA was the first American museum to embrace machine art. The exhibits of the 1930s helped to bring respect to both the art and the museum. Though two of the most important venues for modern art in New York (MOMA and the Whitney) were founded by women, modernity also pushed women in the opposite direction. Many of the most important proponents of the antimodernist movement in art and museums came from women such as Abbie Aldrich Rockefeller and Electra Havemeyer Webb, both of whom collected intensively in American folk arts. Abbie Rockefeller (as well as her husband) had varied collecting interests. Both modern art and folk art, although embodying contradictory ideals, appealed to her, perhaps because they both embraced an aesthetic of simple beauty.

As demonstrated with the Mechanics' Fair in Boston in 1902, local and international fairs became a perfect place for advisors to feature their modern ideas. From the relatively small Mechanics' Fair to the Futurama Exhibition in New York in 1939, domestic advisors used public venues to illustrate their ideas about women and the American home. The Mechanics Fair may have been ahead of its time in advocating modern design, but it was soon joined by other exhibitions from the local to the international level that advocated a similar agenda.

World's fairs provided opportunities for women to demonstrate and observe new ideas in design. They also provided popular subjects for domestic advisors to bring their new ideas to a large audience. At the Century of Progress Exhibition in Chicago in 1933 and at the Futurama Exhibition in New York in 1939, the exhibitors and consumers of the exhibit messages quite purposefully used the term "modern" to emphasize their pride at being headed toward "tomorrow" with new ideas and new technologies. The home was one place where Americans, especially American women, could express these new ideas. Chicago's "Century of Progress" fair in 1933 included a series of home

Dorothy Raley's A Century of Progress *illustrated the household designs featured at the 1933 World's Fair. Exhibits of modern furnishings and decorating abounded at the fair, suggesting that the Victorian Era was officially over. Indeed, this sparsely furnished living room from the "steel house" would have barely been recognizable as a living room to early generations of decorators. Its well-lighted reading and conversation groupings represented the ideal of modern design. (Raley,* A Century of Progress, *66; courtesy* The Winterthur Library, Printed Book and Periodical Collection)

exhibits, which, in the words of observer Dorothy Raley, "completely change the old time concept of the Home . . . because they are Modern in the Nth degree."[18]

Raley's 1934 book featured photographs of the various homes displayed at the fair, including the "Crystal House," "Steel House," and the "House of Tomorrow."[19] "Within a lifetime," she wrote, "American homes have evolved from LABOR-PLACES to EASE-ABODES."[20] This shift, for Raley, represented the symbolic triumph of the modern era. Although the year 1934, right in the middle of the Depression, surely was not a year of "ease-abodes" for everyone, Raley's confidence depicted a domestic fantasy that imagined design to have a transformative power even in the face of a troubled economy.

Advisors raved about the ways that the simple modern style could affect peoples' lives. Dorothy Raley, writing about the 1933 Chicago

World's Fair, declared that the modern era "completely change[d] the old time concept of the home." She made a direct connection between the change in house and furniture design and a change in American women. "Then [the nineteenth century], the housewives were old, bent, and wrinkled at forty; now, modern wives are just maturing into the most glamorous stage of womanhood at that age. And no wonder! Like the automobile, the modern home is a product of the laboratory. But this Machine-Age has not robbed the '1934 Model' of its individuality, its soul, or its charm. The new note in Home-making has come to stay. It is based on Economy, Efficiency, and Beauty."[21] Raley, and other domestic advisors, believed that the clean, simple, modern designs in the home had brought positive change to the lives of women.

The rooms designed for the fairs were the stuff of domestic fantasy. The "House of Tomorrow" was an octagon-shaped room, including a "hall, recreation-cocktail room, hobby room, air-conditioning room, garage, and an airplane hangar."[22] While many women remained unable to access the domestic fantasies they read or heard about, the symbols remained important.[23] The excitement, innovation, and poverty of the 1930s combine to reveal a sense of what might have been and of the degree to which creativity and domestic fantasy could soar even in the face of the harsh reality of the Depression years.

Home arrangement made up an important part of the world's fair in New York in 1939. The fair promoted a certain vision of American culture, and the household played an important role. The Modern-age Furniture company of New York furnished many of the futuristic rooms, including a small table that concealed a liquor cabinet and a "comfortable curved sofa."[24] Visitors to the fair would have little doubt that American designers and cultural leaders intended to look to the future through the furniture displayed in the many household rooms. "We cherish individuality . . . we cherish the democratic principle," wrote observer and critic Emily Genauer about Americans visiting the fair.[25] Visitors would find their democratic values illustrated through the mass-produced furniture they could imagine in their own homes.

Art critic Emily Genauer wrote about the 1939 world's fair in her book *Modern Interiors, Today and Tomorrow.* Emily Genauer, born in 1910, graduated from the Columbia Graduate School of Journalism in 1930 and proceeded to make a career of art criticism in newspapers and magazines.[26] She wrote in praise of modern architecture, such as the Guggenheim Museum in New York, and of modern household design. She wrote for several newspapers in different capacities, such as her role as the editor of the fine and decorative arts sections of the *New York World-Telegram* in the 1930s. Genauer was awarded the Pulitzer Prize for art criticism in 1974 for her work at *Newsday*.

Genauer's 1939 book, subtitled "A critical analysis of trends in contemporary decoration as seen at the Paris Exposition of Arts and Techniques and reflected at the New York World's Fair," celebrated the widespread appeal of the fair. "Millions of persons, coming from all over the globe," she exulted, "have the opportunity to observe [modernism] in full flower. Being a distinctly contemporary expression, a décor that is simple, direct, comfortable, convenient and honest . . . it finds its place very appropriately in the new world of tomorrow."[27] She wrote about her excitement that Americans had begun to participate in modern art and architecture movements. No longer viewing these movements as strictly European, the Americans of the 1930s had begun to look to the future.

Configuring the modern age as "youthful" often helped advisors explain the movement. Anna Hong Rutt declared that "modernism expresses the directness and speed of the youth of today." She labeled the families who chose modernism as a decorating tool as "young, courageous, experimental, impersonal and logical."[28] Alice Waugh, as well, appealed to the next generation. "The modern house with its simple masses and entire lack of applied decoration," she wrote in 1939, "makes almost as great an appeal to the youth of today as do the streamlined car models."[29] As *Good Housekeeping*'s Helen Koues wrote in her book *How to Be Your Own Decorator* in 1939, "Far from being a fad, Modern art and decoration have become a definite part of modern life. . . . The Modern home is especially designed to meet modern requirements of present day living."[30] Using the word several times in one sentence merely emphasized its importance to contemporary readers.

Domestic advisors often promoted modern design and efficiency in tandem. In household goods, streamlining addressed the oft-noted need for sanitation and dust-free surfaces. Streamlining came into vogue around 1930 and began to change the literal shape of objects, both large and small. Part of the appeal may have been technological innovation, which made the rounded corners possible. Corners tended to catch dust, but the streamlined edges helped ease the minds of worried advisors. Amy Rolfe, who opposed most invasions of the factory into the home, praised steel furniture, "for it is so quickly cleaned, so easily kept dust proof and germ proof."[31] She recognized that several aspects of the factory-produced-and-influenced furniture would be assets to the household.

Advisors became astute observers of new materials. New uses for old metals filled household manuals. Elizabeth Burris-Meyer understood that "metal can be lighter to handle than wood and lends itself readily to design."[32] Whereas during the nineteenth century, bronze, brass, silver, pewter, and tin found their way into household accessories, the use of chrome plating changed the look of the twentieth century. Chrome was invented in 1798 by a French chemist. Its assets included color, brilliance, hardness, and resistance to corrosion. Used extensively for armor plating and for projectile covering in World War I, it was first introduced commercially in 1925.[33] Chrome was particularly known for catching light and brightening rooms and was used for chair arms and legs, clocks, and tables. "No word but 'beguiling,'" wrote Emily Post in 1930, "describes many of the toy animals of chromium steel."[34] Metal furniture for household interiors was resisted at first, although showings of tubular chairs and tables at the Chicago World's Fair in 1933 improved its image.[35] Other important metals for furnishings in the machine age included aluminum and stainless steel.

Good Housekeeping's Helen Koues celebrated the new metals and the new woods and textiles being used in modern homes. She delighted in materials such as "glass, cork, metal, rough-textured fabrics, rare woods and synthetic products," finding no problem with new technologies. She appreciated the use of "light, bleached" wood in modern furniture, recommended a coffee table of "clear mirror—especially effective against the rough textured fabric of the carpet," and even pictured a room with a "mirrored wall."[36] Koues was not concerned with preserving traditional materials and arrangements of the past. Rather she scoffed that "we cannot imagine a Swedish Modern chair covered in old satin damask."[37] She rid the home of the old and welcomed the "happy solutions" of modern furniture and arrangements.

Advisor Amy Rolfe deemed electric lighting fixtures as "the most important of all the furnishings of a room" because chrome and other metals responded particularly well to a new emphasis on lighting. With increased use of electric lights in the 1920s and 1930s, the way in which light touched and reflected off of the furniture became important to designers and advisors. "The form, color, and design of the lighting fixtures should all reflect and be in keeping with the general spirit of the room," Rolfe continued.[38] In previous decades, through the teens, many middle-class homes had been fitted with both gas and electric lighting, but by the 1920s and 1930s more and more home builders had accepted—and designed for—the precedence of electric lighting. Light could be better controlled with advances in fixtures and with the gradual removal of gas and kerosene from living rooms and hallways. If the lighting fixture "is inadequate in structural design," wrote Rolfe, "there is a loss of dignity to the whole scheme of decoration."[39]

Advisors noticed the effect of modern home lighting on women's lives. Artificial lighting was especially important in the dark of night, and decorator Edith Rhyne remarked that working women, away from their homes during daylight, had a special relationship to electric lights when they returned to dark apartments. In an article in *Practical Home Economics* in 1935, Rhyne provided photographs of new ways to light a living room and noted that the pictures were taken at night, because "the apartment, being occupied by a professional woman . . . [demanded that] the effect by artificial light was of great consequence."[40]

Domestic advisors utilized the new technologies and new materials to confront the middle-class home from a modern perspective. Burris-Meyer's recommendations included relieving the "overstuffed, heavy appearance" of upholstered furniture with chrome and glass.[41] She educated her readers about the origins of metal furniture, citing chrome-plated steel tubing used for chairs in Germany, and taught that "when metal is treated as metal . . . its own beauty creates an excellent form of decoration . . . its indestructible quality has a definite appeal." Although she did not recommend Bakelite plastic, commenting that "so far, the material seems impractical," she did celebrate the use of other synthetic materials in household furniture.[42]

Acceptance of plastic in household furniture was gradual. The first commercial plastic, celluloid, was invented in the United States in 1868 to substitute for ivory in billiard balls. New plastics, especially Bakelite (1909), Plexiglas, and Lucite (1936) all helped revolutionize the manufacture of American home goods. By the 1940s, plastics had become part of the home as furniture and as accessories. New plastics had important design implications because they could be molded and manipulated in different ways from wood, glass, and ceramics. They also had properties that meant they could be subject to heat, cold, and long years of abuse without breaking. Manufacturing companies such as DuPont, which had spent a century producing only gunpowder and explosives, began to look toward home goods as major new product

Lucite furniture and rayon curtains are the focus of this still from the DuPont corporation's educational motion picture of 1941, "A New World through Chemistry." Furniture and textiles made possible by the chemical laboratory surround this happy woman. In the 1930s and 1940s, new kinds of materials, especially new fabrics, imitation leathers, and plastics, revolutionized the American home. (Courtesy Hagley Museum and Library)

lines. Advisors kept American women aware of advances in industrial design and technology.

Designers realized that Americans could be susceptible to changes in an object's *look*, rather than just in its usefulness. By changing the design every year, household-furnishings companies followed the automobile industry into planned obsolescence. An often-cited example of this trend was the Sears, Roebuck and Company's Coldspot Refrigerator in the 1930s, which did not change in technology but radically changed its design every year. Raymond Loewy and the other industrial designers at Sears added "vertical skyscraper setbacks" in 1935, streamlined corners two years later, and also added different feet, chrome moldings, and other details. This ensured that consumers would consistently pay money for the new designs every year.

New appliances appeared in the advice manuals despite the absence of such objects in most households. "The new one-piece instrument," wrote Emily Post referring to the modern incarnation of the telephone, "can be painted to go with the room and look very well almost anywhere." She recommended that, "whatever we do with our new inventions . . . let us not petticoat our telephones," a direct assault on Victorian "fripperies."[43] Post addressed many electrical appliances in her 1930 manual. She reminded her readers to pay attention to the placement of outlets because many of the new appliances needed to be moved around frequently, such as the "heating pad, say, or a milk-heater."[44]

Despite the enthusiasm, most Americans could not enjoy the products of machine-age design in the early twentieth century. Because of limited access to electricity and because of widespread poverty during the Depression, the great variety of objects and colors that designers and advisors advocated in the interwar period did not become available on a large scale until after World War II.[45] Nearly every American household finally experienced electrical modernization by 1959.[46] Electricity in the 1920s was limited to urban areas and to large businesses, in part because electric-company studies showed that middle-to-lower-income households would not take advantage of an electrical supply, and the investment would not be profitable. In the 1920s, households spent only 8 percent of their total expenditures on household appliances.[47] Although this figure changed in the 1930s, with many families increasing their spending on small appliances, the total number of families with monetary and electrical access to the new consumer goods was limited.[48]

For domestic advisors, modernism often translated into simplicity. "Every article in a room," wrote Maria Parloa in her *Home Economics* of 1910, "should have a reason for being there."[49] In her manual, Parloa went through each room of the house making suggestions for how to recognize and remove extraneous objects. Twenty years later, Emily Post had the same idea. "When furnishing your own house," she wrote, "be sure, first of all, that the colors are harmonious, that the chairs are restful to sit on, that writing tables are well equipped."[50] Like other advisors before and after her, Post clearly articulated that her ideas had less to do with income than with taste. Her instructions for each room followed the basic principle that the family's house would be comfortable only when women made each household decision with the ideals of balance, simplicity, and rationality intact.

Advisors directly related beauty to functionality. "The pitcher that does not pour well cannot be beautiful," claimed Helen Campbell. "The spider-legged table and its insect family of chairs, the things that creak when we sit down and tip over when we get up, these are not beautiful." She had a rigid idea of beauty and claimed that "it is quite possible . . . to believe an ugly thing to be beautiful, through association of ideas, false education, low perceptive faculties, and the like." Her manual was intended to train American women, who "as a whole, have a low national taste"[51] to recognize beauty when they saw it, and then to strive to transfer that beauty to their own homes. Martha Van Rensselaer's 1919 *A Manual of Home Making* included illustrations of "comfortable," practical chairs alongside those "ugly in proportion, erratic in line, over decorated in finish, that should be avoided."[52]

Virginia Terhune Van de Water suggested that her readers strive in every case to "combine beauty with usefulness."[53] The daughter of nineteenth-century advisor Marion Harland (Mary Terhune), Van de Water was born in 1865 into the literary Terhune family of Virginia. Van de Water collaborated with her mother on several projects, including *Everyday Etiquette* (1907) and followed her mother into the field. She dedicated one of her books "to my mother, MARION HARLAND, who, by precept and example, has taught me all that I know of housekeeping and homemaking."[54] Her sister Christine Terhune Herrick also wrote domestic advice, and many other family members were authors. Though Van de Water wrote several texts about the household and about etiquette, she departed from household advice to write *Why I Left My Husband* (1912) and *Women and Bolshevism* (1918). Her domestic-advice manual *From Kitchen to Garrett* merged her mother's nineteenth-century frugality with her own modern sensibility.

"I go so far as to urge every woman," wrote Lillian Bayless Green in 1917, to make the home both "attractive and convenient."[55] Lillie Hamilton French implored each housekeeper to utilize "some closet, or chest of drawers, or store-room, some one receptacle large enough to hold all that is ugly and superfluous."[56] In the ideal house, "the question of utility has governed every arrangement. The useful has been made the ornamental."[57] For these advisors, any object that served no apparent function was ugly.

Charlotte Wait Calkins addressed the modern need for simplicity in decoration. Carpets "should not be bright in color or of large, restless, swirling designs, making the floor appear to rise up. . . . Pictures of dogs are out of place—one does not wish to tread on rose bou-

Domestic advisors of the 1920s believed that even the furniture should be streamlined. Martha Van Rensselaer, Flora Rose, and Helen Canon of the Department of Home Economics at Cornell University in upstate New York provided examples of "types of furniture ugly in proportion, erratic in line, over-decorated in finish, that should be avoided." The home economists cautioned readers to beware of excess decoration and to seek comfort and simplicity in their furniture as well as in their accessories. (Van Rensselaer et al., eds., A Manual of Homemaking, *plate VII; courtesy* The Winterthur Library, Printed Book and Periodical Collection)

quets or dogs."[58] Similarly, "no one should want to rest his head on anything that resembles real rose thorns, tennis rackets, pipes, flags, indian heads, and the like."[59] These design suggestions outlined a specific, restrained mandate for the modern home. Her message was to be subdued in design, counteracting the Victorian era's outrageous patterns. Calkins's recurring theme was that "the house must . . . show an appreciation of comfort, cleanliness, and orderliness. . . . The American in his strenuous life needs beauty in his house."[60]

Advisors presented a series of rules for women to follow when choosing furniture. "For what purpose is it to be used," began Charlotte Wait Calkins. "Is the material appropriate to the use? Is it durable?"[61] She believed that each piece of furniture had to be carefully analyzed to assess its place in the home. "The furnishing of a dining-room," wrote Mabel Hyde Kittredge, "should be very simple." She noted that when a dining room shared space with a living room, furnishings could be more decorative, but "if the room is used only as a place in which to eat, all of the furnishings should suggest this object."[62] Lillie Hamilton French noted quite clearly that, "the dining-room is a place for eating. Its purpose is defined."[63] Furniture should be chosen so as to serve the particular use of the room, and for no other reason.

The "right kind" of living room furniture depended on the function of the room for the family. "Do they read good books?" Kittredge asked, "If so, the book shelves and the library table will tell you so." She noted that "good light" was important only if it served a purpose, that is, if people in the room would be sewing or reading.[64] Dorothy Tuke Priestman rejected traditional notions of propriety in favor of functionality. "Let us be resolved to have our homes in keeping with the lives we lead," she wrote in 1910. "We say it is not suitable to have a workbasket in the parlor. It is if we sew there."[65]

Some advisors thought men and women would like different kinds of rooms. However, unlike the late-nineteenth-century's rigid ideas about men's dining rooms and women's parlors, advisors in the modern era could be somewhat more flexible. Emily Post wrote about "men's rooms."

There is neither sense nor beauty in the popular belief that manliness can be expressed only in the sort of solidity suitable for caging a grizzly bear; that a small room set aside for his personal use must be known as a "den," and be furnished with an overstuffed sofa that would support an elephant and with chairs obviously made for baby hippopotamuses. It is not necessary that the office desk and other objects of wood furniture be either of raw-beef-colored mahogany or of fumed oak, or that the entire color scheme be maroon combined with wet-mud brown.[66]

Post's amusing commentary here on sex-segregated rooms did not mean that she did not have strong ideas about the differences between men and women. Rather, her book was a treatise on practical decorating, practical furnishing, and she had no use for old-fashioned and heavy ornamentation.

Principles of balance brought scientific rules to the living room. Lillian Bayless Green focused on the mantelpiece. After first noting that "the mantle should never be cluttered," she provided certain rules in which the arrangement would be as "symmetrical as possible." Perhaps "a candlestick at either end with a simple clock or vase in the center," suggested Green.[67] In later years, advisors provided even stricter lessons on the properties of symmetry and balance. In 1928, Lois Palmer directed her readers to place all rugs "parallel to the walls; never at an angle to them. It is sometimes a temptation to have a rug reach from one doorway to another, in the direction of traffic, but well-poised people don't yield to it, because they know that such placing makes for bad balance, and will distress others who may see it." She also noted that "an essential of symmetry is to have the major pieces of furniture placed parallel with the walls."[68]

Though advisors stood united on many fronts, including functionality and balance, their most common cause was the elimination of bric-a-brac. Bric-a-brac was a general term that advisors used to refer to a catalogue of decorating errors. While most advisors used the terms "gewgaws," "knick-knacks," and "bric-a-brac" interchangeably, Anna Hong Rutt made a distinction in 1935. The difference was between "knickknacks, which have no artistic merit and are often merely souvenirs, Bric-a-brac, which may have some art quality but are not entirely good, [and] objects of art, which are beautiful in form, color, and texture."[69] Dorothy Tuke Priestman included textiles in her definition of bric-a-brac, complaining about "flimsy, hideous materials, knotted, cascaded, and festooned over mantels, pictures, chairbacks, and bookcase tops."[70] In its broadest sense, it meant "crowded" or "busy," and could even include wallpaper. "I hope that my readers are

Iowa State College's 1917–18 Home Economics Bulletin used this image of an "ill-proportioned, overloaded mantel" to demonstrate the negative effects of "unnecessary ornamentation." Crowded with objects as varied as heart-shaped picture frames, ornate vases, and a miniature American flag, the mantel represented poor taste. Iowa's Agricultural Extension Department joined others around the country in criticizing the pervasiveness of mantelpieces such as this one in American homes. (Bliss, Home Furnishing, *23; courtesy* The Winterthur Library, Printed Book and Periodical Collection)

A display of wedding gifts in a Denver, Colorado parlor demonstrates the proliferation of bric-a-brac that concerned so many domestic advisors in the early twentieth century. These gifts included lamps, figurines, dinnerware, tea sets, vases and other objects that eventually would need to be displayed throughout the home, cluttering surfaces and requiring frequent dusting. Despite the dire warnings of home economists and others, however, middle-class Americans continued to receive mantel clocks, candlesticks and other bric-a-brac as wedding presents throughout the century. (Courtesy Denver Public Library, Western History Collection, X-26016)

not the possessors of, or possessed by, a large variety of bric-a-brac!" wrote Virginia Terhune Van de Water in 1912. "I sometimes wish there was a law against it."[71]

The blanket term "bric-a-brac" included a wide variety of household items. Pottery vases, glass candlesticks, clocks, and other necessary items fell under the umbrella if they proliferated in one room, if they had unnecessarily ornamental casing or design, or often even if they could be considered "cheap." Other items included souvenirs and wedding presents, if too many of them congregated on one table or on one mantel. Dorothy Priestman lamented the popular trend of ornamental gift giving: "How often do we hear someone say, 'My wedding present will be a bit of pottery. It will fill in somewhere and one can't have too many vases.' Can't we indeed."[72] The objects thought of as bric-a-brac could be too many pictures on wall, too many tassels on a curtain pull, or too many pillows on a sofa. Priestman called the objects "collections of weird monstrosities" in 1910.[73] In immigrant homes, the stricture might spread to include religious statuary, crocheted afghans, and other "foreign" and "unnecessary" objects.

As early as the 1880s, some household advisors recommended the elimination of Victorian excess. In 1889, Emma Hewitt wrote:

> Still another law of good decoration declares that there shall be no excess of ornamentation—no useless beautifying, such as a bow around the poker, milk-maid stools in the parlor, and sashes on the table legs; nor is it in good taste to use as ornament, anything perverted from the original purpose, or appropriate service—no hats for coal boxes, men with holes in their heads for salt-cellars and the like monstrosities; to say nothing of such things as the wooden shovel painted with apple blossoms on a sky-blue ground, and hung by an enormous bow beside the hearth, in elaborate, but ridiculous state! This excess of decoration might be called the "American disease," but let us hope that it has nearly run its course, and that we are learning to have beauty *only* where it is needed and appropriate.[74]

Domestic advisors attacked bric-a-brac over a period of half a century, and though women certainly read their advice, they ignored it much of the time and continued to decorate their houses with bows and figurines.[75] But advisors continued the attack.

In 1890, *Good Housekeeping* magazine complained, "It [bric-a-brac] trips you up on the floor, drops down at you from the chandelier and cornices, makes it dangerous to stretch your legs or move your elbows when you sit, and renders it impossible to find a bit of unoccupied wall big enough to lean against."[76] The article went on to suggest that housewives rotate through their bric-a-brac, displaying only a few objects at any one time. Other manuals would recommend banishing all ornament to the attic. Advisors could not find any reason to keep unnecessary belongings or souvenirs around the house. Their message was clear. Lucy Ann Throop declared in 1912, "There is one matter of great importance to be kept in mind and practiced with the sternest self-control, and that is, to eliminate, eliminate, eliminate."[77]

All of the manuals at the turn of the century attacked bric-a-brac and advised that their readers throw it away or hide it. "Eliminate useless articles," wrote Charlotte Wait Calkins. "Be assured that every article that is useless will prove to be ugly."[78] She provided an extended discussion of what is "useless," commenting that "the test of fitness to purpose will make evident the inappropriateness of design of a glass match receiver in the shape of a slipper, a salt dish resembling a chicken, a pin cushion, made to appear, as nearly as possible, like a tomato, or a thermometer gracing a deer's foot."[79] Dorothy Priestman attacked "the old fashioned whatnot" as "responsible for many of the crimes committed in the name of bric-a-brac."[80] While pious sayings and homemade stitchery had been overwhelmingly popular in the nineteenth century, as the new century began, all of that was so much garbage.[81] "Innumerable inappropriate grotesqueries, decoratively intended," wrote Mary Quinn in 1914, "must be severely dealt with and banished . . . to the ash-barrel."[82]

Objects of sentimental value countered modern ideals. Hazel Adler called for the removal of all "objects of sentimental association" from the home. "Heirlooms and souvenirs . . . should find a happy end in a memory chest."[83] Alice Kellogg told her readers that any decorative objects must be "chosen for the enjoyment of those who come into the room, and not be an expression of the individual tastes of the family."[84]

Vociferous anti-bric-a-brac rhetoric became the rallying cry both for advisors who wrote for an immigrant population and for those who wrote for the middle class. For native-born Americans whose ancestors had cluttered their homes to the point of oblivion, bric-a-brac represented a lower-class and tawdry decorating style. These people saw the preponderance of objects and ornament as a class differentiation as well as an ethnic difference. Above and beyond the "foreign" connotations of clutter, domestic advisors emphasized the association between ornament and class. Language about bric-a-brac was a way to annunciate the terms of social superiority that could be gained through simple decoration.

Most advisors dismissed bric-a-brac as clutter that cheapened the look of the American home. They judged the cluttered home, and concomitantly judged the housekeeper. As Dorothy Tuke Priestman wrote in 1910 of those who collected bric-a-brac, the "error . . . is common among a certain class of women."[85] Even one or two cheap objects could destroy the look of a room. Alice Kellogg said succinctly, "bric-a-brac in the cheap meaning of the word is not in good taste."[86] The ornate nature of the piece was important to advisors in rating its social connotations. "The cheaper the fixture, the more ornate it is, as a rule,"

These two pictures give wordless proof of the virtue of elimination.

Though many American women would not have agreed with the sentiment, this basic principle was echoed throughout the pages of domestic-advice manuals in the early twentieth century. Ridding the rooms of America of distracting wallpapers, collections of bric-a-brac, lacy table coverings, and enormous plants was the goal of The Modern Priscilla, *illustrated nicely in this image from the 1925 text. (*Modern Priscilla, *131)*

wrote Lillian Bayless Green with disgust in 1917. She made a connection between ornate fixtures and social inferiority. Green positioned "dignified" American arrangements as the antithesis of old-fashioned "clutter."[87]

Much of the anti-bric-a-brac sentiment was a reaction to the Victorian generation's passion for clutter. Many familiar icons of Victorian home life were attacked along with bric-a-brac. Priestman declared: "The day for hat stands is happily passed. What ungainly ugly pieces most of them were"; and almost in the next breath, "The upright piano is of an unsatisfactory shape," thereby rejecting two of Victoriana's favorite artifacts. In a similar vein, Alice Kellogg exalted that "a reaction has happily set in against the unpleasantly realistic paintings of fish and animals that a few years ago were considered the proper selection for dining room walls." Advisors tried to convince their readers that the modern American home should be free of such old-fashioned artifacts. The domestic fantasy of the turn of the century mandated a simplified home. Showy lace and mantelpieces cluttered with bric-a-brac did not fit that picture. "'No junk!' is the cry of the new interior," Hazel Adler proclaimed, continuing that "homes which cannot free themselves from the clutter of trivial and futile objects are mute declarations of the insincerity of their creator's pretensions to good taste and refinement."[88]

Elizabeth Mainwaring, who wrote the article about the 1902 Mechanics' Fair for *Good Housekeeping* magazine, understood that the major decorating argument of the early twentieth century would concern the modern versus the Victorian home. Her caricatures perfectly outlined the debates of the first several decades of the twentieth century, which could be referred to as the "design wars."

Man and wife: "Now, Mary, that's just the way you fix our house—one mass of cluttering traps. Wish I could have one room as *I* want it!"

"After I took all that trouble to fix your den! And the cozy corner I got up is every bit as pretty as the one here."

"Blamed thing's always coming down on my head. I'd rather have a good easy arm-chair."

"But George, *everybody* has a cozy corner in their den!"[89]

Did everybody have a cozy corner? Many certainly did. And for several decades following this exchange at a public fair in Boston, domestic advisors tried to convince their readers that bric-a-brac, dens, and cozy corners should all be left behind as Americans moved forward into the modern age. That for the most part they failed does not diminish their efforts to prove to middle-class women that modernism did have a place in American homes.

COLOR IS RUNNING RIOT:

CHARACTER, COLOR, & CHILDREN

*The furnishings of a young girl's room may be very much like her
mother's, only still more simple and fresh and dainty. White or ivory
enameled furniture seems especially appropriate. Pieces can often be
decorated in some of the quaint peasant style of painted flowers, and the
same design used throughout the room.*

*In a boy's room, even if he is a very small boy, there should be less effect
of daintiness and prettiness. Use curtains of cretonne in a bold conventional
design rather than a flower-sprigged pattern. Let the furniture be strong
and substantial. Provide some place for him to keep the innumerable
belongings that are dear to the heart of a boy; sets of open bookshelves can
sometimes be built into the room. There should be specimens of his various
collections as he pleases.*

*A man's distaste for feminine frippery and furbelows should be
catered to in the furnishings of his own room. Give him furniture that
is solid and masculine-looking; as the enameled French and slender
mahogany Colonial styles seem most fitted for a woman's room, so the
modifications of Elizabethan oak designs or the modern craftsman
furniture suit the man's room.*
—Modern Priscilla Home Furnishing Book

The 1925 *Modern Priscilla Home Furnishing Book* joined other domestic advisors in the argument that household surroundings would affect each person's character development. This understanding of character formation encouraged people to focus on the long-term effects of decorating decisions. From little girls' bedrooms to the family bathroom, the decoration of each room in the house had long-lasting repercussions.

What kinds of Americans did the readers of twentieth-century domestic advice want their children to become? They wanted well-adjusted kids who understood their roles in the gendered society. They wanted boys whose insect collections could lead to a career in science and girls whose interest in the household would be piqued at an early age. They wanted to preserve a status quo of gender relations, but also to explore new colors and to incorporate modern technology in their homes. Readers of domestic advice plowed through hundreds of pages of commentary on curtain fabrics and other details. With the choices that the modern era offered regarding color palates and materials, the results could vary.

The twentieth century may have provided a scary set of choices to many American women. With sons and daughters facing a consumer world filled with possibility, mothers turned to domestic advice for safety. They looked at books such as *The Modern Priscilla* to guide them on their way to making sure they raised good children and provided good citizens. They wanted to believe that the choice of color on the dining room walls could really effect the future character of the nation, and American middle-class women turned to magazines and books for advice. Advisors themselves navigated their own confusion by providing concrete rules and suggestions. They began a study of the effects of room arrangement on personal happiness, a study that would continue throughout the century.

The Modern Priscilla Home Book prided itself on providing simple directions for positive living. The editors claimed to understand that not all of its readers had grown up in protected, strong-character building environments, and they announced their intentions to fix this problem for the next generation. "The mother who realizes the true significance of home furnishings will never introduce makeshift furniture into her home or be content with anything less than the very best in everything constituting the environment of her children."[1] The future of the nation's children, then, was in the hands of the mothers who decorated their homes. America's children depended on strong furniture, strong colors, and strong gender-appropriate rules. Domestic advisors would help the new generation by providing guideposts for home decorating.

The early twentieth century was a period in which the relationship between household decoration and personality began to make sense. "In this present day of interest in child psychology," wrote Emily Post in 1930, "there are few who fail to realize that children . . . are super-sensitive to beauty in its almost every phase."[2] Although her text did not say much more about the results of academic research, her use of the term "child psychology" indicates its prevalence in the culture. She tried to attract worried mothers to her advice by connecting her advice to the new social science.

Children had been important subjects for "expert advice" since the Progressive Era at the turn of the twentieth century. For example, Progressive Era theories about the effects of recreation on children and adolescents led to the creation of playgrounds and to a new civic responsibility for child development. Public figures such as G. Stanley Hall and Jane Addams had made public stands in favor of properly organized recreation at the turn of the century. Supporters of the "Play Movement" organized the Playground Association of America, arguing that directing children's playtime could contribute to their moral development.[3] In the 1950s, *Good Housekeeping*'s Helen Koues noted that "modern toys and games, like modern ideas, stress the intellectual or 'how to do' side of a child's mind, teaching through play."[4] Throughout the twentieth century, domestic advisors used similar arguments to convince their readers about the importance of household arrangement in children's rooms.

The field of child development grew in the early twentieth century. Social scientists studied the ways in which children learned and created teaching models to correspond with their findings. They began to ask questions about the influences of daily life on the child's future welfare. Since the nineteenth century, childhood had been under the scientific microscope as a separate and vital time of life when the character was formed for the future. With the advent of juvenile detention centers and other "early intervention" methods in the 1870s, criminologists began to discuss what society could do to "save" children before they could be influenced by dangerous elements perceived to be found in certain neighborhoods and among certain groups of people. Domestic advisors picked up on some of the language of the child-development scholars and began to add it into their texts. They built on the worries that many people had about raising children and provided household solutions.

Home economist Hazel Shultz addressed the issue of children's moral and intellectual development. In her 1931 *Making Homes,* Shultz wrote about how to ensure that children were given the proper amount of room and the proper tools as they grew up. Shultz, born in 1891, was by the 1920s a professor in the Department of Home Economics in the Laboratory Schools of the University of Chicago. Her university had been at the forefront of home-economics education at the turn of the century, and Shultz helped turn the focus from nutrition studies to child psychology. Her efforts resulted in many books during the 1930s and 1940s, including *The First Book in Home Economics* of 1936 and a book written for the Home Economics Extension Division on how to teach home study. Her work often emphasized the special role of the educated woman in providing a strong home for her family.

The need for children and adults to simultaneously use the house in their development created certain problems. Hazel Shultz addressed the need for "provisions for developing initiative" in the home. She noted that "because of the necessarily limited size of our homes, members of families must adjust the time and place used to the interests and needs of each other." [5] She included a special section and directions for accommodating children. Providing sketches of children in the home, accompanied by questions such as "Where should a towel rod be placed for this little boy?" and "How is the little girl encouraged to keep her possessions in good order?" gave readers ideas about how to provide for the particular needs of small children. [6]

Shultz emphasized the importance of creating houses that allowed for individuality, an important characteristic for American children. From reading her text, she claimed, "One sees why we develop *individuality* in our homes. If it were not for this desire to have houses and furnishings that meet our individual needs, we might well standardize houses and provide all families with homes exactly alike." [7] However, she made clear in her text that such sameness was not the ideal. She encouraged her readers to discover what made them individuals and to express that in their home decorating. She encouraged parents to nurture such individuality in their children and to provide for the resulting differences in their homes.

1. STOOL for SMALL CHILD   2. CUPBOARD SHELVES and DRAWERS, convenient height for CHILD

Hazel Shultz included many ideas for making homes accessible and appropriate for children. Many domestic advisors ignored children in their texts, but others believed that keeping children in mind when decorating the house would instill a love for home at an early age. This drawing shows how benches (for height) and cupboards (for storage) could help children care for themselves and their belongings. (Shultz, Making Homes, *36; courtesy The Winterthur Library, Printed Book and Periodical Collection)*

In the first several decades of the twentieth century, advisors spent more time discussing children's rooms than ever before. Decorators, home economists, and magazine editors jumped in with statements about the effect of decorating on children's moral development. "A common mistake in furnishing a child's room," wrote Alice Kellogg, "is to fancy that anything that is not wanted in other rooms may be turned to account there." Rather than making the child's room into a "second-rate antique shop," she recommended "a touch of the unique . . . [to appeal to] the plastic nature of the child."[8] Decorators such as Kellogg and her colleague Dorothy Priestman understood that the impressionable nature of children needed to be molded in certain ways, and quite early in life. Priestman directed the "rooms for young people . . . [to be] among the brightest quarters in the house . . . to build that love of home which is to have such an important effect on their future."[9]

Hazel Adler noted that for children, "environment exerts a strong influence upon the formation of tastes, habits, and temperament for the remainder of life."[10] In Elsie Richardson's discussion of bedrooms, she noted that "it has been proved that furnishings and color produce either desirable or disastrous effects upon the sensitive minds of children."[11] The *Modern Priscilla Home Furnishing Book* warned in 1925: "What children see when they are little largely determines their taste in later life."[12] Each girl's "personality, even at a very tender age," warned Blanche Halbert, in 1931, "will be clearly disclosed by the way she cares for her room."[13] The concern continued into the 1950s. Helen Koues noted: "No longer is the average child allowed to 'just grow' like Topsy. Not only do baby doctors and child specialists pass on to eager mothers the new hygiene in bringing up children, but mothers themselves are aware of the influence of environment and realize that the earliest surroundings of the child may have a definite influence."[14] Armed with advice books, American women could control the character of the modern era.

The idea to make boys' bedrooms much different from girls' bedrooms surfaced in the early twentieth century. Differentiating children's rooms from those for adults had been a Victorian phenomenon, and the modern era took the obsession with childhood one step further. Taste makers and commentators of early America had treated children with mild disdain, or as small, underdeveloped adults, and the households and household goods of the period reflected that. However, in the nineteenth century, middle-class houses burst with toys, play-rooms, small chairs, and special objects. Children's nurseries became important in house design, and domestic advisors certainly contrib-uted to the new childhood phenomenon. The early-twentieth-century focus on child psychology emphasized differences between girls and boys, and advisors brought that knowledge to the household, and to the toys and wallpaper in particular. The emphasis shifted from the difference between children and adults to the sexualized differences between boys and girls. Training for their roles must, thought psy-chologists and domestic advisors at once, begin at birth.

The *Modern Priscilla Home Furnishing Book* recommended "simple, fresh and dainty" decorations for a girl's room, whereas a boy's room should have "strong and substantial" furniture.[15] Marjorie Mills, in 1929, suggested "orchid gray paper with silver flowers" for a girl's room, but cautioned that "a boy's room, of course, should be quite dif-ferent." A shift in both design and color was deemed necessary, indi-cating "reds and tans and blacks and blue," along with "substantial ma-hogany furniture."[16] The differences in furnishings and wall color were considered important in order to mold the children to their proper gender roles. Domestic advisors thought that color and design had a strong effect on personal character.

The association between color and gender was for the most part a twentieth century invention. Before factories and dye works could suc-cessfully and cheaply add color to threads and fabrics, clothing colors had been limited. Colors faded easily with repeated washings, and many parents dressed their children in white. At the turn of the twen-tieth century, however, technology and chemical dyes made a rainbow of colors more widely accessible to the middle class. Color associa-tions are not inherent and often take many years to develop. In the first few decades of the twentieth century, many people identified blue with girls because of its "dainty" qualities, and thought pink was ap-propriate for boys because of its vibrant character and closeness to red. However, by the 1940s and 1950s, the strong associations of pink with girls and blue with boys was firmly established in advertising, decora-tion choices, and domestic advice. Half a century later, computer com-panies market pink and blue computers to children in the hopes that the color system remains strong.

Elsie Richardson provided a complete template for furniture choice and arrangement in 1931. In her discussion of children's bedrooms, she noted that "it has been proved that furnishings and color produce

This girl is allowed to daydream about "fairyland" thanks to the ethereal
nature of her room decorations. The Modern Priscilla, *in 1925, recommended*
dainty features for girls, including painted furniture, flowers, and dolls.
(Modern Priscilla Book of Home Decorating, *167*)

either desirable or disastrous effects upon the sensitive minds of children," and she went on to recommend vastly different schemes for boys and girls. "A girl's room should be dainty and bright." She recommended "sateen, tafetta, . . . or dotted swiss" for curtains. For boys, however, only "denims, reps and heavy sunfasts" would do. For a boy's room, "there should be no frills, [or] light fabrics. . . . Convenience and masculinity should be kept foremost in mind." Accouterments for the masculine room included furnishings of dark wood, especially the desk, and a bookcase for "trophies, etc." "Few or no decorative accessories are necessary," she concluded. Boys' temperaments, according to Richardson, tended toward the destructive, so their rooms should be kept clean of items "for boys to soil or mar." [17] By providing this sort of room, American women could be sure that their boys would grow to appropriate, modern manhood.

Most advisors had more to say about rooms for boys, perhaps because their assumed interests in sports and collections held more challenge for the home decorator. Priestman recommended "a prettily-draped dressing table" for girls, and for boys:

> There should be shelves of some sort where the lad can stow away some treasures as his stamp album, his butterflies, his postal collection, or whatever happens to be his hobby, for hobbies in a boy should be encouraged, as they help to bring out his manly traits. The athletic boy should have his weapons about, his fencing foils crossed above the mantlepiece, his gun above the door, his golf sticks in the corner, his cups and his medals here and there. Such a room as this should have strong, heavy furniture, so that in case the boy should take down his boxing gloves and have a bout with his friend nothing would be damaged—unless perhaps the eyes or nose of one of the participants.[18]

The popular journal *House Beautiful* designed a room for "young masters" in 1937.

> Even the young have a right to be masters in their own quarters. If they want to have Jim and Jane and the rest of the members of the Games Club over for an afternoon of hot chocolate and cake and dominoes, they should be able to do so without adult interference. (You can see that we believe in the youth freedom theory.) What they need is a room of their own . . . where they can have company, play games, and study. . . . Each one has plenty of space for seating extra friends—sofas, beds that are covered with durable heavy fabrics, large chairs and small chairs. Then you will see that there are desks, work tables that will fold and take up no space, lots of drawers for gadgets and the inevitable "collections."[19]

The author of the article commented that with a bedroom such as the ones described in the magazine, "no child in the world would want to practice swinging a baseball bat in the parlor."[20] Differentiating between rooms in which certain gendered activities would take place was an important part of domestic advice. The parlor was separated from boys based on their age, but also on their masculinity and assumed, even desired, roughhousing.

The differences between recommendations for boys' and girls' rooms went much deeper than dainty versus rough. Boys' rooms always carried the extra needs of the hobby. The concept of boys having a hobby that they followed from their elementary school years through adolescence found strong advocates in domestic advisors of the 1920s and 1930s. Hazel Shultz even went so far as to say "The pursuit of a hobby is another very common desire, and sometimes necessitates thought in the planning of a house."[21] She provided an illustration of how to alter a closet so as to provide for the insect collection of a fourteen-year-old boy and described his interests in detail: "Beneath the desk can be seen the top of a pile of insect boxes, one of which has been opened and is exhibited on top. With each insect he has the common and entomological names, as well as the place where found. The funnels above his right hand are part of one of his insect traps. . . . On the wall above the bottles is a rare species of moth sent by a friend from the Philippine Islands."[22] Such unusual detail about the particular collection emphasized the importance of the hobby to the development of American boys and to the decoration of the middle-class home.

By the 1950s, most advice books recommended that each member of the family have a hobby. Still focused on boys, Helen Koues suggested, "When it is possible to find the space in attic or basement, it is well to have a real playroom for the boys of the family." Advisors made room for the hobbies of women and girls, as well.[23] Koues included a chapter on "How to Decorate Game and Hobby Rooms" and noted that women might need special space to accommodate a girl's interests in sewing, antiquing, or gardening. When used by men and boys, though, the room should feature "knotty-pine walls . . . [and have] an atmosphere of comfort—almost luxury—but it is simple. There is nothing to break, no rugs to scuff, and man and boy would like it. No frills to bother them—just solid comfort."[24] The common assumption that males would break everything in sight if not protected by the home decorator followed men from infancy to adulthood.

Most domestic advisors believed that personal fulfillment and character development remained important goals of household decoration well after childhood. Home-efficiency expert Lillian Gilbreth used her doctorate in psychology to approach the arrangement of kitchens. She offered her 1927 book to readers as a "philosophy that will make [the home maker's] work satisfying."[25] Christine Frederick also believed that observation of efficiency would lead directly to internal well-being. "The American housewife of today," she wrote, "who can

An open fireplace is cheerful and useful in a hard-to-heat room

for MAN
and BOY

Differences in decorations for men and boys remained fairly constant in the twentieth century. Dark colors, unpainted wood, and game imagery (both animal and competitive) proliferated in rooms designed to appeal to men. Helen Koues's room "for Man and Boy" featured a large fireplace and plenty of space for the men of the family to read and to construct their model planes. (Koues, American Woman's New Encyclopedia of Home Decorating, *330*)

gaze on her shelves of spotless pots and pans, who is refreshed by their gleaming whiteness, who is satisfied as to their safeguarding the family health—she, too will be content and enjoy her housekeeping."[26] The psychological aspect of kitchen design was not incidental to domestic advisors, who believed that room arrangement could lead directly to personal satisfaction.

With a new emphasis on personality and personal fulfillment, advisors felt that the kitchen, considered a room of toil, should instead contribute to the well-being of the modern woman. Modern advisors took their cues from industrial designers, but also found important themes in the studies of social scientists and psychologists. Blanche Halbert included an essay on the kitchen in her book of 1931, noting that "the radio has a definite place in the modern kitchen, contributing not only to the happiness of the housekeeper but to her efficiency." The article, by Greta Gray with assistance by Hildegarde Kneeland of the United States Bureau of Home Economics, went on to comment that "the arm that beats a cake does so with less realization that it is work if the movements are timed to the beat of a waltz." This research was based in part on a study of soldiers, who "forget their fatigue when the band is playing."[27] Advisors felt that women in the kitchen deserved to benefit from the results of psychological examinations based on the experiences of men.

Through careful furniture arrangements in children's bedrooms, hobby rooms, and kitchens, household advisors contributed to a national dialogue about the importance of environmental factors to human development. The subject that received the most attention from home economists and decorators, however, was color. Helen Koues described the obsession of her age: "Color is vital! It is the background against which we live. Consciously or unconsciously, we are affected by our backgrounds—be they bright, gay, soothing, gloomy or merely drab! Above all, don't let your background be drab. This is an age of color. Today our walls are yellow, not cream; dusty pink, not putty; soft blue and green, not gray."[28] New paint and wallpaper technologies meant that the twentieth-century home looked different. Domestic advisors wanted to help their readers navigate all the confusion in color and choose colors that would sustain a strong American character.

For many domestic advisors, color was the best way to express a new era in household design. The use of color to express a particularly modern sensibility began in the first few decades of the twentieth century. Hazel Adler's *The New Interior: Modern Decorations for the Modern Home* of 1916 was an early advocate of modern ideas. Adler suggested both major and minor changes for the middle-class home. As a member of a cooperative kitchen in which women shared the tasks of housework so as not to be burdened by too much drudgery in the home, Adler believed in experimenting with new ideas.[29] She tried to redefine color choices to make new, bold statements. "While we shudder now at the color discords of the Victorian era," she conceded, "we are beginning to realize that a strong and vital people needs to express itself in strong and vital colors."[30] Adler linked the character of the nation with interior decoration.

Domestic advisors interested in color choices followed up on a long history of the psychological affects of color. As early as the eighteenth century, Swedish scientist Emanuel Swedenborg wrote about the direct relationship between color and spiritual qualities.[31] In the late nineteenth century, as color became more easily transferred to fabrics through improved chemical dyes, and to plastics and paints in later years, Americans began to expect color in their lives. Black and white images were used to represent dullness and stagnancy, whereas color opened up a lively world of vibrant and strong emotions. *The Wizard of Oz* built on this image both in print in 1900 and on screen in 1939 with a representation of black-and-white Kansas as compared to the Yellow Brick Road and the Emerald City.

At the turn of the century, color was still seen as suspect by many Americans. The Columbian Exposition's "White City" played on the ideal of white as purity against the colorful backdrop of the midway, with its rides, ethnic populations, and perceived confusion. Dime novels with their bawdy, colorful covers betrayed the emotions within. As color invaded more and more aspects of popular culture, it gradually lost some of its sensational overtones, but color in the household was a gradual process for the American middle class, used to white sanitary kitchens and muted parlors. Though comfortable with clutter, most Americans took several decades to warm to the possibilities of color in the home. But domestic advisors certainly encouraged them.

Color theory was a significant and vital part of many modern, domestic-advice books. Black-and-white texts broke into full color in the modern period. Emily Post's book, along with many others, included a color wheel to help housewives coordinate all aspects of the color of the house. Advisors spent much time convincing their readers of the relationship between emotion and color. Charlotte Wait Calkins advised women to carefully choose the color of each room to project certain feelings. "Yellow is cheery and sunny; red, exciting; blue, depressing."[32] As Elizabeth Burris-Meyer warned her readers, "Many people find undecorated walls, particularly white ones, barren and unpleasant."[33] Readers of domestic manuals came to expect advice on matching the color of the drapes to sofas and carpets, and they expected information on the different characteristics of each color and how that would affect those using the room.

Harriet and Vetta Goldstein went farther than the other domestic advisors of the 1920s in providing a full discussion of color and color theory. In their 1926 work *Art in Everyday Life*, the art profes-

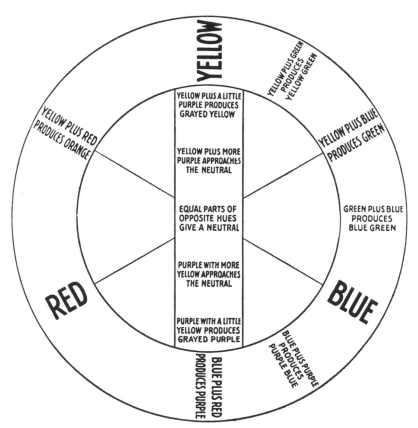

YELLOW

YELLOW PLUS A LITTLE PURPLE PRODUCES GRAYED YELLOW

YELLOW PLUS MORE PURPLE APPROACHES THE NEUTRAL

EQUAL PARTS OF OPPOSITE HUES GIVE A NEUTRAL

PURPLE WITH MORE YELLOW APPROACHES THE NEUTRAL

PURPLE WITH A LITTLE YELLOW PRODUCES GRAYED PURPLE

YELLOW PLUS GREEN PRODUCES YELLOW GREEN

YELLOW PLUS BLUE PRODUCES GREEN

GREEN PLUS BLUE PRODUCES BLUE GREEN

BLUE PLUS PURPLE PRODUCES PURPLE BLUE

BLUE

YELLOW PLUS RED PRODUCES ORANGE

RED

BLUE PLUS RED PRODUCES PURPLE

To make their readers more familiar with choosing colors for home decorating, many domestic advisors provided a color wheel. Depending on the book, these varied between full-color plates and more technical explanations of color theory. Hazel Shultz provided this black-and-white diagram of color properties in her 1931 Making Homes. *(Shultz,* Making Homes, *299; courtesy The Winterthur Library, Printed Book and Periodical Collection)*

sors in the Home Economics Division at the University of Minnesota included a chapter on "How to Know Color," which outlined the "Prang" and "Munsell" systems of color. The Prang System organized colors in concentric circles with gray in the middle. Radiating outward were gray-toned colors, such as gray-green and gray-blue. On the outside of the circle were yellow-green, green, blue-green, blue, etc. The Munsell System was a more complicated diagram "illustrating the three dimensions of color." In the center, again, were variations of gray with the colors radiating outward according to their intensity. Red was the stronger color, reaching a level of ten.[34] The idea that there was a correct way to understand color and that women could learn the rules was an important part of the role of modern domestic-advice books. Part of the idea was to demystify the academic theory and to put it into the hands of middle-class women instead of design professionals. Lois Palmer recommended using construction paper and watercolors to put together a home color wheel.[35]

Color was a new commodity for the 1920s. Although one of the most popular palettes of this period was white, red, black, and silver, in actuality a stunning array of colors was available. The availability of such brilliant colors was in part due to the research scientists who developed quick-drying, inexpensive Duco paint for DuPont in 1924. Duco paint is best known for its application to automobiles, but it also enabled a host of other colorful appliances. DuPont first used the paint for brush handles and toys before convincing General Motors to use Duco lacquer on its 1924 line of cars. The paint, keeping its color through the ravages of heat, water, mud, and age, unlike previous paints, brought color to the American consumer world.[36] Harley Earl, who set up the Art and Color Department for General Motors in 1927, helped bring about the large-scale adaptation of color by major manufacturers. This trend was followed quickly by Chrysler and then by Ford, a company famous, of course, for providing Americans with cars of any color "as long as it's black." Westinghouse, manufacturers of Formica, DuPont, which made Lucite and other plastics, and General Electric employed hundreds of people in product development, many of them in design. Color was an important component of the household artifacts they created.

Interior decorator Elsie deWolfe had unique ideas about the role of color in the home. She wrote one of the early, definitive texts in interior decoration, *The House in Good Taste* of 1910. She also wrote pieces for various magazines and journals, including *Good Housekeeping*. In 1913 she wrote an article as part of a series on "our house interiors" that addressed the color of the dining-room walls. "First of all, I think a dining room should be light and gay," she announced, and "the next thing is the planning of a becoming background for the mistress of the house." Here, deWolfe suggested matching the color of the dining-room walls to the coloring of the home's most important resident. "The color should be selected with due consideration of its becomingness with relation to the hostess. Every woman has a right to be pretty in her own dining room."[37] DeWolfe took the role of color as indicator of personality to an extreme. She believed in the power of color to convey an attitude on behalf of both the house and its hostess.[38]

As these advisors explained to their readers, color became one of the symbols of modern design. "I am sure all of us are grateful," wrote Agnes Foster Wright, "for the present-day use of good, honest, strong color in the decoration of the home."[39] The first issue of *Fortune* magazine marveled over the new opportunity for color choice in objects, such as toilet paper and kitchen appliances, that had never had color before. "In this post-war period of . . . weakened traditions," the editors wrote, "it is not surprising . . . that the American people should gratify its instinct for color by bathing itself in a torrent of brilliant hues."[40] Color could represent national character as well as individual preference.

In 1937, *House Beautiful* encouraged readers to "plan a feast of color for your home."[41] The Ludwig Baumann company advertised "the new vogue of color" with gusto in 1926. The firm sold furniture and other household accessories, boasting "a complete and practical Department of Interior Decoration." As part of that project, the firm produced a manual called *Home Beautiful* that highlighted the best parts of modern design as exemplified in its store. "Gone are the days of unrelieved drab walls, furniture of monotonous shapes and finishes, and commonplace accessories." To this firm, and to the women who worked for its design department, color allowed the home to take on "an individuality and life" not previously available.[42]

Paint companies often hired domestic advisors to write copy for their trade catalogues. The Martin-Senour company noted that "thousands of women have learned the power of color . . . the most powerful single force in decoration."[43] By using the trade catalogue as a domestic-advice manual, the paint company sold paint at the same time as its writing staff disseminated advice. This technique had been used for years by manufacturers of furniture and kitchen accessories, so modern-era women would have been used to reading advice between the price listings of their catalogs. The Sherwin-Williams Company warned in 1910 that "the dominant color used in a room, and the contrasting and combined effects of other shades employed, are not to be reckoned with lightly."[44]

Agnes Foster Wright wrote extensively about color for the Armstrong Cork Company's Linoleum division in 1924. "Color has," she declared, "come into its rightful place as an expression of beauty." She suggested different colors for every room, using the entire color wheel in each home.

> The psychology of color works out a perfect cycle, and through it all we get each color combination in turn. The average nursery has pink and blue, as it should have. The boy's room goes into browns and greens—they suit his khaki and earthy outlook on life. The little miss likes yellow, but adores blue. Her very first beau is sure to tell her that he likes her best in her blue muslin that matches her eyes. The bride wants her old rose bedroom to be dainty, and yet it must not put her robust young husband out of place. The tan living-room must accommodate in its color the grandmother's charming heirlooms and the mother's less graceful and less grateful hand-me-downs.[45]

Her playful look at different color schemes accompanied the serious message that color betrayed important characteristics about each member of the household.

Domestic advisors used color to give emotions to rooms, and they provided specific examples. Amelia Leavitt Hill, author of the 1923 text *Redeeming Old Homes*, gave her opinion on wall color.

> For the living room green is a restful color, and one of which one does not easily weary. Blue is also good, if a dull, rather dark tone be chosen. It is generally not desirable in a room with northern exposure, since it is a cold color in itself. There is, however, a shade of blue, approximate somewhat to the middle tones found in old blue china, which is not conspicuously cold, and which may be used, even in north rooms, satisfactorily. A tan wall covering, like blue, gives an effect of space, and is a bright and cheerful shade for a living room, if selected in a golden tone. . . . The dining room should, according to all the dictates of modern taste, be in blue, decorated with old blue china, if one be fortunate enough to boast any such.[46]

Hill was not daring in her color recommendations and indeed did not provide much room for disagreement. Of course, other advisors would claim that her favorite colors of tan and blue had served their time and that the twentieth century was ready for more.

Elizabeth Burris-Meyer thought the living room should be more exuberant than restful. She wrote in her *Decorating Livable Homes* in 1937: "Colors and textures for a living room that is to be largely *social* in its purpose should be selected to carry out a feeling of gay for-

[*Color Is Running Riot*]

mality." For this proposal, she recommended "vermilion, black, white, citron yellow and gray." While rooms for quiet rest might have more mellow colors, "any room used for social purposes should be decorated with contrasting color." These advisors believed that color had a major effect in determining the attitude and comfort of the people using the room. Her recommendations indicated that color was an important part of the character of either utilitarian or social rooms."[47] Helen Koues wrote that "soft rose and creamy yellow" would be perfect for a living room "to prevent it from seeming too severe."[48] The modern living room, unlike the Victorian parlor, demanded lightness and simple treatment.

Unusual colors often appealed to domestic advisors. "Magenta is the favorite color of modern decorators," wrote Anna Hong Rutt in 1935. "It is a vivid red-purple and is extremely decorative. It is an exciting color, yet the purple element in it makes it mysterious and a bit restrained."[49] Taking risks with modern color schemes was one way that advisors differed from each other. Rutt's basic premise throughout her text was that her readers must understand "the relation of the individual to her surroundings."[50] Her startling use of color was one way that she brought modern individuality into the home.

"Color is running riot," wrote Marjorie Mills in 1929. "Apply your knowledge about it, and you will use it with intelligence."[51] Mills, a domestic advisor who worked for a Boston newspaper, recommended "lovely color schemes that have been worked out by the modernists." She quite directly acknowledged her personal debt to modern designers, but also felt that she had something to say that superseded their work. Domestic advisors took ideas from the available designs and recommended ways for women to incorporate those designs into their home. Mills recommended creative uses of metal furniture with striking color combinations such as "apricot with brown and copper . . . [or] chartreuse and silver with dark blue and jade."[52]

Color played an important role in the decoration of both the kitchen and bathroom. Although Burris-Meyer claimed that "color schemes should be secondary" in these rooms, others disagreed.[53] Amy Rolfe, home economics instructor at the University of Montana and assistant professor of household arts at the University of Missouri, insisted that "the newer kitchens . . . are easier on the eyes than those which are all white." Colorful kitchens "give the woman at the stove or sink the feeling that she is something more than a necessary cog in a highly efficient piece of machinery."[54] Home economics professor Willie Melmoth Bomar emphasized that "the kitchen is no longer a dark dingy place" as it was in the nineteenth century, but also was quick to note that "neither should it be the all-white monotonous place which was the next stop in its evolution." For her, recommending color was a comment on progress, on a change in the meaning of home decoration.[55]

The quandary about an all-white, sanitary bathroom and the colorful, exuberant bathroom, usually led the debate. Devotion to sanitation was important to domestic advisors in this period, but most became convinced that the personal satisfaction gained through colorful fixtures outweighed the sanitary demand for all-white decor. While Mary Quinn summed up the demand for sanitation by insisting that "the first and last impression of a bath-room should always be of its immaculate cleanliness," [56] most advisors believed that the time had come to shake off the obsession with sanitation in favor of modern ideals. "Quite a number of people maintain a preference for an all-white bathroom," commented Priestman, "but it seems to me that a little color gives warmth and cheerfulness." [57]

Bathrooms represented the field of new ideas. As industrial designer Paul Frankl commented in 1927, "Chippendale never designed a bathroom." Freed from the constraints of traditional design, modern designers such as Frankl reveled in their unique opportunity to invent a new style.[58] Domestic advisors also had an opportunity to direct women in the organization, choice of color, and other aspects of these rooms.

Because the bathroom had a shorter design history than other rooms, advisors perhaps felt that it provided a unique opportunity for featuring their modern ideas about both design and psychology. Advisors often felt that every room should "be the outward expression of the spiritual and mental attributes of its occupant," as Amy Rolfe wrote in 1926.[59]

Bathrooms opened up new possibilities, but helped create their own perils. With new decorative accessories, such as mirrors and scales, came new worries about attractiveness and weight that began to preoccupy American women and girls.[60] Fancy bathrooms equipped with bright lights to emphasize every blemish, running water to encourage frequent showers, and scales to enable an obsession with weight consciousness began to be featured in many middle-class homes. Magazine ads encouraged girls to spend more and more time in the bathroom, prettying themselves up for school and dates. The bathroom became an important private area in the house, almost as important as bedrooms. New growth areas in consumer goods, such as cosmetics and hair products, new plastics for hair brush handles and combs, portable mirrors and other toiletries made these items available to the middle class. Domestic advisors seized on the importance of the bathroom and began to emphasize the room in their manuals.

By the 1930s, the bathroom became an important room for domestic advisors. "Bathrooms have become so thoroly [sic] styled that almost a complete line of accessories may be had in . . . chromium or nickel plate, porcelain, glass, and enamel," wrote Christine Holbrook in 1933. Holbrook, as the home-furnishings director of *Better Homes and Gardens*, wrote extensively on interior decoration. Her *Well Dressed Windows* of 1950 included suggestions for color accents. In the 1930s, she focused on the bathroom.

No where has the ensemble idea taken a firmer hold than in towels, bath mats and wash cloths. Seat covers matching the bath mat or rug are both useful and decorative. There is a wide choice of colors and designs that ought to fit comfortably into any style of decoration. The color scheme may be carried to the point of getting a new seat cover in a mother-of-pearl finish and colored faucets for the lavatory and tub. There are no end of delightful color combinations that may be used in the bathroom, providing they do not clash with the adjoining room. They may be more restrained than an old-fashioned flower garden, but they need be no less charming.[61]

Advisors made the bathroom, the ultimate of utilitarian rooms, into a site of both beautiful and practical design ideas.

Domestic-advice manuals and magazines featured color as early as the 1920s and continued to recommend colorful bathrooms for many decades. Universal Sanitary Manufacturing Co., Kohler and Crane, and Standard all displayed bright bathroom ensembles in the late 1920s and 1930s. In the 1930s, Standard Sanitary Manufacturing Co. offered the following colors for sinks, bathtubs, and toilets: "Ming Green, T'ang Red, Clair de Lune Blue, St. Porchaire Brown, Rose du Barry, Ivoire de Medici, Orchid of Vincennes, Royal Copenhagen Blue, and Ionian Black."[62] The Continental and Asian flair to these colors was perhaps an effort to tempt consumers with exotic locales. The Martin-Senour company included "Tibet Grey" among its color choices and also included American colors like "Indian Red."[63]

For domestic advisors, design took precedence over science in the creation of the modern bathroom. With new confidence in modern

"Color is at least half the attractiveness of this practical bathroom," wrote Helen Koues of her green-and-yellow example. Breaking away from the early-twentieth-century sanitized, all-white kitchens and bathrooms, domestic-advice manuals in the 1940s and 1950s featured full-color treatments. Koues's 1954 compendium included this bathroom, featuring brightly painted cupboards and a colorful floor to brighten the look of a white sink and bathtub. The bathroom also included separate storage spaces for each member of the family. (Koues, American Woman's New Encyclopedia of Home Decorating, *facing 544)*

facilities, the reliance on the white bathroom became a thing of the past. Emily Post, in her 1930 *The Personality of a House*, exclaimed that "colored plumbing fixtures are utterly fascinating. I would like very much indeed to rip all white ones out and burst into color through-out."[64] Color was not only a design tool but also a change in attitude about the rooms in question. New ideas about color, and about the meanings of color, transformed the fantasy home.

"The color of a wall must be very carefully considered," wrote home economist Mary Lockwood Matthews in 1926, "because psychologists have found that color affects people in different ways."[65] The 1920s and 1930s found home economists and other domestic advisors rushing to explain the flood of color choices to their constituents. This proved to be a confusing task given the range of colors available and the potential consequences. But throughout the first half of the twentieth century, domestic advisors continued to recommend strict adherence to their rules about color choices. Their main message was: Pay attention to the way the household is arranged because the placement of furniture and the colors of the walls can affect the people who live there as both children and adults.

Chapter 6

OUR OWN NORTH AMERICAN INDIANS:

ROMANCING THE PAST

We of New England are deeply interested in our historic homes, and it is to the lover of the colonial that I wish to show by picture and text the wonderful old mansions that are still in our midst, which have done much to bring New England into prominence in the architectural world of to-day.

Among the old houses there are none so full of interest as those which have been carefully preserved in the same family, handed down from generation to generation. Over the threshold of these homes have passed men and women whose names are linked irretrievably with important events in our nation's history.

These old colonial houses with their beauty of line, their harmony of detail, and their air of dignity, richly repay study by architects and house owners. More and more we turn to them as models for our modern homes. They are a rich heritage from one of the most important pieces of the nation's history, and will ever be cherished for the memories they evoke. Truly American in every respect, they will remain forevermore as revelations of the sturdy spirit, the breadth of mind, the gracious hospitality and the fine ideals of our forefathers who built them.

—Mary Northend, Historic Homes of New England

In the midst of the modernist movement, some domestic advisors turned to the past for inspiration. Mary Harrod Northend, who wrote several books about historic New England homes, believed strongly that Colonial America could be a model for twentieth-century home decorating. She devoted her entire career to traveling around New England, photographing and writing about Colonial homes. Her active years, the first few decades of the twentieth century, paralleled the movement for modern design. Though it might seem like she and her colleagues disagreed with the modernist domestic advisors, in fact Mary Northend wrote for *The Modern Priscilla* and other texts that welcomed new materials such as chromium and plastics. How did both ideals exist simultaneously for domestic advisors?

The thread that held domestic advice together in the first half of the twentieth century was simplicity. Advisors chose particular facets of many different kinds of design movements and put them forward as an alternative to fussy household decorating. They affiliated themselves with the international Arts and Crafts movement, honoring handmade furniture and straight, unembellished lines. They picked and chose among world cultures, identifying particular ones whose designs they saw as straightforward and simple. Most often, these included Japanese and Native American cultures. And they looked to Colonial American houses, especially in New England. All of these movements, as interpreted by domestic advisors, favored understatement, balance, and a sense of honor.

Domestic advisors certainly took liberties with design movements and ancient cultures. Many of them had a limited understanding of the cultures they wrote about, and they used only those aspects of the culture that matched their sensibilities. But they took seriously the idea that their America, the modern world of industrial cities, immigrant populations, and new technology, would be well served through lessons of the past. Their books outlined historical timelines of furniture styles and highlighted important aspects of foreign cultures. They believed that by introducing American women to certain cultural moments and places, they could influence the character of American society.

As evidenced in their writings, domestic advisors believed in the romance of the past. They wrote evocatively about ancient cultures in Asia and America, and poetically about olden times that could be re-created with the correct furniture and wall treatments. Mary North-end was particularly taken with stories of her Colonial ancestors in Massachusetts:

> Chests were an intimate part of the home life in those early times, and viewing their quaintness it is not hard to picture the scenes of which they were a part, when the house mother, in her homespun gown, busily spun at her old clock wheel, drawing the skeins from the chest at her side, while the little ones, seated on rude benches before the open fire, carefully filled the quills for the next day's supply. Mayhap the eldest daughter fashioned on the big wheel, under her mother's guidance, her wedding garments, weaving into them loving thoughts of the groom-to-be, while the song in her heart kept time to the merry whir of the wheel.[1]

Passages like this one appeared throughout Northend's work, high-lighting her ideal vision in which the American home of the past could be superimposed on the present. In her domestic fantasy, by decorating in the style of Colonial ancestors, Americans could find peace in the face of a confusing modern world.

Domestic advisors, determined to eradicate excess ornament and bric-a-brac, turned to many different sources for design. One movement they found particularly appealing was the Arts and Crafts movement. Developed in Europe in the 1850s, Arts and Crafts became popular in America around the turn of the century. Led by John Ruskin and William Morris in England, the American movement introduced figures such as Gustave Stickley and Frank Lloyd Wright.[2] The Arts and Crafts movement offered a sturdy, sincere style that appealed to American domestic advisors. In fact, many had introduced the same ideas decades before Arts and Crafts became popular in the United States. Sponsoring a return to simple decoration in furniture, Arts and Crafts leaders echoed and joined the domestic advisors in their rejection of excess and sentimentality in American homes.

Arts and Crafts design was simple and understated. Architects designed houses to fit into the landscape, and the designed furniture to fit in the house. Many advocates of Arts and Crafts promoted hand-crafted furnishings and decorations. Often seen as a reaction against the factory-produced homes and furniture beginning to become popular in America and overseas in the first part of the twentieth century,

Arts and Crafts had an element of backwards-looking idealism. Just as modernism began to promote new materials, Arts and Crafts' advocates worked with woods and natural fabrics and dyes. As the modern industrial world moved many workers into faceless, unskilled jobs in factories, Arts and Crafts promoted skill in textile and wallpaper design, in furniture construction, and even in calligraphy. Arts and Crafts delighted domestic advisors, many of whom wrote for the movement's journals and praised its leaders in their texts.

Domestic advisor Alice DeWolf Kellogg was one who discussed the Arts and Crafts style. In 1905 she noted, "The mission furniture . . . has made an opening for a simpler fashion in the accessories of furnishing and decoration."[3] For this, she was most grateful. Kellogg, born in 1862, was familiar with several decades of design trends. As an art student in Paris in the late 1880s, Kellogg studied classic works.[4] Educated in Europe, she came back to the United States with knowledge about important art movements throughout history. But she wrote in 1905 about her excitement for "the progressive spirit of the new century and the rapid artistic development throughout our country."[5] Her understanding of old world arts and styles could not dim her enthusiasm for the simple lines and uncluttered interiors of the new century.

Kellogg quoted Arts and Crafts leader William Morris in her 1905 manual, and she explained the ideas of his movement. Continuing the decades-old critique of the Victorian parlor, Morris wrote: "In a country farm house, the kitchen is commonly pleasant and homelike, the parlour dreary and useless." Kellogg called Morris "one who has given inspiration to all departments of the house" and agreed with him that the goal of home furnishing should be to make the house simple and livable.[6] Kellogg's career as a writer on interior decorating branched out to include several books about American holidays. She wrote about Arbor Day, Memorial Day, Thanksgiving, May Day, Flag Day, and the Fourth of July. Her ideas included recitations, school celebrations such as tableaux and drills, and songs. Kellogg's ideas about the home remain an important legacy, but during her career, she intertwined her home-decorating tips with her tips for patriotic celebrations. She wrote several books between 1897 and her death in 1911, some of which appeared in several editions, and she contributed many articles to women's magazines.

Women's magazines provided one way for middle-class women to access both the ideas of domestic advisors like Alice Kellogg and of major architects. Though some architectural movements concentrated on public buildings, Arts and Crafts architects designed many single-family homes. Many Arts and Crafts followers published layouts of homes in popular journals such as *House Beautiful, Ladies' Home Journal* (LHJ), and Stickley's *Craftsman* in the first decades of the twentieth century. *Ladies' Home Journal* printed model-house plans between 1900 and 1902 that included designs from Frank Lloyd Wright.[7] LHJ had a circulation of over one million in this period, and this wide exposure meant that the architectural language of Arts and Crafts could be brought to people all across the country.[8]

Furniture design and construction joined with home building as important aspects of Arts and Crafts. "Craftsman" furniture, often called mission furniture, became popular in America around 1900. Chairs in this style had straight, unembellished spindles between the armrest and seat, and beds included this feature in the head and footboards. Helped along with positive reaction from domestic advisors, Gustave Stickley's craftsman furniture became the first, popular, modern-American style in the twentieth century. Whereas the English Arts and Crafts style had been handcrafted and was therefore unattainable by much of the population, Stickley introduced machine-made furniture of similar style to the United States by 1900, which remained popular for several decades. He rejected most ornamentation, claiming, "The piece is . . . first, last, and all the time a *chair*, and not an imitation of a throne, not an exhibit of snakes and dragons in a wild riot of misapplied wood-carving."[9]

Because craftsman furniture tended to be relatively unembellished, domestic advisors approved. The craftsman design included no frills, lace, or fringe—no extras. Advisors loved the simplicity of the lines and the design. Alice Kellogg recommended the style for the den, especially if it "belong[s] exclusively to the man of the house." To her, the masculine quality of the room demanded "mission furniture, [with] its rich, deep tones of its brown or green finish, and its expression of simplicity."[10] Dorothy Priestman similarly cautioned that "mission furniture . . . would be out of place with a pale, flowered wallpaper, lace curtains and damask hangings."[11] In fact, advisors promoted Arts and Crafts ideas throughout the entire house, considering the heavy mission furniture to be incompatible with such Victorian mainstays as lace and damask.

Mission furniture got its name from the Spanish mission churches of California. Joseph McHugh, the first to make furniture in this style, was said to have been inspired by a chair he had seen in an old San

[*Our Own North American Indians*]

Seat to the Crafters Library Set.

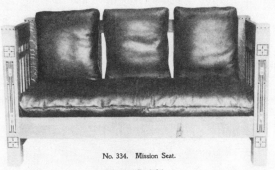

No. 334.   Mission Seat.

Quartered Church Oak.
Marquetry Panels of Imported Colored Austrian Woods.
Old Brass Trimmings. Spanish Roan Skin Cushions, Hand Laced, in the following tans:
No. 3 Dark Red; No. 5 Dark Green; No. 38 Dark Brown.
Extreme Height, 35 inches.   Width, 67 inches.   Depth, 30 inches.

Price, Any Oak Finish...................................$96 00.

THE SHOP OF THE CRAFTERS
AT CINCINNATI

Arm Chair to the Crafters Library Set.   Morris Chair to the Crafters Library Set.

No. 331.   Mission Arm Chair.   No. 333.   Mission Morris Chair.

Quartered Church Oak.   Quartered Church Oak.
Marquetry Panels of Imported Colored Austrian Woods. Marquetry Panels of Imported Colored Austrian Woods.
Spanish Roan Skin Cushions, Hand Laced, in the following tans: Spanish Roan Skin Cushions, Hand Laced, in the following tans:
No. 3 Dark Red; No. 5 Dark Green; No. 38 Dark Brown.   No. 3 Dark Red; No. 5 Dark Green; No. 38 Dark Brown.

Price, Any Oak Finish.......................$45 00.   Price, Any Oak Finish.......................$48 00.

The Crafters recommend their pieces in the dull waxed finishes, such as Weathered, Fumed, Flemish, Austrian or Early English shades.
When ordering be sure and state finish of wood and color of leather wanted.

12

Mission furniture was popular at the beginning of the twentieth century.
Sold in stores throughout the country, the furniture had distinct characteristics,
such as dark upholstery and simple, straight lines. Many domestic advisors appreciated the
unembellished style, though others thought it was too heavy for the modern living room.
(Shop of the Crafters Catalogue, *12; courtesy* The Winterthur Library,
Printed Book and Periodical Collection)

Francisco church. The name, however, caused great controversy, since Stickley, the most popular maker of this furniture, rejected the notion that he copied his designs from California missions. Manufacturers continued to use the term "mission" to imply that the furniture was an historical style, benefiting from American nostalgia for the Old West. Alice Kellogg praised the furniture:

> The "mission idea" has . . . made a powerful impression in American homes, and the substitution of the straight line for the curved, the absence of applied ornament, and a simple in place of a complex construction have made a distinct advance in furniture. In its original setting—in the mission buildings in California—this furniture was most primitive in pattern, but by various modifications it has been rendered comfortable and fills a field for which hitherto there had been either inadequate or inartistic provision.[12]

It was precisely this association with the primitive West that caught the attention of many advisors as well as many American consumers. The actual history of the furniture was less important than its association with haciendas and ranchos filled with exotic Spanish characters.

Some advisors seemed wary of bringing mission furniture into every American home. Amy Rolfe was an instructor of home economics at the University of Montana in Bozeman. In her 1917 text, she taught her readers about mission furniture, but cautioned that it might not be appropriate for every region.

> The mission furniture originated some thirty years ago in a little mission church in California. The church was a humble frame structure and the chairs made for it were of the simplest, straight-line construction possible. Because they were so simple they seemed to possess an element of beauty, and the public soon recognized this fact and called for other straight-line designs in inexpensive furniture. . . . Mission furniture is often wrongly used, however. . . . While mission furniture may seem very much at home in a western house, it may be entirely out of place in a house of the middle west, and surely would be incongruous in a colonial mansion of the east.[13]

Advisors remained cautious about recommending western styles to their eastern readers. Though Rolfe lived and worked in Montana, she was hesitant to recommend mission furniture for everyone. Despite some caution, however, the Old West became a popular theme for home decorating in the early twentieth century.

The turn of the twentieth century welcomed a new interest in Western history that fit right in with mission furniture. Books like Helen Hunt Jackson's *Ramona* (1884) introduced thousands of Americans to the romance of the Spanish West and promoted tourism in the region. *Ramona* described the tragic story of a half-Indian woman raised in Spanish society and her Indian lover. Though intended as a critique of racism, the book instead created legends about the culture of Southern California. In the several decades after the publication of the book, during which it was constantly reprinted, people organized "Ramona Pageants," set up a fictional birthplace, and made it a pilgrimage site.[14] The book has been the subject of several movies, the first one by famed director D. W. Griffith. The craze over *Ramona* revealed an American longing for romantic historical legends within the United States.

One unintended result of the wild popularity of *Ramona* was that Americans began to turn to the West for inspiration for their home decorating. With the idea that the frontier had "closed" and that Americans had reached their manifest destiny of inhabitancy from coast to coast, came a fascination with the ancient cultures that had populated the region before the United States moved in. Domestic advisors joined the movement by recommending certain Spanish styles in the home. Emily Post recommended, with various caveats, the Spanish method in her 1930 *Personality of a House*. "Handled with taste, knowledge and *restraint*, the Hispano-American house, in a hot climate, is ideal. Its overthick walls are designed to keep out the heat; its doorless openings encourage the circulation of air; its untrimmed surfaces are beautifully suitable to the embellishment of tropical foliage; its patio—especially one that is arcaded on its northern side—grants a shaded outdoor retreat."[15] Mission furniture and Spanish architecture gave domestic advisors examples of what they considered ancient and romantic styles to recommend to readers eager to bring a sense of the past to their homes.

American Indian cultures were among the most popular "foreign" cultures in domestic-advice manuals. Domestic advisors joined a larger movement called "Romantic Nationalism" in which a country's identity is expressed through the adaptation of the arts of indigenous cultures.[16] Artist Alice Kellogg saw the possibilities of Native American items for middle-class home decorating. "A better idea is to secure some decorations from our own North American Indians, rugs, pottery, and baskets, each offering a field rich in national and artistic inter-

Contrasting with the patterned carpet underneath, this Navajo rug demonstrates one way in which middle-class Americans brought "exotic" Native American cultures into their home-decorating schemes. This family parlor featured an American flag along with the rug and included no shortage of accessories and decorative touches. The Navajo rug was probably not unusual in middle-class homes in Colorado, given that nearby Native American cultures became part of the cultural lore of the Southwest. (Courtesy Denver Public Library, Western History Collection, X-22919)

est. A Navajo blanket of bright colours when hung against the wall will look brilliant by artificial light; or it may be made of utilitarian value if thrown on a lounge for a cover, or laid on the floor as a rug."[17] The embrace of "our own" Indians demonstrates the sense of ownership that white Americans felt toward the people who first inhabited their country. Kellogg and others wrote about Indian arts as if the artifacts of these cultures could impart some of their simplicity to the complicated American life that had taken over their land.

Many domestic advisors wrote about Native American arts as a disappearing way of life. Dorothy Tuke Priestman noted that "the Indians too have taught us much about basketry, and those who have made a collection of old baskets have found it very interesting to study the quaint, curious patterns which are symbolic of the life of this passing race."[18] Priestman sounded almost like an anthropologist studying an ancient culture. Her recommendations had little to do with the actual decorative qualities of the pieces, but rather with their symbolism. Indian baskets represented hard work and a simple culture, both things that Priestman wanted to bring into her house-decorating plans. She liked the romance that the artifacts brought with them.

Southwestern cultures, such as the Pueblos and Navajos, provided domestic advisors with a native architecture to discuss. Charlotte Calkins, in her call for national leadership in design, argued that the Pueblo cliff dwellings represented the only truly American architecture. "Americans lead in the comforts and equipment of the home, but in domestic architecture aside from the purely American type of the Pueblo Cliff dwellers, they have not . . . given to the world much that is original and expresses truly the life of the people."[19] In the first few decades of the twentieth century, with dozens, even hundreds, of Native American tribes to choose from as decorating models, most domestic advisors described the worlds of the Navajo and the Pueblo Indians of the Southwest.

Architect Mary Jane Colter used Pueblo ideas in creating houses and train stations for the Fred Harvey Company. Colter, born in Pennsylvania in 1869, worked as an art teacher before accepting her first job with the Fred Harvey Company in New Mexico in 1902. The Harvey Company led tours, by railroad and later by automobile, through the Southwest, introducing tourists from the East to the natural and built environments of New Mexico and Arizona. While on vacation, tourists ate at specially designed restaurants and stayed at special hotels. They were served by "Harvey Girls," uniformed waitresses from all over the country who made the tourists feel at home in the new settings. Mary Jane Colter spent her entire forty-year career designing and building tourist destinations for the Harvey Company. Her first building was the Alvarado Hotel and Indian Museum in Albuquerque, and she went on to design many more hotels, restaurants, and gift shops. Many of her buildings, including the Lookout and the Watchtower at the Grand Canyon, and the Painted Desert Inn at the Petrified Forest, both in Arizona, are still standing today.

Colter's buildings appropriated construction techniques and interior decorating from native New Mexicans. She used adobe walls and incorporated sand painting and blanket weaving to make her buildings look more authentic, and she also employed Hopi builders and craftspeople. Colter's buildings introduced tourists to southwestern culture. She used the Southwest's ideology of simplicity as a symbol for the region. She created vacation spaces that were specifically set up to be different from the busy homes of her East Coast patrons.[20] Her designs helped sustain an interest in southwest Indian art objects that fueled a heavy trade. Visitors bought pots, baskets, rugs, and other home decorating items from Pueblo Indian women who laid out their wares on blankets in front of Colter's buildings. Her sensitive use of Hopi designs and themes were echoed with varying degrees of authenticity in homes across the country.

Many advocates of Arts and Crafts design looked as far away as Asia to find a culture worthy of respect and emulation. When recommending a style to feature in the American home, advisors searched for ancient cultures that prioritized simple design. Known for a sense of balance and harmony, Japanese design, as interpreted by American writers, became a strong partner to Arts and Crafts ideals. Alice Kellogg recommended "a Japanese vase" for a hallway or reception room.[21] "It is interesting," Charlotte Calkins wrote in 1916, "to take color schemes for interiors from shells, birds, flowers, fruit and Japanese . . . prints."[22] These decorators saw the quiet design of Asian art as a positive complement to their rededication of the simple American home.

Many manuals included suggestions for how to use Asian designs in American settings. *The Good Housekeeping Discovery Book* of 1905, a compendium of "practical hints from the experience of hundreds of housekeepers and home-makers," included suggestions for a "Japanese Tea." "The reception rooms may be adorned by lanterns, fans, parasols, screens, all of Japanesy style. . . . Scatter cherry blossoms in great snowy masses to light up shadowy corners." The hostess would have to buy many items to decorate her home. The finishing touch was for her to don a kimono and do her hair in "Japanese style, adorned with half a dozen tiny bright fans."[23] Using "Japanesy" style in household decorations was a way to solidify the housewife's commitment to American culture by making Asia seem more exotic.

While Japanese culture provided a good example of the simplicity domestic advisors worked so hard to achieve, they approached other Asian cultures with more trepidation. Oriental rugs inhabited a rather troubled space in the domestic-advice manuals. Some praised their unique qualities, emphasizing their exotic nature. Amy Rolfe wrote in 1917: "Oriental rugs have a power of fascination and a peculiar mystical quality which stirs the imagination and emotions more, perhaps, than any other item of household furnishing. Each rug, laboriously made by hand, represents months or years of patient work, and necessarily reflects the changing moods and mind of the maker. Each piece of fabric has received a personal touch which gives it almost a life and personality in the family circle." [24] Trade booklets, such as one from Sherwin-Williams paint company in 1911, included educational remarks concerning the "classification of Oriental rugs" into categories of "Persian, Turkoman, Caucasian [and] Turkish." [25]

However, many advisors cautioned against welcoming these foreign items into the home. "In the well furnished American home, far, far removed from the original setting of tropical sky and barbaric splendor, have these weaves a place?" asked Maud Ann Sell in 1918. Her answer was "most emphatically in the negative." [26] Lois Palmer cautioned in 1928 that the rugs' history might be too foreign for the American home. "Having been designed and made to be used in tents where there was little or no furniture," she wrote, "and by people who spent a large part of their time out of doors, these rugs are extremely difficult to use in modern interiors." [27] Her problem with the Oriental rug was that it was too primitive for Americans, and she cautioned against bringing this questionable cultural artifact into American homes.

Advisors' fascination with Asian cultures was supported by some of the largest distributors of household goods in American cities. In New York City, A. A. Vantine's advertised rattan and wicker furniture, and the store catalogues included drawings of Caucasian models in kimonos, their houses draped in Asian fabrics. They even offered a tearoom where women could have lunch during their shopping trips.

> On the Mezzanine is The White Cloud Tea Room—the most interesting place in which to lunch or tea in all the great shopping district of Fifth Avenue. Here the most delightful Oriental atmosphere prevails. Seated amid picturesque and colorful furnishings and decorations, courteously served with either American or Oriental dainties by Chinese and Japanese maids in native costume, one feels as though one were really in the Far East. Up here among the many quaint lanterns and overlooking the fascinating displays on the main floor, how easy it is to plan an Oriental room or sun porch or special corner in one's home—and we may add, never a day goes by without some patron doing just this very thing. [28]

Vantine's produced trade catalogues as advertisements of their wares to their middle-class clientele. The catalogue included items from many different Asian cultures, including "Russian Brass Candlestick,

I **Wonder** what to give—the things
that tell
Of ages past, of arts now lost ;
That show the skill we moderns love?
Forsooth, there's but one spot I know—

"Vantine's"

Oriental Lamps

L AMPS of Bronze, Syrian Brass, Porcelain, Pottery,
Wicker Glaze. Brazier Lamps, tall Floor Lamps in
Bronze and Brass. Bracket Lamps. Student Lamps.

Electroliers in Bronze, Brass,
Iron and Gilt.
Helmet and Shields.
Mosque Lanterns converted.
Reading Lights.
Drop Lights and Chandeliers.
Port Cochere Lights,
and special ideas for dens and
cosey corners.

THE VANTINE GEISHA LAMP SHADE
FROM $2.50 TO $5.00

Lamp Shades

in Metal, Shell, Paper. Bent, Leaded, and Art Glass. Globe Shades
in Eastern shapes and pagoda effects, trimmed with glass, shell,
silk and Syrian brass fringe.

*Stores like Vantine's that sold household accessories with a foreign flair depended on
an audience of American women who read about other cultures in books and magazines.
Although most domestic advisors would have disapproved of the bric-a-brac that Vantine's
sold, they introduced readers to the concept of getting inspiration from other countries for
American decorating. Vantine's, a New York City establishment, built upon the desire for
exoticism by advertising "the things that tell of ages past, of arts now lost." The company's
Wonder Book featured lamps inspired by Syria, Arab mosques, and even one called
"The Vantine Geisha lamp shade." (Wonder Book, A. A. Vantine and Co.; courtesy
The Winterthur Library, Printed Book and Periodical Collection)*

Brass Korean Candlestick, Moradabad Brass Candlestick" alongside Mah Jong sets and incense sets. The store claimed to offer "something different and unusual" for every customer.[29] The "Wonder Book," produced by Vantine's in 1910, advertised ideas for "nooks" in the home to correspond with the Indian, Oriental, Turkish, and Moorish goods for sale in the store.

Stores like Vantine's helped promote a fascination with exotic, foreign cultures. Proliferating all over the nation in the first part of the century, these stores provided consumers with a wide variety of "curios" for their homes. Many Americans considered these trinkets and decorations to be a safe way to bring foreign cultures inside their homes. Domestic advisors, always trying to limit the bric-a-brac, tried to steer their readers toward simple Japanese prints, but often the sheer amount of items available proved hard to resist for American consumers. Stores with names like "Wah Fung Curio Co." and "Japanese Curio Co." sprang up in cities like Denver and in tourist destinations such as Manitou Springs, Colorado. By 1915, a total of twenty-six stores appeared under the heading "Curios" in Denver, including the "Mexican and Indian Curio Co."[30] These stores sold all sorts of items, from rugs, to prints, to figurines. They counted on American women reading about particular cultures in domestic-advice manuals and then ignoring the restrictions on bric-a-brac in their homes.

Whether writing about nearby New Mexico or faraway Japan, domestic advisors stimulated interest in other cultures. They used their knowledge of world history to identify those cultures that exhibited sufficiently exotic decorating while remaining true to the Arts and Crafts principles of simplicity and balance. The southwestern Native American cultures and the Japanese, as interpreted by domestic advisors, served these purposes perfectly, and artifacts from these cultures became quite popular in American homes. However, by far the most popular design trend in the first several decades of the twentieth century was American Colonial. Deeming even Pueblo and Spanish Californian cultures as too foreign, many advisors turned to historic New England and devised a romantic nationalism of their own.

Despite turn-of-the-century interest in the West, most Americans still believed that the history of the United States began and ended in New England. Proponents of the "New Englandization" of history, as it has been called, rewrote the history of America to exclude early

Inspiration for several decades of American Colonial decorating, the New England kitchen was a popular venue at Philadelphia's Centennial Exposition in 1876. The kitchen featured women clad in Colonial garb and seated amidst every possible representation of Colonial life, including an enormous hearth. The kitchen inspired generations of Americans to fill their homes with turned chairs, pewter plates, and spinning wheels to emulate the quaintness of the past. (Saunders, The Great Centennial Exhibition, *542; courtesy The Winterthur Library, Printed Book and Periodical Collection)*

exploration and civilization in the Southwest and Florida. They invented their own creation myth. Often, history books opened with the landing of the pilgrims at Plymouth, Massachusetts, and described the early years in the English colonies as the first story of U.S. history. The New England colonists, and to a lesser degree those of Virginia and the rest of the mid-Atlantic, became stand-ins for a wide array of historical counterparts. Their lives defined the entire colonial adventure, and early American history became reduced to their experiences, loosely interpreted. Their household decorations, though often misrepresented by museum executives and domestic advisors alike, took on power as sole representations of early America.

The Colonial Revival began as early as 1876, with widespread interest in the New England kitchen at Philadelphia's Centennial Exposition. The movement picked up speed at the turn of the century and continued into the twentieth. Helped along by industrial mass production of reproduction wallpaper and paint colors, American women brought the Colonial Revival into their homes. Many domestic advisors actively encouraged this view of America and wrote eloquently about the importance of preserving Colonial American history and ideals through household decorating. Just as women could bring values of simplicity and even a little exoticism into their homes with Japanese prints or Navajo rugs, so could they use Colonial-inspired chairs and tables to demonstrate their commitment to what they thought of as American values. This had only a little to do with any actual Colonial ancestor and much more to do with the perception that, as Americans, New England settlers were their ancestors by birthright.

The phrase "American Colonial" illustrates the trend in household furniture that took over American homes in the 1920s. The use of both words together conveyed the duality of the idea of patriotism and history. Elizabeth Burris-Meyer included a chapter on incorporating history into furniture choices and tried to educate her readers about the historical styles. "Few types," she said, "surpass the American Colonial."[31] She encouraged her readers to learn about historical-period household arrangement in order to make their homes conform to an idealism of the past.

In the early twentieth century, as before and since, many Americans associated patriotism with a reverence for Colonial New England. Domestic advisors helped this trend along by relating household artifacts to values of simplicity and honor. New England settlers represented certain characteristics that many found lacking in contemporary culture. Early settlers symbolized moral sanctity, hard work, and strong family ties. People thought of eighteenth-century New Englanders as strong-willed people of faith committed to patriarchy and propriety, and as talented craftspeople. They thought of the material goods and buildings that remained from that culture as having value because of their associations with such people. The coverlets, wallpapers, pewter pitchers, and lanterns of Colonial New England re-created for people what they considered to be a simpler time.

Although men dominated the furniture-design industry, the Colonial Revival created places for many women artists. Women especially heeded the call to return to handicrafts in an age of machines. They formed societies and groups to manufacture accessories from baskets to blankets. Domestic advisors included the female-dominated aspects of Arts and Crafts in their manuals. Hazel Adler praised the Blue and

Helen Koues picked up on the trend for early American decorating in her 1926
How To Be Your Own Decorator. *She recommended the "homely comfort" offered by
the simple furniture "typical of the homes of our ancestors." This room featured a rocking
chair, wooden settle, and a pot on a crane in the hearth. In the 1939 edition of her book,
Koues elaborated on the idea with a "Colonial Williamsburg" room, complete
with upholstered chairs modeled after the newly opened tourist attraction.*
(*Koues,* How to Be Your Own Decorator *[1926], 8; courtesy
The Winterthur Library, Printed Book and Periodical Collection*)

White Society of Deerfield, Massachusetts, for "the separation of the good old design from its later elaboration with unnecessary spirals and ornaments." She recommended using these designs "in the decoration of the modern home." The Blue and White Society made needlework designs on textiles such as bedspreads. Adler admired the Blue and White designs for being "expressive of certain important phases in American life and character," namely, the Colonial period.[32] Similarly, Dorothy Priestman commented: "The Arts and Crafts movement has given a stimulus to basket making, and has helped to put this craft on a higher plane."[33] Interestingly, although the advisors rejected most ornamentation, they appreciated these hand-made crafts. Colonial crafts represented proper values for domestic advisors, who relished almost anything that carried the moniker "Colonial," whether embroidery or door frames.

Proponents of the American Colonial ideal made New England material culture popular to people as different as prestigious museum collectors and ordinary housewives. When domestic advisors wrote about the style, they joined (and probably accelerated) a movement already in progress. The popularity of New England colonialism reached a peak in the 1920s and continued to be strong throughout the twentieth century. Major collectors such as John D. Rockefeller Jr. at Colonial Williamsburg (1926) and Henry Ford at Greenfield Village (1929) started to give early American artifacts a prestige they had not enjoyed before. Advisors picked up on this fashion and taught American women how to incorporate the popular style into their homes. *Good Housekeeping*'s Helen Koues demonstrated the style in 1939: "With the Williamsburg feeling in furnishings sweeping the country, Good Housekeeping Studio furnished a house in Baltimore with attractive reproductions of the period and the documented fabrics similar to those used in Williamsburg."[34]

It would be difficult to overestimate the effect that museums like Colonial Williamsburg had on American household design. With tourism building throughout the twentieth century, more people than ever had the opportunity to visit house museums and outdoor historical parks. These venues tended to emphasize the beautiful material culture of early America and present artifacts in their most magnificent state. Museums in the houses of governors, other politicians, and famous authors, mostly men, proliferated throughout the country. Patriotic groups such as the Daughters of the American Revolution operated museums in the houses of the signers of the Constitution, such as the Steven Hopkins house in Providence, Rhode Island. Walking through these houses, tourists could see elaborate glassware used by George Washington and view elegantly canopied beds and recently reupholstered chairs. Entire streets of houses filled with colonial furniture, such as at Deerfield, Massachusetts, and Williamsburg, Virginia, continued to open and attract visitors from the 1920s throughout the century. On-site gift shops selling items such as paints in trademarked Colonial Williamsburg colors encouraged them to go home and replicate the houses' grace and elegance.[35]

American Colonial design incorporated several important themes of the Arts and Crafts movement. Domestic advisors advocating the future-looking, unembellished style of the twentieth century felt little conflict in also advocating Colonial furniture and accessories. They conceived a way for the New England style to fit in with their idea of sturdy, honest furniture. As early as 1900, advisor Bertha Hynde Holden expressed her desire that the day would soon come when Americans would learn to appreciate "the sturdy chest and chair, the mellow brass and pewter, the old time when the craftsman worked out his inner conviction."[36] Although she was ahead of the curve, Holden's sentiments fit quite nicely with the later decades of the twentieth century when Americans did begin to honor the craftspeople of an earlier age.

Throughout the twentieth century, domestic advisors explained how to integrate antiques into modern homes. In 1917, Alice Kellogg wanted her readers to be careful of the antiques they used, choosing ones that had a direct relationship with American ideas.

> There is so much interest in old furniture nowadays that a bedroom fitted up in antique pieces or their reproductions makes a pleasant change from modern fittings. An old four-poster may be made comfortable with wire springs and a hair mattress; an old chest may hold the hand-woven linen and blankets; a low-boy take the place of a dresser, and a high-boy become the chiffonier. . . . A corner or square washstand may be equipped with an old blue china bowl and pitcher, and a candle-stand, work table, rush-seated chairs and rag carpet carry out the quaint ideas of the past.[37]

And several decades later, the "quaint ideas of the past" still held importance for decorators. Narcissa Chamberlain wrote in 1953, "The adaptability of 18th century styles to modern living . . . [preserves] our American inheritance of good taste . . . developed in New England houses from our beginnings."[38] She clearly linked the Colonial styles with a specifically American sense of good taste and good breeding. As for what came later, she had nothing good to say, pointing out that the Victorian era "degenerated to a point of meaningless ornament and knick-knackery about which the less said the better."[39]

Mary Harrod Northend's many books and articles contributed to the reverence for the American Colonial style, especially in New England. Northend was born to a prominent New England family in 1850. Through her family's associations, she gained access to historic homes in the North Shore (north of Boston) region of Massachusetts. Her interest in Colonial homes and furniture led her to a successful career in photography and domestic advice. She began writing in 1904 and began publishing photographs of Colonial architecture and accessories soon thereafter. During the next two decades, before her death in 1926, Northend made more than 35,000 photographs of Massachusetts homes. She wrote eleven books and published what probably amounted to hundreds of articles in magazines, such as *McCall's, Outlook, Century,* and *Good Housekeeping.*

Northend's collection of photographs of houses and their contents was "considered one of the most valuable private collections in the country."[40] In her books, she described the history of certain artifacts, like doorknockers, and then indicated that the renaissance of these styles would demonstrate Colonial American values, such as independence and ingenuity, in modern homes. Northend focused on those items in the eighteenth-century homes that she felt best encapsulated American values. The furniture and accessories of the Colonial era were important to preserve, according to Northend, because of their tie to the early New England settlers rather than because of any inherent decorative or design value. She recommended decoration by association.

Northend manipulated her homes and furniture to conform to her idea of what the American Colonial style looked like. As Charles Arthur Higgins wrote about her in 1915, "She often spends from an hour to an hour and a half in one room, arranging small insignificant details, to make a complete whole" before she took a picture. She spent this hour analyzing and arranging the room. She took her own ideas about the past and used old furniture to make her point that American Colonial furniture could express certain values. To her, manipulating doorknockers, candle molds, window treatments, china, glassware, silver, pewter, furniture, and draperies could express her sentimental affection for the Colonial era. She carefully placed spinning wheels and cooking pots so that the room would look as if the Colonial woman of the house had just stepped away from her spinning and cooking.

By manipulating the furniture, Northend participated in one of the basic pastimes of the Colonial Revival. Though historians certainly had their part to play, other enthusiasts often decorated Colonial homes and museums. Based on stories they had heard from their older relatives, or on what they thought must have been the proper arrangements, they organized parlors, kitchens, and hallways rather arbitrarily. Collectors who specialized in one type of chair, for example, might furnish a room with twelve mahogany dining chairs with ball-

Mary Northend, photographer and author, took this photograph in a Massachusetts home, probably around 1910. The photo demonstrates her love of Colonial artifacts, such as the spinning wheel and skein winder near the hearth. In this image, she also arranged a round table with a lamp in the center of the room, typical of nineteenth-century arrangements. Northend's books and articles used images like this one to show modern women how to use Colonial artifacts and nineteenth-century decorating in their own modern homes. (Courtesy The Winterthur Library, Decorative Arts Photographic Collection)

and-claw feet, though such an arrangement would have been unusual in the 1700s. Proponents of the Colonial Revival, though they craved authenticity, were more concerned with the symbolism of the furniture than with literally reproducing ancient living rooms.

Northend felt that "there is a charm about old furnishings that cannot fail to appeal to all lovers of the quaint and interesting." She wrote her books because she believed that "hitherto little appreciated relics [would now be] reinstated with all their original dignity."[41] Although some would deem this type of sentimentality "antiquarian" later in the century, Northend had a genuine desire to have an influence on American homes, and she played her part by educating women about Colonial furniture. She praised Colonial architecture, with its "beauty of line . . . harmony of detail, and . . . Air of dignity" and declared the

Colonial homes she photographed and wrote about as "truly American in every respect." Should there be any doubt of what that meant to her, she elaborated that the homes and their furnishings and accessories "will remain forevermore as revelations of the sturdy sprit, the breadth of mind, the gracious hospitality, and the fine ideals of our forefathers who built them."[42]

Mary Northend and other female domestic advisors used Colonial furniture to express their patriotic commitment. As Northend wrote in 1909, "Homes constructed by the early settlers in this country . . . possessed, almost without exception, one feature of comfort and cheeriness which is sadly lacking in modern homes. . . . The enormous open fireplace with its huge logs and high-backed wooden settles around which the family life of the sturdy pioneers centered."[43] Northend connected the fireplaces and the settles (Colonial benches), which she photographed again and again, with family life and sturdiness. In her photographs, she manipulated furniture because she wanted to find a way for middle-class American families to re-create the ideal of family life that she held so dear and that she associated with the Colonial era.

The affection domestic advisors felt for Colonial furnishings continued well into the twentieth century. Many decorating books encouraged New England families to restore their old homes, and they provided tips for accurate decorating. Samuel and Narcissa Chamberlain wrote such a book together in 1953. The Chamberlains, who lived in Paris during the 1920s, certainly were familiar with many different historical periods in architecture. Samuel Chamberlain was an artist and architectural illustrator who drew rural buildings in France and England, as well as closer to home in Colonial Williamsburg. He and his wife shared a deep affection for the beauty and simplicity of Colonial architecture and furnishings, and they worked on several books together, including one called *Southern Interiors of Charleston, South Carolina* (1956). But one of their first loves (and most popular subjects) was New England.

Narcissa Chamberlain picked up where Mary Northend left off and wrote extensively about the inherent values of Colonial decorating in the 1950s.

These pictures have been gathered together that you may see in authentic and original form the rooms of the past, their charm and practicality, and the beauty and changing style developed in New

England houses from our beginnings. This is a guidebook for the home owner or decorator who wishes to preserve in practical modern surroundings our American inheritance of good taste. . . . It is not necessary to cook over the open hearth (though it can be fun too!) nor to read by candlelight, in order to profit by what the past has to offer.[44]

Chamberlain brought the Colonial Revival into the postwar era. Her 1953 book, *Old Rooms for New Living: How to Adapt Early American Interiors for Modern Comfort*, chronicled her efforts, with her husband, to renovate their "famous old house" in Marblehead, Massachusetts. Her sentiment was clear: "The adaptability of 18th century styles to modern living is evident."[45]

Mary Northend described the Sherburne house in her 1914 *Historic Homes of New England:*

> A fine example of mahogany is shown in a beautiful secretary standing at one side of the room, and through its traceried-glass doors are caught glimpses of curious shells and bits of pink and red coral—brought home by some seafaring Sherburne—as well as numerous Indian relics. It has also a few old books left from a rare collection. Each chamber shows wonderful four-posters, hand-knotted spreads, odd candlesticks, foot-stoves, and powder-horns, each piece enhancing the flavor and romance that clings to every nook and corner of the old house. All these relics, as well as the fire-buckets hanging in the rear hall, have been in the family for generations.[46]

Her descriptions suggested that the power of New England could seep into modern, suburban homes with simply the placement of a spinning wheel or other Colonial accessory. Though she loved the old houses she found in Massachusetts towns, she realized that many of her readers had to adapt her ideas to their own ordinary homes. By transporting the items from Colonial America, they could bring the fantasy of simpler times inside. Whether mission furniture or Colonial fire buckets, artifacts from old-fashioned cultures could bring romance to the modern American home.

Chapter 7

TOGETHERNESS & THE

OPEN-SPACE PLAN

Meet a Modern American Husband and Father

*Here's Ed Richtscheidt of Pines Lake, NJ, his wife Carol and their three
children. They live in a gray shingle split-level house with three bedrooms,
one bath and an unfinished basement room that will one day be the game
room. On the North side of their lot, where they plan to build a barbecue,
Ed has made a play yard for the children.*

*We're introducing Ed and his family because, like millions of other
married couples today, they're living the life of McCall's, a more casual but
a richer life than that of even the fairly recent past.*

*Today the chores as well as the companionship make Ed part of his
family. He and Carol have centered their lives almost completely around
their children and their home. Every inch of their home and yard is lived
in and enjoyed. And it's a very happy place.*

*Carol appreciates a hand with the dishes, as well as a chance to talk
things over without interruption. She's proud of the color scheme Ed
mapped out for the house, admits she never could have found such
handsome draperies.*

— "Live the Life of McCall's*"*

In May of 1954, the editorial staff of a popular women's magazine encouraged its readers to "Live the Life of *McCall's*" with a several-page photo essay on family life.[1] "Thanks to our heritage of freedom," the editors wrote, "men, women and children are achieving it *together*. They are creating this new warmer way of life not as women *alone* or as men *alone*, isolated from one another, but as a *family* sharing a common experience."

The article featured a photo essay depicting New Jersey couple Ed and Carol and their split-level house. Before Ed headed off to meet his carpool to the office, the family made breakfast together, each smiling moment captured by the photographers at *McCall's*. The clear message was that the couple shared their home and its responsibilities.

Ed liked to "putter around the house." But the article, under the headline "The Man's Place Is in the Home" also listed household activities that Ed did not like, including: "Dusting, vacuuming, finishing jobs he's started . . . washing pots and pans and dishes . . . [and] doing the laundry." The article did not list activities that Carol disliked. To reassure readers that the magazine did not intend to overturn a traditional hierarchy, *McCall's* was quick to mention that "for the sake of every member of the family, the family needs a head. . . . This means Father, not Mother."[2] The article clearly stated that Ed was "a part of his family" in ways that his own father had not been, but also set boundaries on the lengths Ed was willing to go. "One chore against which Ed consistently rebels is vacuuming. He considers it women's work."[3]

The article continued to outline the possible "manliness issues" that could arise when fathers participated in the housework and childcare. "Often the different kinds of lives [Ed] leads come into conflict. Sometimes, when he's particularly preoccupied with a problem of his own, the kids just plain annoy him. And he feels like slamming the door and going off for a long walk by himself, or sitting down to a good game of cards with the boys."[4] Togetherness had its limits, and *McCall's* allowed men the option of physically leaving the house. Togetherness in the home was not intended to threaten a power structure, but to pay tribute to a new kind of domesticity.[5]

Advisors in the 1930s and 1940s began to use the family unit as an organizing principle of the American home. Advisors used the word and the idea of "togetherness" in the postwar era to pursue women's dedication to freedom through prioritizing home life. The *McCall's* article and others built on this new attitude and gave it a name. Advisors used the idea of togetherness to recommend a major change in the building and decoration of American middle-class homes.

Women's magazines such as *McCall's* helped to create and perpetuate the togetherness fantasy. Magazines about the household were often called "shelter" magazines.[6] While *Ladies Home Journal* had enjoyed a circulation of over one million in 1906, *McCall's* circulation reached almost five million by the early 1960s.[7] Many of these magazines had long and venerable histories of mass circulation. Most of these magazines had mainly women writers and a largely female readership.[8] Women's magazines in the mid-twentieth century gave domestic advisors a popular platform. Women's magazines flourished, and women both wrote and read these articles.

Major women's magazines published many of the domestic-advice manuals in midcentury. Many magazines strictly segregated their staffs by gender, hiring the women in decorating positions. In 1954, *Ladies' Home Journal* employed Cynthia McAdoo Wheatland as the interior decoration editor and Margaret Davidson as the homemaking editor.[9] The editor of *Woman's Home Companion*, Henry Humphrey, hired women to write his *Women's Home Companion Household Book* in 1948. Harriet Burket, Aline Jordan, K. Joyce Ryan, and Mary Ellen Slate provided the advice for the book, since Humphrey expressed "temerity in advising [women] about the performance of their important duties."[10] The editors of *McCall's* joined together to produce *McCall's Decorating Book* in 1964, and another magazine got into the game with *Better Homes and Gardens' Guide to Entertaining* in 1969.[11] Through these books, magazines provided domestic advisors with more space to explain their ideas. Magazine articles on decorating could occupy a page or two; the *Woman's Home Companion* manual was a full 889 pages of advice.

Often, in the spirit of togetherness, domestic-advice books in the mid-twentieth century featured the talents of a husband-and-wife team. Hazel Kory Rockow, Ph.D., was the senior home economist at Brooklyn College when she coauthored *New Creative Home Decorating* with her husband Julius Rockow, an interior decorator.[12] As a family team themselves, the Rockows had much respect for the role of home decorating in family life. "This new attitude may well be one of the

Many domestic advisors embraced the "togetherness" theme of household management in the 1940s and 1950s. This "do-it-yourself" couple is doing it together as they complement each other's knowledge of power tools and design. Magazines and manuals promoted the ideal of husband-and-wife decorating, introducing the idea that the household could bring the family together. (Humphrey, Woman's Home Companion Household Book, *201)*

healthiest developments in the field of present-day marital and family relationships," they wrote. This was no small claim, but the Rockows went further. "Beautiful homes inculcate ideas and values that make for a decent, upright society." [13] Linking home decoration with "upright society" and family life, even if it was a fantasy, was an important goal.

Domestic advisors urged women to embrace the family to the exclusion of most anything else. In the advice manuals and magazines, any job or volunteer work outside the home was peripheral to the task of homemaking. While close to twenty million women did have paying jobs or careers in the 1950s, as some women had in every other decade of American history, the editors of the popular magazines underplayed this aspect of their readers' lives and livelihoods.[14] Charlotte Adams was an unusual domestic advisor in that she wrote her text for working women. "The 1950 census," she wrote in her introduction, "showed that more than half the employed women in the country are married."[15] "It would be ideal," she wrote, "if the housework were shared equally with their husbands. But let us not venture into the realm of unreality."[16] Adams' manual was unusual in that it identified and spoke to working women, but it did not veer away from the notion that women would ultimately always be in charge of family and home life, and it addressed its commentary on the home to women only.

The 1950s saw a housing boom in America, and family togetherness became part of the new housing designs. In part because of new government financing and widespread affluence, this was a period of increased housing starts.[17] Advisors suddenly had a broader audience. This housing frenzy was limited to the middle class and included thousands of returning soldiers and their families. The U.S. government presented them with free education and good rates on housing loans, providing a challenge for a new generation of home builders and a new audience for domestic advice.

Congressional legislation helped to encourage the national obsession with the home. The Servicemen's Readjustment Bill (The GI Bill) of 1944 and the Interstate Highway Act of 1956 pushed millions of former soldiers into white-collar jobs (after a free college education) and then into the brand-new suburbs.[18] The new roads led to the new suburbs, providing a way for the white middle class to commute to the cities. The Federal Housing Administration forced many new families to build new homes by discouraging repairs of existing structures and instead providing much better financing for new housing starts.[19] This meant that advisors had to invent a conception of the home to appeal to the new suburban residents.

The most famous postwar homebuilder was William Levitt. He became a household name after his company cleared potato fields in Long Island, New York, and built thousands of new homes. On one day in 1949, he signed 1,400 contracts with families.[20] Levittown homes included such family-oriented features as a picture window where the housewife could watch her children playing and an attic that could be expanded to make room for future children. Levittown changed the way many Americans thought about homes. Despite the loss of individuality that accompanied such massive building programs, people appreciated the family-centered values that the new houses represented.

Domestic advisors hoped that women would make their houses conform to new ideals. Although Charlotte Adams admitted that "most of us are 'stuck' with the quarters in which we live,"[21] many middle-class families did have the opportunity to help design their future homes, or at least to choose from a selection of designs. Federal home financing in this era changed to a great extent the relationship that middle-class women had with their homes by increasing the control over the primary locations of various rooms. "This is a good sign," wrote Hazel and Julius Rockow in 1954. "It enhances the likelihood that women, no longer content with drab and listless homes, will contribute new and interesting ideas."[22] Women could exert control over their homes by choosing the floor plans.

The open-space plan was the combined result of technology and ideology. New methods of house fabrication made the open-space plan possible, eradicating the need for beams and supporting walls at small intervals. The Prairie School of architecture advocated open space in the home in the 1910s and 1920s, and the bungalow style of the early century used one large room as a focus for the family activity in the household. However, these homes usually included enclosed dining rooms in the floor plan. Open-space advocates even challenged this formal dining space in midcentury.[23] The loss of the dining room — often considered a masculine space — reoriented the home toward the feminine parlor, now called the family room. As housing starts improved beyond architects' wildest expectations, the so-called ranch house enjoyed its most popular period.

In the 1950s, the architectural trade magazine *House and Home* flaunted pictures of new floorplans along with explanations of new techniques and building fabrics. In 1953, *House and Home* presented the "most influential house" of the year. "Many of America's top builders," claimed the article, "believe that this is the house the public will accept." This admission that the public had a strong voice in the creation of this home is interesting, as it suggests that Americans had an idea — which was perhaps different from the conventional wisdom of architects — of what comprised a good house. Although the article touched on aspects of roof construction and discussed new types of plywood, the main thrust of the article concerned the floor plan. It was the floor plan that "people are waiting to buy."[24] It was an open-space plan.

The open-space plan was easily recognizable to readers of shelter magazines. In fact, women's magazines and domestic advisors had an important role in creating the market for the open-space plan. This is the house "they have been reading about—not only in *Life* but in other magazines. . . . An open floor plan . . . with excellent circulation and an unusual amount of livability," noted *House and Home*.[25] This plan, then, was not simply a conceit of architects, but was a project that American women had been reading about and waiting for. There was a direct relationship between the new house plan and the women's magazines.

The American middle-class public was ready for the open-space plan. They loved the "Trade Secrets" house of 1953 and jammed the model houses in cities across the country, from Delaware, to Texas, to Ohio, to Tennessee. According to architect Thomas Riskas of Phoenix, Arizona, "The Trade Secrets House has attracted the largest single-day crowd in the history of model home opening, and since then, traffic has been heavy."[26] The March issue of the magazine raved: "The Trade Secrets House has aroused more enthusiasm in more cities than any builder house ever erected. In every city where the house has opened to the public (15 so far), record-breaking crowds poured through it. Huge crowds, long lines and traffic jams are now old stories; so is the almost unanimous approval."[27]

So what was the most influential house of 1953? At the most basic level, the floor plan usually dictated an L-shaped living area with a dining area at one end. The *House and Home* example included a large living room with many options for usage. "A new kind of flexibility in room planning . . . will let different families use it in different ways. The rear of the living room has a study-bedroom on one side marked off by a folding partition. On another side of the living room is the dining room combined with an activities room. On the third side is a paved terrace. All of this large space can be separated from the living room or become part of it."[28] Another section of the article named it a "combined dining room and all-purpose family room."[29] The noncommittal attitude of these descriptions—almost a carte blanche to use the room in any of a number of different ways—made this one-size-fits-all plan more palatable to the middle class. Each family could, *together*, make decisions about how to use each room.

The new houses embodied togetherness. One-story, with a short flight up and a short flight down, the house became known as the ranch, or split-level house. Families sacrificed privacy and noise reduction in favor of more room for family-oriented activities. Instead of concentrating on an expanded nursery so the children could play together, the open plan created the expanded living/activity/dining room so that the entire family could play, read, work, eat, and watch television together. In many suburban tracts, the houses were built onto a poured-concrete base and had no basement. Other fancier subdivisions did include a separate basement "rec room." The house was built to be self-consciously devoid of servants or other help. By limiting closed-off spaces to sleeping rooms (often shared) and bathrooms, the house demanded togetherness. It was the concrete arena in which family drama would be played out.

The open-space plan emphasized the role of women in the home. The kitchen moved to the front of the house, giving it more stature, and the living room often opened up onto the back yard with a sliding door or picture window. Both of these innovations were designed to make child care easier for the woman in the home as she worked inside and watched her children through a window. Both of these innovations also gave the woman at home more responsibility and less privacy.

Advisors often compared the open-space plan to the Colonial "keeping room." This one room housed all family activities except cooking. As Mary Davis Gillies wrote in her *Popular Home Decoration* of 1940, "So effective were their designs that we still copy the originations of our forbears."[30] Narcissa Chamberlain's manual claimed to illustrate how modern women could "profit by what the past has to offer."[31] As they had in the earlier part of the twentieth century, domestic advisors used "Colonial America" as a symbol of high ideals. The open-space plan allowed them to reference their Colonial ancestors who, similarly, had lived most of their lives in one room.

Domestic advisors criticized the Victorians' use of household space. As Annette J. Warner wrote in 1919, "The large living-room of the modern house is an attempt to amalgamate into a single space the interests formerly represented by separate rooms, such as reception-room, music-room, parlor, sitting room and library."[32] The breakdown of room differentiation occurred because of new ideas about family interaction, which continued throughout the twentieth century. Hazel and Julius Rockow noted in 1954, "The past two decades have brought a twofold development in modern architecture. Large, many gabled homes have given way to compact, efficiently planned homes. The decrease in the size of dwellings has led to a reduction in the number of individual rooms, until today the twelve or fourteen room home is comparatively uncommon."[33] Upper-middle-class homes of the nineteenth century had libraries, sunrooms, porches, nurseries, sewing rooms, and a plethora of pantries and turrets. Separating activities and people through the discrete spaces of separate rooms was an idea that had worked in previous eras but that contradicted the new ideals of the 1950s. Advisors now focused on the trauma to the family caused by a cramped series of rooms. Ray and Sarah Falkner, in their *Inside Today's Homes* of 1954 noted that "the space enclosed literally shapes our lives" and wrote that in homes with closed-in spaces, "family frictions develop [and] tensions find no release." They recommended "adequate, efficient space" as the antidote to most problems in family life.[34] Advisors literally believed that the open space would give families the room they needed to find happiness.

Domestic advisors helped to displace the dining room from American domestic space. As Elinor Hillyer wrote in her *Mademoiselle's Home Planning Scrapbook* in 1946, "A dining-room is a hotly debated question nowadays—to have or to have not." Her conclusion was that the dining room had been underused for decades and would not be a great loss to the house. Because she wrote her manual for young women, new brides, and therefore new homemakers, she felt free to recommend a fresh approach. "Frankly, it's no matter of fashion; it's a matter of straight economics, plus smaller families, lack of household help, and changing living patterns. . . . The dining-room, occupied by the average family at best only three hours a day, was soon under fire. . . . Many young people choose to let the dining-room go for the present; dine in one end of the living room, or in an alcove off the kitchen or pantry."[35] The dining room had been a statement of formality in the middle-class home for over a century. Dining-room furniture, such as tables, matching chairs, and sideboards, had been important features of the household. Eliminating the dining room from the home in favor of the open-space plan was a major declaration of "changing living patterns," as Hillyer understood.

Advisors' waning enthusiasm for the dining room led them to advocate the "dinette set." Furniture that was small enough to fit in the smaller areas became popular along with the open-space plan. However, Gladys Beckett Jones criticized the dinette in 1946 because it "lacks the possibility of extending the seating space." Jones, in her *Manual of Smart Housekeeping*, realized that "the dinette or dining al-

"The warm friendly room above does double duty," wrote Elizabeth Halsey of this image. Photographs of portable furniture like this rolling cart helped domestic advisors explain how to switch over from more familiar house floor plans with separate rooms into the open space plan of the 1950s. (Halsey, Ladies' Home Journal Book of Interior Decoration *[1959], 141)*

cove serves the same purpose as the conventional dining room," but found this situation "regrettable." In her opinion, "a permanent dining room promotes the establishment of good eating habits and table manners" for children, and she lamented its loss. However, so that she would not appear to be too critical of a room rapidly disappearing from architects' plans, she did suggest that the dining room "may be used for other purposes than dining."[36] Her recommendation was not to get rid of a separate dining room, but to make that room a multipurpose space that would be useful to all members of the family as a study or sewing room.

Open-space plans provided decorating challenges. As Ethel Davis Seal wrote in 1919, "The question has arisen as to just how one should go about combining the living and dining room without making a hopeless mess of things."[37] Early twentieth-century advisors found family life to be important, but the complete open-space plan was not widely implemented by architects until the postwar era. In 1933, Christine Holbrook turned to the basement as a "room which all the family can enjoy—a room which might be called a 'second living room.'" Holbrook recommended the use of "the new studio couches" in the space, and even "a compact little kitchenette."[38] Her suggestions for the second living room sound remarkably similar to what advisors would later recommend for the upstairs open space. Holbrook had

Though the open-space plan was often prized by domestic advisors, the limited privacy and mandated formality of the upstairs space often encouraged more creativity in the basement. The growth of teen culture in the 1940s and 1950s also gave home decorators inspiration to create a special room for youthful entertainment. Far away from the work-related spaces of upstairs kitchen and study, the "rec room" provided families with a sense of a vacation getaway within the confines of the household. (Halsey, Ladies' Home Journal Book of Interior Decorating *[1954], 224*)

begun a national movement to prioritize family space over all other spatial considerations in the house, but because architectural design had not incorporated her concept, she placed this room in the basement.

Advisors often discussed basement playrooms, also called "rec rooms" or "rumpus rooms," as important to family life. In the 1930s and 1940s, advisors creatively identified the basement as a room large enough for family activities. "In the basement is an illustration of what can be done with a room not ordinarily used," wrote Dorothy Raley in 1934.[39] In her 1939 *How to be Your Own Decorator*, Helen Koues, a writer for *Good Housekeeping*, celebrated the basement. "With hosannas to the modern new automatic heating systems," she wrote in 1939, "our cellars have new personalities. Sans coal bins, dust and discarded paraphernalia, we now have new space, where we can let ourselves go in creating a room for recreation and games. We can make it primarily a room for games with a big open space for ping pong table, or put a shuffle board design in the floor. Or, we can make it a comfortable room for lounging, for card games—an extra living room for the children."

Koues recommended furniture "sturdy in construction and genuinely comfortable." She decorated her prototype basement playroom with casual furniture, and identified it as an "extra living room." Her greatest praise of the room was that, in contrast to the rest of the 1930s' home, it had "big open space."[40]

Gladys Beckett Jones identified "the modern playroom or rumpus room" as a "particularly desirable place" in 1946. However, she identified a major flaw in the use of this room to encourage family development. "Little children do not like to be isolated from their elders," she wrote, "and they are happier playing in a ground-floor room."[41] Although in previous and future eras, or to a different sensibility, "isolation" from the family would be precisely the point of a separated playroom, the mid-twentieth-century advisors thought that the household should encourage family togetherness. When *McCall's Decorating Book* discussed a place for children in a new home, they noted that "you will want to include a . . . play area."[42] The use of the word "area" indicated that the children would be best off in a part of a room that adults also used. The basement, since it provided an isolated space, was not a suitable room for the American family.

Ray and Sarah Falkner emphasized the family's need of the open-space plan. They refused to treat the living room as "an isolated unit" and instead emphasized "the group activities for which the room is intended."[43] The family needs must dictate, wrote these advisors, the specific decoration of the room. As the Falkners told their readers, "Group-living space is for everyone, and all should share in its planning. Perhaps the most common mistake is to regard the living room as the woman's domain, possibly with one corner fitted up for the man of the house. It then becomes a 'nice room' planned primarily to elicit admiration from women guests. Heartening family life does not thrive under such circumstances." For the Falkners, the most important part of home decorating was the emphasis on the family. "Planning for all is not easy," they cautioned, "but is healthy fun."[44] These advisors believed that their readers should decorate their homes with the "togetherness" ideal of the family in mind. The home, in their view, must be accessible to the entire family.

Many advisors recommended specific groupings of furniture to make the room useful for everyone in the family. Furniture groupings received much attention in advice manuals of the mid-twentieth century because the living space was so large that it needed smaller cen-

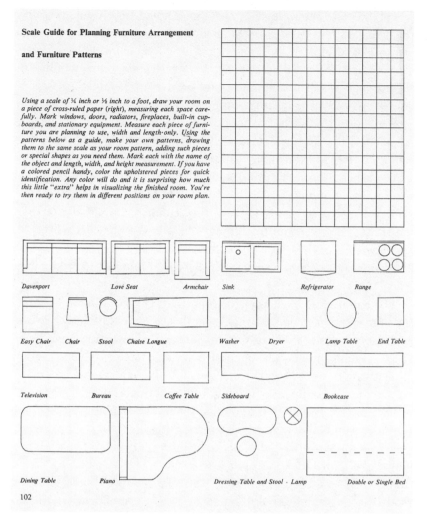

Scale Guide for Planning Furniture Arrangement

and Furniture Patterns

Using a scale of ¼ inch or ⅛ inch to a foot, draw your room on a piece of cross-ruled paper (right), measuring each space carefully. Mark windows, doors, radiators, fireplaces, built-in cupboards, and stationary equipment. Measure each piece of furniture you are planning to use, width and length-only. Using the patterns below as a guide, make your own patterns, drawing them to the same scale as your room pattern, adding such pieces or special shapes as you need them. Mark each with the name of the object and length, width, and height measurement. If you have a colored pencil handy, color the upholstered pieces for quick identification. Any color will do and it is surprising how much this little "extra" helps in visualizing the finished room. You're then ready to try them in different positions on your room plan.

Davenport   Love Seat   Armchair   Sink   Refrigerator   Range

Easy Chair   Chair   Stool   Chaise Longue   Washer   Dryer   Lamp Table   End Table

Television   Bureau   Coffee Table   Sideboard   Bookcase

Dining Table   Piano   Dressing Table and Stool · Lamp   Double or Single Bed

With new homeowners baffled by how to organize their lives within an open-space plan, domestic advisors tried to make it easy. Providing graph paper and cut-out furniture was one way for advisors to give their readers some creativity within the restrictions of the floor plan. Many magazines and texts encouraged women to experiment with furniture arrangements, giving them clues and hints about conversation groupings and convenient arrangements, but leaving the final decisions open. (Halsey, Ladies' Home Journal Book of Interior Decorating *[1959], 102)* ters of interest. The wide-open space gave domestic advisors room for many suggestions in relation to furniture groupings. The open-space plan was a revolutionary change since it was so amorphous as to require dedication to make it appropriate for each individual family. The sheer openness of the plan must have been overwhelming for women unused to decorating large rooms for so many different activities. The advice books rose to the challenge.

In 1948, the *Woman's Home Companion Household Book* noted that "the grouping, not the amount of furniture, is really the most important consideration." The editors noted that "balance, symmetry and naturalness" composed the rules to apply to any furniture group.[45] "It isn't really necessary, any longer," they claimed, "to put the table in the center" of the room for dining. "This is the old, formal way."[46] The advisors in this book recommended a more organic, free-form methodology to room organization based on movement rather than on custom.

The Falkners advised a "major conversation group" and a "secondary conversation group" for the open-space plan. The major group would incorporate "the family multi-purpose . . . center for music, television, reading, and buffet suppers." They also included "a desk group in the living room . . . out of traffic's way." If the room seemed *too* open, the Falkners recommended adding "screens, draperies or . . . room dividers," but they seemed to think that separate groupings for different activities would allow the entire family to use the room comfortably.[47]

Advisors recommended versatile furniture. Elizabeth Halsey listed items, useful for large, multipurpose rooms. "The low coffee table . . . could easily be turned up to make a standard-height dining table, or a card table opening to seat ten people. . . . A chest of drawers was no longer purely a bedroom bureau, but . . . [could] go into any area of a modern room as a sideboard, bureau, or night table."[48] Halsey made direct comparisons between the furniture and the American way of life, as "flexibility is very important to us today." She was clear about the relationship between a decorative scheme and a methodology for living. "Ideas about a fixed place to dine at home have undergone many changes in modern times,"[49] she asserted. The dinette she presented in her book was her social commentary on modern living.

Advisors delighted in recommending new ideas for the open-space home. "Today," wrote Hazel and Julius Rockow in 1954, "the living room is a happy combination of the front parlor, drawing room, library, music room and often the game room of fifty years ago." This change

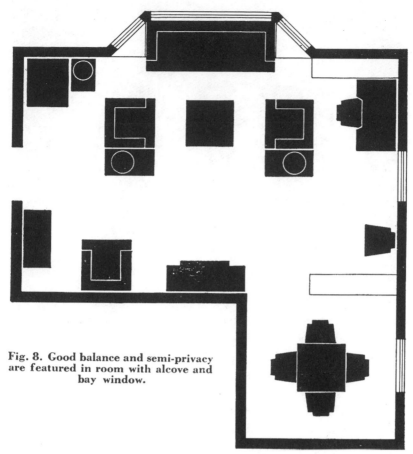

Fig. 8. Good balance and semi-privacy are featured in room with alcove and bay window.

Though only admitting to "semi privacy," this floor plan suggested a way for families to achieve some separation of the living room and the dining room within the L-shaped open plan. New furniture such as the dinette set became popular as people no longer had room for a full-sized dining room table.
(Woman's Home Companion Household Book, 56)

from rigid rules concerning the purpose of each room meant freedom of choice and the freedom, perhaps more significantly, to change over time. "The notion that a home is decorated only once to last for a lifetime," the Rockows remarked, "arose out of a psychological reflection of earlier scarcity economies and is now outdated." [50] The freedom of the fifties carried over into the home, freeing house designers from outdated restrictions on their creativity.

Dual furniture had been controversial among domestic advisors before the 1950s. While folding gaming tables and other dual-purpose

Convertible furniture, though certainly not new in the 1950s, enjoyed a renaissance as people strained to make their floor plans more flexible. The daybed gave people the ability to use the living room on a daily basis without having to provide a special room just for guests. (Halsey, Ladies' Home Journal Book of Interior Decorating *[1959], 43)*

furniture enjoyed popularity in the eighteenth century, advisors of the nineteenth century did not approve. "Let me urge you," wrote Margaret Sangster in 1898, "not to be deluded into the purchase of a folding-bed. . . . It is neither one thing nor the other, masquerading in the daytime as a cabinet or a bookcase in a clumsy way and fooling nobody." [51] But the same furniture can be influenced by different ideologies over time. Because Sangster, and other advisors in the 1890s, worried about the honesty of furniture, they did not care for the qualities of dual-purpose furniture that would become more important in the early and mid-twentieth century.

Dual-purpose furniture began to be treated in advice manuals with a positive regard in the 1930s and 1940s. The Ludwig Baumann furniture company argued as early as 1926, "It has remained for the twentieth century to develop two-purpose furniture in such a variety and so excellent in design that a living room, say, may be converted in a twinkling in to a completely appointed dining room or sleeping room." Although Baumann was selling its "smart occasional pieces" to a public not yet prepared with open-space plans, advisors had already begun to see the advantages of multipurpose furniture. Studio couches, so named because they could save space in a one-room apartment by becoming alternately a bed and a couch, enjoyed unprecedented popularity during the era of the open-space plan.

Domestic advisors illustrated the connection between the home and the outdoors, an important new frontier. *House and Home* claimed that the sliding-glass door giving onto the "paved rear terrace . . . will introduce many families in northern cities to a new kind of indoor-outdoor living." [52] Families could now move many activities outside. "Today's terrace is often an extra living room," proclaimed *Good Housekeeping* in 1952.[53] Ray and Sarah Falkner, in their *Inside Today's Home* of 1954, declared that readers should design their living rooms with attention to the outdoors. "How does [the living room] relate to the other areas in the home?" they asked, "to the sun and the wind, to the outlook and the outdoor living space?" [54] But the outdoor connection to the living room also gave women more responsibility for being in all places at all times. The proximity between the kitchen and the patio allowed a mother to "watch her children playing indoors or outdoors, [and] keep an eye on the front door." [55]

The open kitchen was one radical aspect of the open-space plan. This innovation was a sharp break from the ideal of sequestered kitchen work. Often women doing their own cooking lived in homes where this task was separate from the rest of the house. The open kitchen for the middle-class family was a major departure. In homes throughout the nineteenth-century landscape, kitchens existed in the back of the house, separated from the rest of the home by a corridor, pantry, or other seldom-used room. Bringing the kitchen up to the front of the house was a bold statement, predicated on a century of waning outside help for the middle-class housewife. The cooking surface was open so that the housewife could look over the counter and see the children playing in the family area. When guests filled the open space, she could interact with them while preparing their meals.

Advisors saw the kitchen as one of the most important spaces in the house. *The Woman's Home Companion Household Book* noted in 1948, "As a homemaker a large percentage of your time is spent in the kitchen. It is a very important room, for it is the most vitally concerned with keeping your family alive." [56] The open kitchen provided a way for a woman to be "together" with her family and yet still be separated. The open kitchen gave a woman a place from which to watch the rest of her family, but it did not change the gendered nature of the room.

The "trade secret" house included the option to have the kitchen open or closed. "Most families" will want the open kitchen, claimed the January 1953 issue of *House and Home*. After the model home opened to the public and the magazine could gather data, the editors came back in February with some results: "Somewhat surprisingly, almost universally the women liked the unconfined kitchen (except in the deep

The popular "command-post kitchen," touted by House and Home *magazine in 1953, provided a way for a parent to watch her children and cook at the same time. The command post provided more flexibility but also more responsibility. In this photograph, bar stools at the kitchen counter allowed both informal dining space and also a way for children and guests to keep the cook company during meal preparation. (Halsey,* Ladies' Home Journal Book of Interior Decorating *[1959], 195)*

South, where servants are still available) and the idea of being part of the household while preparing meals."[57] Women who planned to cook their own meals wanted to feel part of the action, but those with hired help wanted to be sure the servants were not part of the family's built-in "togetherness."

Advisors and magazine editors tried to make the open kitchen palatable to women. Model homes and magazine perusing helped architects figure out what would please "the average housewife . . . since she is the one who casts the deciding vote when the family buys." In 1953, *House and Home* determined that this typical woman "wants control of the house. She wants a command post, not a foxhole. . . . So, she takes naturally to a well-planned 'open' kitchen."[58] These army terms, used here during the Korean War when many would-be homeowners sat overseas in foxholes, illustrate the "home front" attitude of Americans at this time. In order to fight the cold war and in order to build consensus during a confusing time, women had to be part of the war effort. The transformation of the kitchen into a command post placed women in charge of the preservation of American democracy at home.[59]

Advisors configured the open kitchen as rejection of the efficiency kitchen. "Science as applied to kitchens should be taken in small doses," wrote Mary Davis Gillies in 1940, "and then only when well sugar-coated."[60] In the mid-twentieth century, advisors tried to make the kitchen into a family space rather than a laboratory. They looked to ways to add, as the *Woman's Home Companion Household Book* suggested in 1948, "a livable note to the kitchen."[61] Bringing the family into the home meant, in many cases, taking the scientist out.

Advisors celebrated the return of the family kitchen. Gladys Beckett Jones deemed the new kitchen "the socialized kitchen" in 1946. She critiqued the work of efficiency experts who, since the turn of the century, had recommended the "uninterrupted working surface . . . [in] efficient compact kitchens." These experts, she cautioned, may have provided a clean workspace, but they forgot the importance of the family in their zeal. "Certain human values have been overlooked," she proclaimed. "The kitchen should have been planned to meet family needs." Her recommendations for the socialized kitchen recommended that "the dining room and kitchen can be converted into one large kitchen-dining unit for family use as a general work and playroom." She noted that making the kitchen accessible to other rooms of the house would ensure that "the family group be held together."[62] Jones, and other advisors, strongly believed that the very nature of the kitchen should emphasize the family life within the house.

Advisors believed that the open kitchen would have direct implications for the status of women in society. "Today's housewife," claimed the architectural editors of *House and Home* gleefully, "is once again the center of the family life, no longer in solitary confinement." This article did not recommend moving women out of the kitchen but moving the kitchen itself. This rhetoric did not change the status of women; it instead changed their proximity to the rest of the family. It used "togetherness" as a tool to convince the American woman that this kitchen would help her "get companionship from the rest of her family."[63] Similarly, a 1955 *McCall's* article on prefabricated houses claimed that the model shown, with a giant "25-foot kitchen-activity room" in fact "emphasizes family life."[64]

Advisors argued that women worked outside the home only to improve their family life. *Look* magazine claimed that women worked "less toward a 'big career' than as a way of . . . buying a new home freezer."[65] As Elizabeth Sweeny Herbert wrote in an article about freezers in 1954, "This is the kind of freezer that could change your

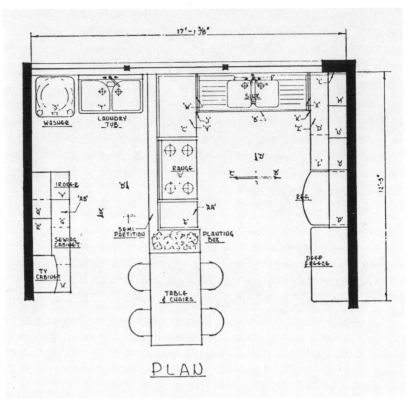

PLAN

Deep freezers showed up everywhere in the 1950s and 1960s, from advertisements in Good Housekeeping *to kitchen floor plans in domestic-advice manuals. The ideal of the well-kept family who would always have enough food appealed to many home economists and home decorators. In this floor plan for an ideal kitchen, the deep freezer found a place in what many considered to be the most important room. (*Koues, American Woman's New Encyclopedia of Home Decorating, *522)*

whole life."[66] The freezer was an icon of freedom and plenty. Advertised incessantly in women's magazines, the home freezer represented the American home and served as a defense against the troubles in the outside world. Significantly, the freezer delineated the American woman as an important part of that defense. A woman working for a freezer was a woman who supported her family.

Advertisers tried to represent the freezer as an appliance that could strengthen family bonds. Vance Packard commented in his *The Hidden Persuaders* in 1957 that freezers represented "the assurance that there is always food in the house; [since] food in the house represents security, warmth and safety."[67] The new, larger, colder freezers theoretically freed up much of the housewife's week for other tasks, giving her more time to spend on the many levels of responsibility for her family. Women could sustain family life by baking birthday cakes for the whole year at once and then revealing them one by one as the occasion warranted.[68]

Advisors used the freezer as a symbol of the strength of the American family. While it might seem farfetched to cast the home freezer as a major icon of American life, the 1959 "kitchen debates" in Moscow highlight the international scope of the connection between household appliances and national pride. Vice President Richard Nixon traveled to Moscow in July of that year to meet with Nikita Khrushchev. The two strolled through an exhibit of American technology and proceeded to have a discussion about the relative merits of communism and democracy.[69] Perhaps not surprisingly, given the home-based focus of the era, the discussion centered on washing machines and efficient kitchens instead of on bombs and other nuclear weaponry.[70]

In Nixon's way of thinking, the global political position of the United States had everything to do with the American dedication to the family. He considered the home to be not only a defense against Communism, but also America's best virtue. Although Nixon did not refer to—and probably had little direct knowledge of—the women's magazines and manuals that supported his rhetoric, he had succinctly outlined the domestic policy of the cold war that had already been the subject of hundreds of articles by domestic advisors.

In the postwar era, domestic advisors put their own positive spin on togetherness. Their enthusiasm helped mute the crises that both men and women felt brewing within the domestic sphere. Domestic advisors, from magazine editors to decorators, privileged the home above all else in American society. The open-space plan provided advisors with a concrete emblem of their work. Outwardly portraying domesticity as an answer to communism and to other international threats, the advisors turned inward to the home and enveloped both men and women in their plans. That there were cracks in this ideal would become more apparent as the decade wore on.[71]

Some advisors began to express their discontent with the open-space plan. Loss of an attic, as well as of other formerly basic private spaces, were points of concern. The attic had been the subject of many domestic-advice treatments in the earlier part of the twentieth century. Mary Northend's "Making the Attic Livable" appeared in *House and Garden* in 1919 and claimed that "additional space is an absolute necessity" and could be found in the attic. She suggested many uses for the room, from a retreat for the father of the family, "giving him a den or study where he can be quiet and can fuss around with his hobbies," to "additional room for guests." The attic could provide a place for anybody to "be completely isolated from the family life." [72] Because of the emphasis on family life in the mid-twentieth century, the attic had been abandoned and any privacy it offered disdained. However, advisors did understand that this loss could be severely felt.

"Whatever happened to the attic?" questioned *Good Housekeeping* in 1955. "Where do you go when you're moody or mad? The fine architectural lines of the open-plan contemporary house, which has no nooks or crannies to catch dust and possessions and no dangerous stairs to trip up the unwary in the dark, couldn't be more practical or beautiful. But the modern house is so unmysterious, so open and above board!" That there was nowhere to put "the Christmas tree ornaments between Christmas trees . . .the letters that should have been thrown away, the cap and gown, the wedding dress, the ballet tutu, the fencing foils" seemed to be a solvable challenge. But *Good Housekeeping* was quite circumspect on the question of the need for a personal retreat. "Now we live in uncomplicated houses that presuppose life to be uncomplicated," the editors wrote, but they noted that "life has not changed much." There are still complications; people still get "moody and mad," and they "simply don't know where to go." [73] The article ended there, but readers surely got the sense that there would be more questioning to follow.

In 1958, *Look* magazine pointed out that the open plan produced a real lack of privacy, especially for women. In the weekly "For Women Only" section, the editors questioned whether women could find solitude in their own homes. "To some, the American bathroom has become a sanctuary for the psyche." A state of affairs in which the only refuge is the bathroom was certainly cause for concern. But even this small hideaway was no good. As *Look* pointed out, "In big families . . . [the] bathroom inevitably resembles a three-ring circus more than it does a retreat." [74] The article suggested, rather than an abandonment of the open plan, a system of "room dividers" for privacy. But the magazine did identify the problem.

Betty Friedan's *The Feminine Mystique* of 1963 provided a strong critique of the open-space plan. She specifically blamed the open-space plan for the problems of women in the mid-twentieth century.[75] Friedan began by interviewing the staff at *McCall's*, who were credited with starting it all in 1954. "Suddenly, everybody was looking for this spiritual significance in togetherness, expecting us to make some mysterious religious movement out of the life everyone had been leading for the last five years—crawling into the home, turning their backs on the world," a former editor remembered. "But we never could find a way of showing it that wasn't a monstrosity of dullness."[76] Even the very creators of togetherness found it a difficult doctrine to defend. They realized that if men took over the women's sphere and women still faced limited career opportunities, there was nothing left for them to do. The architecture of family life did not permit any physical space for women to have any existence separate from the family.

Friedan took on the open-space plan. She delved deeper into the problem of the bored, listless housewife, labeling the open-space plan as one cultural culprit in this societal devaluation of women's lives.

> Take, for instance, the open plan of the contemporary "ranch" or split-level house . . . which has been built in the millions from Roslyn Heights to the Pacific Palisades. They give the illusion of more space for less money. But the women to whom they are sold almost *have* to live the feminine mystique. There are no true walls or doors; the woman in the beautiful electronic kitchen is never separated from her children. She need never feel alone for a minute, need never be by herself. She can forget her own identity in these noisy open-plan houses. The open plan also helps expand the housework to fill the time available. In what is basically one free-flowing room, instead of many rooms separated by walls and stairs, continual messes continually need picking up. A man, of course, leaves the house for most of the day. But the feminine mystique forbids the woman this.

The open-space plan, touted for years by domestic advisors, was exposed by Betty Friedan as a trap rather than a celebration of family life.

Friedan connected women's lives directly with their domestic architecture. She wrote about a woman she met who had indicated a desire to be a writer. "But when I saw [her] house," Friedan continued, "I wondered where . . . she would put a typewriter." Friedan noted that most of the women she spoke to remained in their suburban homes.

When they realized that their lives needed to change, "this moment of personal truth was . . . likely to be marked by adding a room with a door to their open-plan house."[77]

According to Friedan, the architecture of women's lives failed them in the suburbs of the 1950s. The much-touted embrace of the family had removed an aspect of privacy from women's lives. The open-space plan followed directly the mandates set out by domestic advisors, by magazine editors, newspaper columnists, interior decorators, and professional architects. Experts, both women and men, had praised the new floorplans. Friedan's was a specific critique on decades of domestic fantasy. Although she blamed the phenomenon on men and the male-dominated magazine staffs of the 1950s, domestic fantasy had been pursued by women for over a century and a half.

Domestic advice in the mid-twentieth century both created and perpetuated the fantasy of togetherness. Advisors in this era continued their wide cultural appeal to middle-class American women. The exposure of the problems of the open-space plan caused advisors in later decades to develop new ideas. The open-space plan perhaps suffered in the minds of some women. But significantly, women did not reject the importance of domestic advice. For over a century, women have recognized that domestic advice is for the most part fantasy, imagination, and desire. The base reality of life has not interrupted the flow of domestic fantasy in America. Domestic advisors celebrated the many lives of women by continually reinventing them.

Conclusion

This is not a story that ends in the 1950s. At the turn of the twenty-first century, domestic advice remains front and center in American culture. At any bookstore today, dozens of works on subjects such as entertaining, housekeeping, and interior decorating fill the shelves. Stories about the home are everywhere. Domestic servants, a problem for nineteenth-century domestic advisors, continue to rile the public, as female candidates for federal Cabinet positions must withdraw due to implications of hiring household help illegally. Massive stores such as Home Depot encourage both men and women to engage in a constant state of home improvement. Threats of germs continue to plague homes as Americans search for special sponges and mops that claim to eradicate these invisible pests. Shopping for the home has gone beyond what A. A. Vantines offered in early twentieth-century New York to include exotic dishware at Pier 1 or pseudocolonial apothecary chests at Pottery Barn. People still strive to bring other cultures into their homes; the Turkish cozy corner or ubiquitous Navajo rug in turn-of-the-century middle-class homes have often been replaced by Kenyan salad tongs, Shaker baskets, or Colonial sleigh beds sold at Crate and Barrel.

Domestic advisors of the turn of the twentieth century carry on a long tradition of women writing about the home. They picked up certain aspects of nineteenth- and early twentieth-century advice manuals and updated and expanded them into complete volumes. Lydia Maria Child's idea for a budget decorating book, *The American Frugal Housewife*, has been updated in many different forms, from Emilie Barnes' *Beautiful Home on a Budget* (1998) to Lauri Ward's *Use What You Have Decorating* manual (1999). Just as early nineteenth-century advisors told their readers to refrain from having a show parlor, modern decorators admire sincerity in domestic arrangements. Lifetime Television's Katie Brown claims to offer "affordable advice" in her book *Katie Brown Entertains*. Books such as Marion Talbot and Ellen Richard's *Home Sanitation* have new versions that take up the early home economists' call for strict attention to clean, healthy homes. The creators of the Boston Cooking School would appreciate such modern magazines as *Cooks Illustrated*, which address the material science of food preparation. Advisors who discussed the psychology of the home would be heartened by Alexandra Stoddard's work, including *Creating a Beautiful Home*, given that she addresses the way that different home arrangements can affect happiness and well-being.

Indeed, each theme addressed in early advice manuals has a counterpart on today's shelves. There are advisors who explain the intricacies of Southwest design, modern color schemes and materials, and special rules for children's rooms. Books in the *Simple* series instruct people to rid their homes of clutter, indeed of any decoration at all, and trends such as "shabby chic" help new homeowners who prefer the lived-in look. Shelves and shelves of books in home decorating—and even self-help—sections of bookstores testify to the sustained interest in domestic activity through the end of the twentieth century.

Many writers turned to other cultures to discover new and old rules about the meanings of household arrangements. Just as early twentieth-century domestic advisors such as Hazel Shultz explored the ways that color and furniture arrangement could affect the psychology of both children and adults, so do their contemporary counterparts. For example, the main foundation of the Form School of Feng Shui concentrates on the ways that objects and furniture are arranged in the house, and the flow of "ch'i," usually translated as positive energy. The ch'i of each individual house is modulated differently, but certain basic rules should be followed. The central idea of Feng Shui, as one practitioner and Feng Shui consultant explains, is "to bring you and your home into harmony."[1] Feng Shui texts echo the domestic advisors of the early twentieth century who instructed their readers on use of color and choice of furnishings. Feng Shui is a series of beliefs about the importance of decoration and stability in people's lives. The basic principles correspond in many ways to the domestic fantasies of generations of American domestic advisors.

Many domestic advice texts today include cooking and entertaining advice. Barbara Smith's first book, *Entertaining and Cooking for Friends*, came out in 1995 after she had already achieved some level of fame as a model and restaurateur. She now has three restaurants: in New York City's theater district, in her hometown of Sag Harbor on Long Island, and at Union Station in Washington, D.C. Smith's book, according the cover notes, brought "a jazzy rhythm, an urban energy, and a global perspective" to beach parties and Valentine's Day dinners. "Being a model is about fantasy," Smith once noted, "and so is entertaining."[2]

B. Smith's eagerly awaited 1999 *Rituals and Celebrations* divided the year into twelve special rituals. The celebrations included parties for Christmas and Kwanzaa, as well as a Juneteenth celebration and a special ritual for a young girl's rite of passage to adulthood. B. Smith expands the ways that domesticity can encompass new approaches to time-honored traditions. Her book fills a new market niche, but while Smith "thinks the book has particular appeal to African Americans," she also believes "there's something in it for everyone."[3] Smith brings national issues that are important to her, such as acceptance and enthusiasm for African American culture, into the home. The success of her restaurants and of her books on entertaining attest to the appeal of these subjects.

Cheryl Mendelson, author of the 1999 tome *Home Comforts: The Art and Science of Keeping House,* delivers meticulous instructions on housekeeping tasks. Mendelson emphasizes her dual roots in the introduction, noting that her Appalachian grandmother and her Italian grandmother had different roles to play in her domestic education. Her book carefully describes rules such as how long certain foods can remain fresh in the cupboard and how often bed sheets should be washed. She recommends cleaning out the freezer every week—when in fact most families are lucky if they get to it once a year. She offered her book as an encyclopedia of sorts, noting that in the past, mothers passed these things on to their daughters, but that many people today live in total ignorance of the basics of home maintenance. Her bestseller served as a reference tool in a similar way to nineteenth-century tracts such as the *Domestic Cyclopedia,* which attempted to answer every question and to predict every need of the homemaker—even if today's homemaker is perceived as a part-timer.

Martha Stewart, the most prolific and successful of the modern domestic advisors, is chairman and chief executive officer of Martha Stewart Living Omnimedia. She has captured the public's imagination and achieved new heights in the proliferation of domestic advice. In her first letter to stockholders of her newly public company in 1999, Stewart wrote: "I set out to create a company that would provide impeccable content, assiduously created, and useful products, responsibly designed and manufactured for the widest possible audience in order to enliven, enhance, and better everyday living."[4] Martha

Martha Stewart's first book, Entertaining *(1982), introduced readers to her ideas about beautiful table settings, innovative projects, and complex cuisine. Her later texts included cookbooks as well as wedding planners and guides for home decoration.*
(Courtesy Random House, Inc.)

Stewart takes her work as a domestic advisor seriously. "Our goal," she wrote in 1997, "is to teach, to inform, and to inspire all of you."[5] The 1990s "domestic diva" believes that she has something of value to offer American homemakers.

Stewart's domestic-advice career grew in the 1980s and 1990s. Her role as a domestic advisor began when she worked as a caterer in Connecticut in the 1980s. Her first book, *Entertaining,* came out in 1982 and launched a domestic-advice career of unprecedented proportion. In its thirtieth printing, *Entertaining* has sold more than 600,000 copies. Stewart has since published more than thirty books, ranging from *The Wedding Planner,* to *Martha Stewart's Gardening,* to *Martha Stewart's Christmas.* Her magazine *Martha Stewart Living* began publication in

1990, and in September 1997, she started production of a television show of the same name. Special editions of her magazine, for weddings, babies, and holidays, appear annually. She also appears regularly on the cable TV Food Network and on various morning talk shows. Her radio and newspaper appearances called "Ask Martha" are syndicated in regions across the country. She markets products for the home in several ways, from her Martha Stewart Everyday lines at Kmart to her Martha by Mail project kits and luxury items.

In 1997 Stewart left Time-Warner and began her own corporation, Martha Stewart Living Omnimedia. The company's 1999 annual report noted revenues of $145 million in the publishing department, $31 million from television, and $20 million from merchandising. From the high-end catalogue and internet sales, the company increased its revenues dramatically to $36 million in 1999.[6] These are numbers that most domestic advisors in history could not have imagined. Though domesticity has always been popular, Martha Stewart has also made it profitable. Altogether, she is perhaps the most famous female brand name in the American consumer world, and she continues to expand her holdings and projects.

Martha Stewart addresses most of the issues that domestic advisors of the past found important. In an article about the decorative use of household flags in the July/August 1999 issue of *Martha Stewart Living* (MSL), the magazine celebrated both patriotism and historically-inspired decorating. "Magnificent both in what it stands for and in how it looks," read the article, "the flag is synonymous with the ideals on which this country was founded." The article went on to emphasize the historic links of the practice of using flags by noting that "Martha's Federal-style house in Westport, Connecticut, was built around 1805. Here, the placement of a single contemporary . . . flag at each window befits the symmetry and dignity of a federal house."[7] Victorian-era advisors had similar links in their works to emblems of religion or patriotism.

In the late nineteenth century, home economists addressed the ways that air and water entered and left the home, and one hundred years later, Martha Stewart addresses the same subject. "A house's plumbing system has three related networks of pipes," the magazine explains, echoing generations of home advisors before it, "The first, the water-supply network, brings fresh water into the house and distributes it to the fixtures. The second, a drain and waste network, removes used water and waste. The third, a venting network, provides air to the system."[8] This explanation, and others that acquaint readers with the inner-workings of their homes, echoes the texts that brought male-dominated information systems to women.

A 1997 article brought readers to the familiar world of American antiques, just as Mary Northend had done for her early twentieth-century readers. "Nothing connects us to the tables and traditions of colonial America," according to Martha Stewart, "quite like the warm satiny touch of this lustrous metal. History and pewter are as insepa-rable as the metals that make the alloy. . . . Everybody ate and drank from pewter."[9] And MSL also brings readers to Lillian Gilbreth's and Christine Frederick's more modern ideas for the efficiency kitchen. The ideal kitchen, declared MSL in 1995, would shine in the areas of "utility, durability, and good, clean looks." This kitchen was "rational-ized by experience to the simplest lines, greatest ease of use, highest safety standards, and lowest maintenance. Laboratory tables are avail-able in standing or sitting heights."[10]

Modern design, important to domestic advisors such as Dorothy Raley, also finds its place in MSL. While Raley wrote about the dawn of the machine age in 1934, Martha Stewart describes metal furniture more than six decades later. "I love the simple and pure lines of the fur-niture," writes Stewart. "This furniture is perfectly suited to meet the needs of the modern home. Anonymous as it is, this mass-produced furniture is carefully, sensibly, and thoughtfully made. A piece that catches your eye can be made to look perfectly at home anywhere."[11] Manuals such as the *Woman's Home Companion Household Book* of 1948 celebrated the creative use of color. Stewart introduced her line of Everyday Colors at Kmart in 1997 and noted that "it will be accompa-nied by a series of color menus with suggested complements for all 256 paints in the collection." The editors of *Martha Stewart Living* learned from advisors before them and continue the teaching that "color can still be used to give each room a distinct character. . . . When all colors harmonize, a house will be a joy to behold."[12]

Stewart includes a column called "Remembering" in each issue of her monthly magazine. Using nostalgic references to her home-town of Nutley, New Jersey, or to her early years at "Turkey Hill" in Connecticut, she evokes an era or a historical moment when she felt at peace because of certain domestic ideals. Whether a remem-bered recipe, a family anecdote, or a household project, these inci-dents remind readers of their ultimate goal, to find domestic harmony through creativity and ingenuity. When Martha Stewart remembers her past, real or imagined, it gives readers a point of reference. Martha Stewart's "Remembering" columns are affecting because they are a link to the past. Just like the domestic advisors before her, she discusses patriotism and religion, science and order, color, antiques, and other cultures. She focuses on furniture and wall paper, on kitchen efficiency and bedroom decoration. In fact, her entire repertoire is this type of link, looking backward to over a century of women writing about the home.

But she is also a link to the future. When Martha Bruere admonished her readers in 1912 to "follow the spinning wheel into the world," she could never have imagined what it would mean to host an empire of domesticity. The image of Stewart toasting her initial public offering (IPO) at the New York Stock Exchange with fresh-squeezed orange juice and homemade brioche caught so many people's attention specifically because of the perceived clash between the public sphere of stock trading and the private sphere of the home. Stewart's success— and, indeed, the success of the vast numbers of books and videos on home entertaining, cooking, and decorating—compels both spheres because it harks to the past, a world of moral parlors, unholy cozy corners, and basement rec rooms, and because it brings domesticity out of the home and into the world.

One year I watched Martha Stewart on TV making her own wrapping paper from old, brown paper bags and gold spray paint. Poor Martha, what a mess! She went to so much trouble, too: cutting the bags, spraying curlicue designs, waiting for the paint to dry. It took quite a long time—and then when she wrapped her gifts, they looked so homely!

I could have told her that a jumbo roll of wrap was on sale at Ocean State Job Lot for only $1.00 but who was I to spoil her Christmas?[13]

This letter, written in response to the *Providence Journal-Bulletin*'s appeal to readers on the occasion of Martha Stewart's visit to the Rhode Island Flower and Garden Show in 1996, expresses what many feel is Stewart's excessive obsession with do-it-yourself homemaking. Why would any rational person who could buy wrapping paper for one dollar attempt to make it herself? Why would any woman who understands that she has opportunities outside the home give more than a moment's thought to setting the table, making the bed, or painting pale blue moons on the bedroom wall?

Stewart's projects, in fact, bring domestic fantasy to a level that many consider absurd. Who could possibly have time to make the complicated acorn wreaths, lavender potpourri bags, or ravioli from scratch? With recipes for crackers and breadsticks, and with instructions for wine-bottle-cork bulletin boards and decorative-glass bottle soap dispensers, Martha Stewart brings domesticity to a new level of complicated craft that even her nineteenth-century counterparts did not imagine. To many contemporary observers, the Martha Stewart phenomenon is actually worse than absurd. In its creation of an unattainable ideal, it sets women up for failure.

Many women share the sentiments of parodies such as "Is Martha Stewart Living?" and "Martha Stewart's Better Than You at Entertaining." Stewart's recipes are too complex, they say, her homemaking ideas too time-consuming. Did anybody really make candles out of coral-toned melted paraffin and quahog shells or dye toile in hibiscus-flower tea to achieve a perfect "dusky pink hue" with which to re-upholster a side chair?[14] A recent issue of the satirical newspaper *The Onion* parodied a woman who performed tedious household chores as if they were crafts. She made her own soap, but this was not the only "arduous 19th-century chore" she did in her spare time. "There's nothing more pleasurable than spending a lazy Sunday afternoon churning butter," she enthused. The article noted that this woman's "love of grueling chores was inspired" by Martha Stewart.[15]

Indeed, Martha Stewart's success in post-1970s America is mind-boggling to many observers. To her critics—and there are plenty—her ascension to popular acclaim simply does not seem possible. In the decades since Betty Friedan questioned the feminine mystique and the open-space plan in 1963, many individuals have joined in her call to liberate women from the household. Movements to help women find opportunities outside the home have ranged from demands for day-care and flexible work schedules to the 1990s "Take Our Daughters to Work," an annual day of programs geared to introducing career possibilities to new generations of girls. In the 1970s, sayings such as "A woman's place is in the house . . . and in the senate" brought attention to the changing role of women in American society specifically by emphasizing the fact that women were no longer associated solely with homemaking. Magazines like *Ms.* introduced a generation of women to new ideas. The women's liberation movement, often referred to as the largest social movement in the history of the United States, has radically changed both opportunities and realities for American women.[16]

To be a feminist and a subscriber to *Martha Stewart Living*, then, can be a complicated proposition. One feels the need to qualify the interest in domesticity with a twist on the *Playboy* reader's insistence that he only buys the magazine for the articles. "I only buy *Martha Stewart Living* for the pictures," one could say, or for the recipes, or for the gardening tips. Domesticity has become almost a dirty pleasure, an interest for which one must apologize in public settings. To many, *Martha Stewart Living* seems to bring women back into some kind of 1950s suburban nightmare. Even if, as the editor claims, "you'll never find articles in the magazine about getting a man, dieting, or fixing your hair,"[17] you will find articles about how to load a dishwasher and how to cut heart-shaped croutons for Valentine's Day. Stewart's enterprise of hyperdomesticity is as scary to some as it is comforting to others.

As Stewart gained popularity among American women, her critics got louder. Martha Stewart became as associated with old-fashioned domestic drudgery as Typhoid Mary is with contagious disease. A 1995 article in *New York* magazine noted that Stewart "embodies a direct threat to three decades of received ideas about motherhood, wifehood, home, career. . . . Martha Stewart has become an icon largely by headmistressing a vision of old-school female control."[18] One of Stewart's harshest critics, Jerry Oppenheimer, hammered her in his unauthorized biography for being insincere, harsh, and conniving. He found fault with her nostalgic re-creation of her marriage and family life and took offense when she wrote about these subjects in her magazine because she was divorced and, he claimed, estranged from many family members.[19] *Spy* magazine's Greg Easley claimed he would uncover "the *real* Martha Stewart—a cruel, money-losing, chronic delegator."[20] Daryl Royster Alexander of the *New York Times* called Stewart "the latest guru on the labor-intensive life style,"[21] noting that her directions "pale next to" those for eighteenth-century cookbooks, but invoke the same type of housework-as-drudgery image. Journalists often search for a historical precedent to make their point that Stewart's work revives an old second-class standard for women. Christopher Caldwell, for instance, wrote in the *Weekly Standard* in 1996 that "Stewart is less a latter-day Emily Post than an upmarket Heloise."[22]

The *New York Times*'s Patricia Leigh Brown called Stewart "a latter-day Mrs. Beeton in Armani,"[23] and in January 1996 the *London Times* echoed this nomenclature by designating her "the guru of graceful living, a *fin de siècle* Mrs. Beeton."[24] English advisor Isabella Beeton wrote elite advice for women in the early nineteenth century, and this comparison makes a statement about Stewart's class pretensions. Many commentators have noted the similarity between the backgrounds of Ralph Lauren (born Lifshitz) and Martha Stewart (born Kostyra) as children of immigrants who set a standard for modern Americans that is ultimately based in the values of English gentry.[25] Stewart is often seen as somehow illegitimately using her married name to blend in with WASP culture, though in more recent years she has emphasized her Polish roots by, for example, inviting her mother onto her television show to make Pierogi.

Articles about Martha Stewart proliferated in many different newspapers and journals throughout the 1990s. Headlines such as the *New Republic*'s "Money, Time, and the Surrender of American Taste: Les Trés Riches Heures de Martha Stewart" (1996) addressed her role in the production of class elitism.[26] Her rise to corporate success was chronicled in *Business Week*'s "Martha Inc.: Inside the Growing Empire of America's Lifestyle Queen" (2000), and a 1998 *New York Times* article asked, "Is Martha Stewart a colonialist tool? An American populist? Or is she merely a flyspeck on the damask tablecloth of history?"[27] Martha Stewart has been a feature of articles in media outlets ranging from the erudite *New Yorker* to the somewhat more hip *Providence Phoenix*, in which Beth Wolfensberger presented "ten helpful hints for anyone who isn't quite loving her yet."[28] Wolfensberger's humorous article noted that "the natural human impulse" in response to Stewart's projects is to "freak out" and "then to feel that a) you are a faulty, disorganized creature, or b) that Martha is insane."[29]

The 1998 annual meeting of the Modern Language Association (MLA) and the 1999 annual meeting of the American Studies Association (ASA) brought critiques of Martha Stewart into the scholarly realm. A proposal for a special session on Stewart at the MLA questioned how her work, "produced by the culture of late capitalism," serves to "construct notions of whiteness and middle-class heterosexual identity." These scholars attacked her "aggressive heterosexual performance" as a representation of "imperialist nostalgia."[30] In other words, they wondered whether Martha Stewart's concentration on middle-class married women's homemaking skills was working to bring women back in time to an era of fewer opportunities. Stewart, insisted many, was part of a national backlash against women's rights.

Indeed, historians have joined other critics in seeking to separate the history of women from the history of domesticity. While early works such as Nancy Cott's 1977 *The Bonds of Womanhood* discussed the role of nineteenth-century women in the home, women's history scholarship soon moved away from the home toward the hospital, the factory, the saloon, and the department store. In their work, historians have searched for places where they could see the connection between women and the home being broken. "While we can learn much about individuals from the houses in which they lived," wrote public historian Page Putnam Miller in 1992, more effort should be spent researching and interpreting "sites that were workplaces and meeting places." [31] The editors of *Writing the Range: Race, Class, and Culture in the Women's West* noted in their introduction that when women's historians first began writing histories in the 1970s and 1980s, they explored the important areas of "domestic work and childbearing." However, the editors remained hopeful that "as more women become historians" they will discover "new areas of research and new ways to think about gender and history." [32] Many found the association between women and the home to have been problematic in American history because of the traditional value placed on the marketplace over what transpired in the home. "Why are we still talking about domesticity?" complained one women's history scholar to me as I told her the topic of my research. "Let's move on."

This book is my answer to that question. It has addressed domestic writing as a way of seeing and understanding American culture. The hundreds of domestic-advice manuals spanning over 150 years of history that I read during the course of my research convinced me beyond a reasonable doubt that these books and their authors were connected with the most important cultural dialogues of their day. Domesticity gives these writers a way to interact with and to help construct national ideologies. Catharine Beecher used the home as the base for education in a wide range of subjects, from ventilation to religion. Chemist Ellen Richards developed a women's laboratory at MIT and brought her teachings into the home, and social activists Mabel Hyde Kittredge and Florence Nesbit attacked what they saw as the degrading combination of poverty and ignorance of domestic life. Home economists such as Helen Campbell and Marion Talbot believed that the study of domestic rules and regulations would help women find a voice in the political arena. Mary Northend took her talent as a photographer into the home, and Mary Jane Colter built hotels in the Southwest, both of them creating domestic fantasies around historic re-creations. Helen Koues brought her knowledge of color and balance to domestic spaces, such as kitchens, bathrooms, and hobby areas. All of these women took domesticity into new places and in new directions.

Domestic advisors discussed the role of women in education, in social action, and in science. These authors were also professional architects, photographers, social workers, teachers, interior decorators, scientists, and psychologists. They came to their study of domesticity not because it was the only thing out there for them, but because it was one of a whole set of issues that they found compelling. These were people concerned with clean air, nutrition, and health, with patriotism, education, and art. Domesticity was for them—and continues to be for others—a way to navigate through their complicated world.

Even as the women's movement has changed the way Americans think about jobs, children, healthcare, and equality, it has not quelled the interest in domesticity. Domestic-advice manuals and the homes they describe are embedded in social and cultural contexts that make these texts a fruitful platform from which to study American history. These texts, though they may make both historians and the general public uneasy, can teach us about the way in which the home is a place where national ideologies of class, race, and gender are expressed in *things*, such as bric-a-brac and wicker chairs. We should pay attention to the history of domestic advice not because it circumscribes the small, private world of middle-class women, but, quite to the contrary, because it illuminates national priorities, addresses public dilemmas, and reminds us that what we have in our homes connects us to the larger culture.

Notes

INTRODUCTION

1. Martha Stewart, discussion with the author, February 22, 1996, Westin Hotel, Providence, Rhode Island.

2. Jones, "Mad about Martha," G1.

3. Ibid., G2.

4. Letters to *Providence Journal-Bulletin*, Providence, Rhode Island, January 1996. Features writer Keren Mahoney Jones wrote a query for the newspaper, encouraging local readers to share their thoughts about Martha Stewart. Keren Mahoney Jones, discussion with the author, January, 1996.

5. For more on advertising as "Zerrspiegel" (funhouse mirror), see Marchand, *Advertising the American Dream*.

6. Of the 115 domestic-advice manuals used in this book, 74 were published in New York and 26 in Boston.

7. Eunice Beecher, *All around the House*, 1.

CHAPTER ONE

1. See Davidson, *Revolution and the Word*.

2. Evans, *Born for Liberty*, 72. See also Kelley, *Private Woman, Public Stage*. Kelley found that "literacy among adult whites" reached 90 percent in the early 1800s (vii).

3. Baym, introduction to *The Lamplighter*, xii.

4. *Charlotte Temple* was published in over 200 editions in America, most of these in the nineteenth century. Douglas, introduction to *Charlotte Temple*, viii.

5. Child, *The American Frugal Housewife*, 101.

6. See Sklar, *Catharine Beecher*; Baer, *The Heart Is Like Heaven*; Clifford, *Crusader for Freedom*; Bruce Mills, *Cultural Reformations*; Karcher, *The First Woman in the Republic*; Antoinette May, *Helen Hunt Jackson*; Mathes, *Helen Hunt Jackson and her Indian Reform Legacy*; Tonkovich, *Domesticity with a Difference*; Finley, *The Lady of Godey's*; Rogers, *Sarah Josepha Hale*; Vigneron, *Studying for Survival*; Okker, *Our Sister Editors*.

7. Helen Jackson, *Bits of Talk about Home Matters.*

8. Cummins, *The Lamplighter,* 401.

9. Harland, *Common Sense in the Household,* 1.

10. See Rowson, *Charlotte Temple* (1794), Cummins, *The Lamplighter* (1854), and many other women's novels of this period. Susanna Rowson noted in her "author's preface" that the book was written "to your own children . . . [and] the many daughters of Misfortune who, deprived of natural friends, or spoilt by a mistaken education, are thrown on an unfeeling world." At the end of chapter 1, Cummins noted to her readers that the heroine was in trouble. "Poor little, untaught, benighted soul! Who shall enlighten thee?" These entreaties to the reader were common in sentimental novels, and also in domestic advice in the nineteenth century.

11. Harland, *Common Sense in the Household,* v.

12. For more on Amelia Simmons's cookbook, see Nylander, *Our Own Snug Fireside,* 212.

13. Child, *The American Frugal Housewife,* 83–84.

14. Eunice Beecher, *All around the House,* 7.

15. Ibid., 5.

16. Catharine Beecher and Stowe, *The American Woman's Home,* 13.

17. *American Female Poets,* 359.

18. Elizabeth Ellet, selected bibliography: *Euphemio of Messina; A Tragedy, Translated from the Italian* (1834); *Poems, Translated and Original* (1855); *The Queen of American Society* (1870); *Summer Rambles in the West: Narrative of a Trip in 1852 through Michigan, Illinois and Minnesota* (1853); *The Women in the American Revolution; Women Artists in All Ages and Countries* (1859).

19. These journals included *Home Circle* (Philadelphia), *Home Monthly* (Boston), *Hours at Home* (New York), *Household Journal of Popular Information, Amusement and Domestic Economy* (New York), *The Household Magazine* (Providence), *Household Monthly* (Boston), *The Housekeeper's Annual and Lady's Register* (Boston), *The Housekeeper's Friend* (Providence). These are only some of the dozens of household journals published in the 1860s, 1870s, and 1880s.

20. *Home Almanac,* 1.

21. Gardner, *The House That Jill Built,* vii.

22. Eastlake, *Hints on Household Taste,* 85.

23. Catharine Beecher and Stowe, *The American Woman's Home,* 16.

24. Ellet, *The New Cyclopedia of Domestic Economy,* 16.

25. Eunice Beecher, *All around the House,* 5. Eunice was married to Henry Ward Beecher, Catharine and Harriet's brother.

26. Eunice Beecher, *The Home,* 67.

27. Hewitt, *Queen of Home,* 401–2.

28. Hale, *The Good Housekeeper,* 126.

29. *Practical Housekeeping*, 423.

30. Ibid., 465.

31. Leslie, *The Housebook*, 304.

32. Ellet, *The New Cyclopedia of Domestic Economy*, 26.

33. Julia Wright, *The Complete Home*, 438.

34. Hewitt, *Queen of Home*, 297.

35. Ibid., 301.

36. Catharine Beecher and Stowe, 16.

37. Julia Wright, *The Complete Home*, 258.

38. Ibid., 259.

39. See McDannell, *Material Christianity*.

40. See Bushnell, *Christian Nurture*.

41. Helen Jackson, *Bits of Talk about Home Matters*, 234.

42. *Home Circle*, 84.

43. Spofford, *Art Decoration Applied to Furniture*, 232.

44. Ellet, *The New Cyclopedia of Domestic Economy*, 21.

45. See Ames, *Death in the Dining Room*, 8.

46. Ellet, *The New Cyclopedia of Domestic Economy*, 21.

47. Langford, *The Hearthstone*, iv.

48. Ibid., 38.

49. Ibid., 39–40.

50. Spofford, *Art Decoration Applied to Furniture*, 192.

51. Cook, *The House Beautiful*, 45.

52. See Garrett, *At Home*, and Grier, *Culture and Comfort*.

53. See Bushman, *The Refinement of America*.

54. See Ames, *Death in the Dining Room*.

55. Clarkson and Clarkson, *Household Decoration*, 5. In addition to her advice manual, Lida Clarkson wrote two books on art, *Brush Studies* (1886) and *Easy Lessons in Drawing and Painting* (1889).

56. Susan Brown, *Home Topics*, 491.

57. Ibid.

58. Ibid., 500.

59. *Household Conveniences*, 3.

60. Ormsbee, *The House Comfortable*, 191.

61. Whipple, *The Housekeeper's Book*, 15.

62. Ellet, *The New Cyclopedia of Domestic Economy*, 21.

63. Langford, *The Hearthstone*, 373.

64. Child, *The American Frugal Housewife*, 90.

65. See Roger Moss and Winkler, *Victorian Interior Decoration*, 87–88.

66. Child, *The American Frugal Housewife*, 90.

67. Stowe, *House and Home Papers*.

68. Eunice Beecher, *All around the House,* 7.

69. Langford, *The Hearthstone,* 39.

70. Ellet, *The New Cyclopedia of Domestic Economy,* 21.

71. Catharine Beecher and Stowe, *The American Woman's Home,* 94.

72. Hewitt, *Queen of Home,* 108.

73. Museums holding Bridges's works include the National Museum of American Art in Washington, D.C., the Art Institute of Chicago, and the Brooklyn Museum, which featured Bridges in their 175th anniversary exhibit entitled "Masters of Color and Light: Homer, Sargent and the American Watercolor Movement."

74. Hewitt, *Queen of Home,* 109.

75. Catharine Beecher and Stowe, *American Woman's Home,* 91.

76. Church, *How to Furnish a Home,* 7.

77. Eunice Beecher, *All around the House,* 7.

78. Ibid.

79. Ormsbee, *The House Comfortable,* 11.

80. Ibid., 131.

81. Ellet, *The New Cyclopedia of Domestic Economy,* 21.

82. Julia Wright, *The Complete Home,* 165.

83. Babcock, *Household Hints,* 127.

84. Ellet, *The New Cyclopedia of Domestic Economy,* 21.

85. Babcock, *Household Hints,* 127.

86. Julia Wright, *The Complete Home,* 397.

CHAPTER TWO

1. The book *Home Sanitation: A Manual for Housekeepers* was published in several different editions, beginning with Richards's 1898 version (Boston: Home Science Publishers) and continuing with 1904 and 1911 versions by Talbot, Richards and "the Sanitary Science Club of the Association of Collegiate Alumnae" (Boston: Whitcomb & Barrows). The book was reissued in 1917 by Marion Talbot alone after Richards's death in 1911.

2. See Hoy, *Chasing Dirt.*

3. See D'Emilio and Freedman, *Intimate Matters.*

4. See Tichi, *Shifting Gears,* and Tomes, *The Gospel of Germs.*

5. Campbell, *The Easiest Way in Housekeeping and Cooking,* 8.

6. Ibid., 121.

7. See Henry, "Reporting 'Deeply and at First Hand,'" 18–25.

8. Bancroft, *The Book of the Fair,* 939. Bancroft noted that these women spoke "at a separate session of women," and were followed by Catherine Coman of

Wellesley College, "showing that not only were women's wages steadily advancing, but during the present century the occupations open to women had increased a hundred fold."

9. Campbell, *Household Economics*, 185.

10. Ibid., 237.

11. Ibid., 243.

12. Justin Morrill Land Grant Act of July 2, 1862, chap. 130, 12 stat.503.7 U.S.C. 301 et.seq. chap. 130, sec. 4(6).

13. See Lynn Gordon, *Gender and Higher Education*, 99–100.

14. As quoted in *Journal of Home Economics* 27:2 (February 1935): 273. Also see Stage and Vincenti, *Rethinking Home Economics.*

15. Apple, "Liberal Arts or Vocational Training?," 90.

16. In 1994, responding to pressure from both inside and outside the organization for a rethinking of the professional goals of home economics, the AHEA officially changed its name to the American Association of Family and Consumer Services.

17. Farmer, *Boston Cooking School Cookbook.*

18. Parloa, *Home Economics*, 55.

19. Kincaid, "Miss Parloa at Home," ii.

20. The Women's Laboratory lasted until 1883, when MIT built new laboratories with space for women. For more on Ellen Swallow Richards's work at MIT, see the MIT Museum, Cambridge, Mass.

21. For more on Ellen Richards, see Levenstein, "The New England Kitchen," Horowitz, "Frugality or Comfort," and Cravens, "Establishing the Science of Nutrition at the USDA."

22. The University of Chicago, to recognize Breckinridge's importance to the city of Chicago in general and to the University of Chicago in particular, named a building after her. The building, currently a coeducational dormitory, was originally a place for visiting women to stay on campus.

23. Talbot and Breckinridge, *The Modern Household*, preface.

24. Ibid., 1.

25. Mary Matthews, *The House and Its Care*, viii.

26. Clavert and Smith, *Advanced Course in Homemaking.*

27. Mary Matthews, *The House and Its Care*, 22.

28. Ibid., 120.

29. Justin and Rust, *Home Living*, xi.

30. New York State College of Home Economics at Cornell University, Tenth Annual Report, 1935 (640.6, C815a, 10th, 1935), 46.

31. Ibid., 9.

32. Peyser, *Cheating the Junk Pile*, 211.

33. Ibid., ix.

34. Ibid., xi.

35. Campbell, *Household Economics*, 2–3.

36. Ibid., 8.

37. Ibid., 2.

38. Talbot and Breckinridge, *The Modern Household*, 84.

39. Ibid.

40. Grauel, "Priscilla Club of Domestic Science," 36.

41. Frederick, *Selling Mrs. Consumer*, 167.

42. See Rutherford, "An Uncommon Life," 42.

43. See Frederick, *Come into My Kitchen*.

44. Gilbreth, *The Homemaker and Her Job*, 95–96. Thank you to Jane Lancaster for sharing with me her insights on Lillian Gilbreth.

45. White, *Housekeepers and Home-Makers*, 45.

46. Balderston, *Housewifery*, 48–49.

47. Gray, "The Kitchen," 475.

48. Ibid., 462.

49. Burris-Meyer, *Decorating Livable Homes*, 15.

50. *Modern Priscilla Home Furnishing Book*, 143.

51. See Blaszczyk, "Where Mrs. Homemaker Is Never Forgotten."

52. Betty and Pat, who appear on Reynolds Wrap commercials and on that company's website, are home economists. Betty worked in the Betty Crocker Test Kitchen and as a home economist for the Quaker Test Kitchens. She manages the Reynolds Kitchens in Virginia. Pat was a home-economics teacher and extension home economist in Minnesota before becoming the senior home economist for Reynolds Wrap in 1990. The two dispense helpful kitchen tips on TV and develop new products for Reynolds. Many of their ad campaigns, such as the "missing mom" commercials in 2000, focused on women's use of Reynolds Wrap to save time in the kitchen (see <www.reynoldskitchen.com>).

53. The link with Good Housekeeping gave Armour foods credibility. The Good Housekeeping Institute introduced its "Ironclad Contract" in 1902, in which every advertisement in the magazine came with a full guarantee. In 1909 the company introduced the "Seal of Approval," which told consumers that the kitchens and workshops of domestic advisors had been busy testing each product.

54. Jean Adams, *The Business of Being a Housewife*, 2.

55. Ibid., 55.

56. "The Good Housekeeping Seal: New Look, Same Promise," the Hearst Corporation, 1997.

57. For more on Maltby, see Blaszczyk, "Where Mrs. Homemaker Is Never Forgotten."

58. Ibid., 168–69.

59. See Annmarie Adams, "The House and All That Goes On in It," 165–72.

60. Frederica Shanks student notebook, The Winterthur Library: Joseph Downs Collection of Manuscripts and Printed Ephemera.

61. Ibid.

62. Ibid.

63. Campbell, *Household Economics*, 75.

64. Richards and Talbot, *Home Sanitation*, 19.

65. Ibid., 54.

66. Catharine Beecher and Stowe, *American Woman's Home*, 63.

67. Ibid., 59.

68. Van de Water, *From Kitchen to Garrett*, 162.

69. Parloa, "Stuffy Houses," 123.

70. Parloa, *Home Economics*, 60.

71. Ormsbee, *The House Comfortable*, 137.

72. Susan Brown, *Home Topics*, 536.

73. French, *Homes and Their Decoration*, 53. Thank you to Robin Veder for sharing with me her insights on plants in the home.

74. See Tomes, *The Gospel of Germs*, 11.

75. Ormsbee, *The House Comfortable*, 96.

76. Baxter, *The Housekeeper's Handy Book*, 11.

77. Parloa, *Home Economics*, 41.

78. See Tomes, *The Gospel of Germs*.

79. Krout, *Platters and Pipkins*, 126.

80. Richards and Talbot, *Home Sanitation*, 55.

81. Ibid., 54.

82. *Modern Priscilla Home Furnishing Book*, 185.

83. Kittredge, *The Home and Its Management*, 38.

84. Parloa, *Home Economics*, 46.

85. *House and Garden*, January 1919, 41.

86. "The floor of a kitchen should be painted," wrote the Beecher sisters in 1869, "or, what is better, covered with an oilcloth. To procure a kitchen oilcloth as cheaply as possible, buy cheap tow cloth, and fit it to the size and shape of the kitchen. Then have it stretched, and nailed to the south side of the barn, and, with a brush, cover it with a coat of thin rye paste. When this is dry, put on a coat of yellow paint, and let it dry for a fortnight." (Catharine Beecher and Stowe, *American Woman's Home*, 371.)

87. Lois Palmer, *Your House*, 22.

88. *Modern Priscilla Home Furnishing Book*, 74.

89. Agnes Wright, *Floors, Furniture and Color*, 74.

90. See Tomes, *The Gospel of Germs*.

91. Frederick, *Selling Mrs. Consumer*, 22.

92. See Dutton, *DuPont: 140 Years.*

93. *Modern Priscilla Home Furnishing Book,* 47.

94. Richards and Talbot, *Home Sanitation,* 7.

CHAPTER THREE

1. Richards and Talbot, *Home Sanitation,* 181.

2. Nesbit, *Household Management,* 20.

3. Ibid.

4. Zinn, *The Twentieth Century,* 84.

5. See McClymer, "Gender and the 'American Way of Life,'" 3–20. See also Ewen, *Immigrant Women in the Land of Dollars,* 156–63; Diner, *Erin's Daughters in America;* Romo, *East Los Angeles,* 140.

6. French, *Homes and Their Decoration,* 70.

7. "Letters on Houseworkers on New Apparatus," *Good Housekeeping,* January 1913, 135.

8. See McCarthy, *Noblesse Oblige;* Muncy, *Creating a Female Dominion;* Sklar, *Doing the Nation's Work;* Pascoe, *Relations of Rescue.*

9. Evans, *Born for Liberty,* 150. Other important women-dominated good works organizations included the National Consumers' League, the National Association of Colored Women, the National Council of Jewish Women, and the National Council of Catholic Women.

10. See Schneider and Schneider, *American Women in the Progressive Era,* 107.

11. See Trolander, *Settlement Houses and the Great Depression,* 34.

12. Rosenberg, *Divided Lives,* 29. See also Linda Gordon, "Women, Maternalism and Welfare," 63–86.

13. Bruere, *Increasing Home Efficiency,* 290.

14. See Martha Bensley Bruere, *Report, Buffalo, November 14th to 15th, 1934,* Franklin D. Roosevelt Library, Hopkins Papers, Box 65. This is a report to Federal Emergency Relief Administration director Harry Hopkins, who sent out reporters to investigate conditions around the country. The reporters were instructed to collect information from social workers (http://newdeal.feri.org/texts/449.htm).

15. Ibid.

16. For more on Martha Bruere, see Horowitz, "Frugality or Comfort," 239–59.

17. Bruere, *Laughing Their Way: Women's Humor in America* (1945); *What Forests Give* (Forest Service, USDA, 1938).

18. Nesbit, *Household Management,* 4.

19. Ibid., 16.

20. Ibid., 4.

21. Kittredge, *The Home and Its Management*, 4.

22. Ibid., insert.

23. For more on Kittredge, see her obituary in *The New York Times*, May 9, 1955. "Crusader for School Lunches Here Is Dead"; also "Mabel Hyde Kittredge," *Journal of Home Economics* 47:10 (1955): 753.

24. Kittredge, *The Home and Its Management*, 17.

25. Wald, *The House on Henry Street*, 108.

26. The "family" was made up of a guard who worked at the fair and an unrelated Irish widow with her three children. These and all other details are recounted in Barnes, "Katharine B. Davis and the Workingman's Model Home of 1893," 1–20.

27. See Ava Clark, *Adventures of a Home Economist*.

28. Kittredge, *Housekeeping Notes*, 1.

29. Ibid., 16.

30. Ibid., 70.

31. Bertha Smith, "The Gospel of Simplicity," 84.

32. Ibid., 90.

33. Ibid., 84.

34. Barker, *76 Historic Homes of Boulder, Colorado*, 155–56.

35. For more on Theodosia Ammon's "Gwenthean Cottage," see the *Boulder Daily Camera*'s Focus section, Sunday, August 26, 1973.

36. Gillespie, "Labor-Saving Devices Supplant Servants," 132–34.

37. See Jensen, "Crossing Ethnic Barriers in the Southwest," 169–80, and Jellison, *Entitled to Power*. The first home demonstration agent assigned under the Smith-Lever act went to work in Illinois in 1915 (Jellison, 16).

38. For more on the Spanish-speaking extension agents, see Jensen, "Canning Comes to New Mexico."

39. Van Rensselaer and Canon, *A Manual of Homemaking*, 81.

40. As quoted in Harris, "Grace under Pressure," 231. For more on home-extension clubs, especially in the Midwest, see Holt, *Linoleum, Better Babies and the Modern Farm Woman*.

41. For more on Gilbert, see her papers at the Center for Southwest Research, General Library, University of New Mexico.

42. Gilbert, *We Fed Them Cactus*, ix.

43. See Tey Diana Rebolledo, "Introduction," in Gilbert, *We Fed Them Cactus*, xv.

44. Bruere, *Increasing Home Efficiency*, 168.

45. Whitcomb, "Children of Many Nationalities Receive Practical Instruction," *School Life*, March, 1926, 138–39. As quoted in Romo, *East Los Angeles*, 141.

46. Romo, *East Los Angeles*, 141.

47. Joselit, "A Set Table."

48. *Di Froyen-Velt*, April 13, 1913, 5. See Schreier, *Becoming American Women*, 116. *Di Froyen-Velt* is available at the YIVO Institute for Jewish Research, New York.

49. See Schreier, *Becoming American Women*, 113–17.

50. See, for example, "A Chinese Dinner of Six Courses," *Good Housekeeping*, February 1, 1890, 149. "Nothing that they cook is better done than their rice. Even the Chinese laborers in their camps, manage to cook rice to a degree of perfection that an American housewife might rival, but could not surpass."

51. Baxter, *The Housekeeper's Handy Book*, 83.

52. Wilson, "Table Embroideries Adapted From Hungarian Pottery," 10.

53. Richmond, "Making Money at Home," 3.

54. Nesbit, *Household Management*, 24.

55. Tedrow, "A Home Improvement Unit in an Indian School," 236.

56. Ibid.

57. Brigham, *Box Furniture*, 43.

58. Ibid.,1.

59. Kittredge, *Housekeeping Notes*, 12.

60. Ibid.

61. Ibid., 9.

62. Ibid., 37.

63. French, *Homes and Their Decoration*, 77.

64. Shultz, *Making Homes*, 24.

65. Ibid., 24.

66. Kittredge, *The Home and Its Management*, 79.

67. For changes over time in images of families surrounded by material goods, see Garrett, *At Home*, and Seale, *The Tasteful Interlude*.

68. See Roger Moss and Winkler, *Victorian Interior Decoration*.

69. Montgomery Ward catalog, 1895, 347. Lace curtains were advertised alongside lambrequins: short, ornamental drapes usually used on the tops of windows or doors.

70. For more on middle-class consumption at the turn of the century, see Marilyn Moss and Browne, *Making the American Home*; Foy and Marling, *The Arts and The American Home*; Foy and Schlereth, *American Home Life*; Grier, *Culture and Comfort*.

71. Babcock, *Household Hints*, 96.

72. Kittredge, as quoted in Bertha Smith, "The Gospel of Simplicity," 84.

73. Merriam-Webster Dictionary. "Lace-curtain, adj, (1934)."

74. J. T. Farrell. *Young Manhood*, 282 (1934). The phrase has been used in conjunction with other immigrant groups (according to the Oxford English Dic-

tionary: in 1949 *Saturday Review of Literature*, 3:1 [June 1949], "Mrs. Rusky's folks were lace-curtain Jews; they had a piano and a Polish maid"), but is more frequently used as "lace-curtain Irish."

CHAPTER FOUR

1. Mainwaring, "The Two Rooms," 423.

2. Ibid.

3. See Huyssen, "Mass Culture as Woman"; Pollock, "Modernity and the Spaces of Femininity"; Kardon, ed. *The Ideal Home*; Felski, *The Gender of Modernity*.

4. See Sparke, *As Long as It's Pink*.

5. *Modern Priscilla Home Furnishing Book*, 2.

6. See Jones, *Manual of Smart Housekeeping*.

7. Priestman, *Home Decoration*, acknowledgements.

8. For more on Emily Post, see Edwin Post, *True Emily Post*.

9. Emily Post, *The Personality of a House*, 9.

10. Ibid., 312.

11. Throop, *Furnishing the Home of Good Taste*, 129.

12. Le Corbusier, *The Decorative Arts of Today* (1925), as quoted in Sparke, *As Long as It's Pink*, 104. Richards, "Modernism in Furniture," 447.

13. Rutt, *Home Furnishing*, 6.

14. Ibid., vii.

15. Ibid., 6.

16. Richards, "Modernism in Furniture," 447.

17. Wilson et al., *The Machine Age in America*, 43. For more on the Machine Age, see: Drexler and Daniel, *Introduction to 20th Century Design*; Morningstar, *Flapper Furniture and Interiors of the 1920s*; Bush, *The Streamlined Decade*; Meikle, *Twentieth Century Limited*; Sparke, *The Plastics Age*; Terry Smith, *Making the Modern*; Kardon, *Craft in the Machine Age*; Kaplan, *Designing Modernity*.

18. Raley, *A Century of Progress*, 6.

19. Ibid., 10.

20. Ibid., 13.

21. Ibid.

22. Ibid., 71.

23. Marchand, *Advertising the American Dream*.

24. Genauer, *Modern Interiors*, 52.

25. Ibid., 25.

26. Emily Genauer's papers are held at the Archives of American Art, Smithsonian Institution, Washington, D.C.

27. Genauer, *Modern Interiors*, 11.

28. Rutt, *Home Furnishing*, 6.

29. Waugh, *Planning the Little House*, xiii.

30. Koues, *How to Be Your Own Decorator*, 91.

31. Rolfe, *Interior Decoration for the Small Home*, 114.

32. Burris-Meyer, *Decorating Livable Homes*, 176.

33. Wilson et al., *The Machine Age in America*, 312–14.

34. Emily Post, *The Personality of a House*, 509.

35. The landmark display of the Wakefield Rattan Company's wicker furniture at the 1876 World's Fair in Philadelphia caused a major boost in the sales of wicker furniture. For more on wicker, see Adamson, *American Wicker*.

36. Koues, *How to Be Your Own Decorator*, 25–27.

37. Ibid., 29.

38. Rolfe, *Interior Decoration for the Small Home*, 138.

39. Ibid. Light had been an inspiration for design in the past. For example, the brass tacks on eighteenth-century upholstered arm chairs helped reflect candlelight on dark nights. For more on nineteenth-century lighting, see Garrett, *At Home*, 140–62.

40. Rhyne, "Still Life in the Home," 103. Rhyne was a professor in the department of Home Economics at Montana State College.

41. Burris-Meyer, *Decorating Livable Homes*, 159.

42. Ibid., 178–79. For more on plastics, see Fehrman and Fehrman, *Postwar Interior Design*.

43. Emily Post, *The Personality of a House*, 317.

44. Ibid., 320.

45. See Tobey, *Technology as Freedom*, 5.

46. Ibid., 2.

47. Ibid., 21.

48. Ibid., 20–29.

49. Parloa, *Home Economics*, 35.

50. Emily Post, *The Personality of a House*, 441.

51. Campbell, *Household Economics*, 110.

52. Van Rensselaer and Canon, *A Manual of Homemaking*, 84.

53. Van de Water, *From Kitchen to Garrett*, 78.

54. Ibid., dedication page.

55. Green, *The Effective Small Home*, iii.

56. French, *Homes and Their Decoration*, 42.

57. Ibid., 65.

58. Calkins, *A Course in House Planning and Furnishing*, 45.

59. Ibid., 63.

60. Ibid., 37.

61. Ibid., 55.

62. Kittredge, *The Home and Its Management*, 37.

63. French, *Homes and Their Decoration*, 22.

64. Kittredge, *The Home and Its Management*, 48.

65. Priestman, *Home Decoration*, 69.

66. Emily Post, *The Personality of a House*, 395.

67. Green, *The Effective Small Home*, 108.

68. Palmer, *Your House*, 77.

69. Rutt, *Home Furnishing*, 298.

70. Priestman, *Home Decoration*, 73.

71. Van de Water, *From Kitchen to Garrett*, 78.

72. Priestman, *Home Decoration*, 103.

73. Ibid., 73.

74. Hewitt, *Queen of Home*, 64.

75. See Ames, *Death in the Dining Room*.

76. *Good Housekeeping*, January 18, 1890, ii.

77. Throop, *Furnishing the Home of Good Taste*, 129.

78. Calkins, *A Course in House Planning and Furnishing*, 64.

79. Ibid., 63.

80. Priestman, *Home Decoration*, 73.

81. See Ames, *Death in the Dining Room*, 97–149.

82. Quinn, *Planning and Furnishing the Home*, 54.

83. Adler, *The New Interior*, 38.

84. Kellogg, *Home Furnishing*, 18.

85. Priestman, *Home Decoration*, 75.

86. Kellogg, *Home Furnishing*, 233.

87. Green, *The Effective Small House*, 75.

88. Adler, *The New Interior*, 38.

89. Mainwaring, "The Two Rooms," 423.

CHAPTER FIVE

1. *Modern Priscilla Home Furnishing Book*, 1.

2. Emily Post, *The Personality of a House*, 390.

3. For more on the psychological significance of play for children in the Progressive Era, see Cavallo, "Social Reform and the Movement," 509–22. G. Stanley Hall was influential in the development of the field of psychology, especially the Child Study Movement, between the 1870s and 1920s.

4. Koues, *The American Woman's New Encyclopedia*, 287.

5. Shultz, *Making Homes*, 37.

6. Ibid., 36.

7. Ibid., 37.

8. Kellogg, *Home Furnishing*, 94.

9. Priestman, *Home Decoration*, 153.

10. Adler, *The New Interior*, 114.

11. Richardson, "Important Considerations in Furniture Selection and Arrangement," 442.

12. *Modern Priscilla Home Furnishing Book*, 179.

13. Richardson, "Important Considerations in Furniture Selection and Arrangement," 442.

14. Koues, *The American Woman's New Encyclopedia*, 294.

15. *Modern Priscilla Home Furnishing Book*, 179.

16. Marjorie Mills, *Home-Makers Guide*, 66.

17. Richardson, "Important Considerations in Furniture Selection and Arrangement," 442.

18. Priestman, *Home Decoration*, 153.

19. "Quarters for Young Masters," *House Beautiful*, July 1937, 26.

20. Ibid.

21. Shultz, *Making Homes*, 28.

22. Ibid., 29.

23. Koues, *The American Woman's New Encyclopedia*, 289.

24. Ibid., 330.

25. Gilbreth, *The Homemaker and Her Job*, vii.

26. Frederick, *Come into My Kitchen*, 21.

27. Halbert, *The Better Homes Manual*, 479.

28. Koues, *The American Woman's New Encyclopedia*, 4.

29. For more on cooperative kitchens, see Hayden, *The Grand Domestic Revolution*, and Allen, *Building Domestic Liberty*.

30. Adler, *The New Interior*, 41.

31. For more on early color theory, see Bridget May, "Advice on White," 19–24.

32. Calkins, *A Course in House Planning and Furnishing*, 39.

33. Burris-Meyer, *Decorating Livable Homes*, 334.

34. Goldstein and Goldstein, *Art in Everyday Life*, 184–203 (Figs. 155 and 157). For an example of specific teachings about color, see "The Selection and Harmonious Combination of Color," *Practical Home Economics*, 13:4 (April 1935): 109.

35. Palmer, *Your House*, chap. 1.

36. See Dutton, *DuPont: 140 Years*, 296–300.

37. deWolfe, "A Light, Gay Dining Room," 203.

38. Elsie deWolfe's biographer Jane Smith has credited the decorator with

being "the first person who pulled up the blinds, let in the sunshine, cleared out the smelly tasseled curtains within curtains. . . . She simply cleared out the Victoriana and let in the twentieth century." See Jane Smith, *Elsie deWolfe*, introduction by Diana Vreeland, xii.

39. Agnes Wright, *Floors, Furniture and Color*, 5.

40. "Color in Industry," *Fortune*, February 1930, 110a.

41. *House Beautiful*, June 1937, 1.

42. *Home Beautiful*, 14.

43. *Home: Simple Ideas for Its Decoration*, 8.

44. *Your Home and Its Decoration*, 24.

45. Agnes Wright, *Floors, Furniture and Color*, 5.

46. Hill, *Redeeming Old Homes*, 142.

47. *Home Beautiful*, 14.

48. Koues, *How to Be Your Own Decorator*, 66.

49. Rutt, *Home Furnishing*, 39.

50. Ibid., 309.

51. Marjorie Mills, *Home-Makers Guide*, 124.

52. Ibid., 66.

53. Burris-Meyer, *Decorating Livable Homes*, 15.

54. Rolfe, *Interior Decoration for the Small Home*, 30.

55. Bomar, *Social Aspects of Housekeeping*, 22. Bomar taught home economics at East Carolina Teachers College and went on to be the head of the Home Economics Department at Kansas State Teacher's College in the 1930s, from where she published her next book, *An Introduction to Homemaking and its Relation to the Community*. Philadelphia: W. B. Saunders, 1932.

56. Quinn, *Planning and Furnishing the Home*, 162. See Lupton and Miller, *The Bathroom, the Kitchen, and the Aesthetics of Waste*, 33. For more on the scientific use of white porcelain in turn-of-the-century bathrooms, see Tomes, *The Gospel of Germs*.

57. Priestman, *Home Decoration*, 144.

58. Frankl, "Baths and Bath Dressing Rooms," 51. Chippendale furniture, popular in England and the American Colonies in the mid-to-late eighteenth century, was named for Thomas Chippendale, a London cabinetmaker. He published a volume of his designs, *The Gentleman and Cabinetmaker's Director*, in 1754. For more on the derivation of the Chippendale style in Europe and the United States, see Bowman, *American Furniture*. Chippendale's work enjoyed a revival in the United States in the 1920s with the new interest in Colonial style, so his name would have been familiar to many *House and Garden* readers.

59. Rolfe, *Interior Decoration for the Small Home*, 164.

60. See Brumberg, *The Body Project*.

61. Holbrook, *My Better Homes and Gardens Home Guide*, 91.

62. Lupton and Miller, *The Bathroom, the Kitchen, and the Aesthetics of Waste*, 32.

63. *Home: Simple Ideas for Its Decoration*.

64. Emily Post, *The Personality of a House*, 379.

65. Mary Matthews, *The House and Its Care*, 161.

CHAPTER SIX

1. Northend, *Colonial Homes and Their Furnishings*, 106.

2. For more on the Arts and Crafts movement, see Kaplan, *The Art that Is Life*.

3. Kellogg, *Home Furnishing*, 126.

4. See Blaugrund and Bowie, "Alice D. Kellogg: Letters from Paris."

5. Kellogg, *Home Furnishing*, preface.

6. Ibid., 71.

7. See Dethier, "The Spirit of Progressive Reform."

8. Boris, *Art and Labor*, 54.

9. As quoted in Bowman, *American Furniture*, 151.

10. Kellogg, *Home Furnishing*, 51. The characteristic color was produced by "ammonia fumes reacting with the tannic acid in the wood" (Bowman, *American Furniture*, 151).

11. Priestman, *Home Decoration*, 38.

12. Kellogg, *Home Furnishing*, 126.

13. Rolfe, *Interior Decoration for the Small Home*, 100.

14. The Ramona Pageant began in 1923 and is held annually in April and May in the Ramona Bowl in Riverside County, California. The pageant, featuring a cast of hundreds, is one of the longest-running outdoor plays in the United States (see <www.socialhistory.org/Biographies/hhjackson.htm>).

15. Emily Post, *The Personality of a House*, 44.

16. See Kaplan, *Designing Modernity*, 19.

17. Kellogg, *Home Furnishing*, 51.

18. Priestman, *Home Decoration*, 110.

19. Calkins, *A Course in Home Planning and Furnishing*, 9.

20. See Kaufman, *National Parks and the Woman's Voice*, 25.

21. Kellogg, *Home Furnishing*, 18.

22. Calkins, *A Course in Home Planning and Furnishing*, 37.

23. *The Good Housekeeping Discovery Book No. 1*, 16.

24. Rolfe, *Interior Decoration for the Small Home*, 51.

25. *Your Home and Its Decoration*, 63.

26. Sell and Blackman, *Good Taste in Home Furnishing*, 55.

27. Palmer, *Your House*, 255.

28. *Entrance to Vantine's*, 5. Thank you to Mari Yoshihara for sharing with me her insights on the meanings of Asian artifacts in American homes.

29. Ibid., 28.

30. *Colorado State Business Directory* (1915), 1309.

31. Burris-Meyer, *Decorating Livable Homes*, 337.

32. Adler, *The New Interior*, 8.

33. Priestman, *Home Decoration*, 110.

34. Koues, *How to Be Your Own Decorator*, 41.

35. See Rossano, *Creating a Dignified Past*.

36. Holden, "Tenement Furnishings," 312.

37. Kellogg, *Home Furnishing*, 92.

38. Chamberlain, *Old Rooms for New Living*, 1.

39. Ibid., 7.

40. *Boston Herald*, December 18, 1926, in clipping file of the Decorative Arts Photography Collection (DAPC) at Winterthur Museum and Library, Winterthur, Delaware. Winterthur received the Northend collection of glass negatives in or before 1964 and maintains an open collection of hundreds of Northend's printed photographs of Colonial New England homes.

41. Northend, *Colonial Homes and Their Furnishings*, 92.

42. Northend, *Historic Homes of New England*, 263.

43. Northend, "Colonial Fireplaces and Fire-Irons," 488.

44. Chamberlain, *Old Rooms for New Living*, 1–2.

45. Ibid., 2.

46. Northend, *Historic Homes of New England*, 128.

CHAPTER SEVEN

1. "Live the Life of *McCall's*," 27–35. The magazine's editor, Otis Lee Wiese, took credit for bringing the genre of "women's service magazines" to a new level. "Throughout the bright days of the 20s and the twilight of the 30s—the long years of the war, the bitter peace and the Korean conflict—in fact, right up to this moment, *McCall's* has been sensitive to your needs as women first.... *McCall's* has been striving to widen your horizons, inspire you to lead lives of greater satisfaction, help you in your daily tasks" (27).

2. "Live the Life of *McCall's*," 27.

3. Ibid., 34.

4. *McCall's*, May 1954, 61.

5. For more on 1950s in America, see, among others: Lerner, *America as a Civilization*; Satin, *The 1950s*; Zinn, *Postwar America*; Witther, *Cold War America*;

Jezer, *The Dark Ages;* Kaledin, *Mothers and More;* Oakley, *God's Country;* O'Neill, *American High;* Fehrman and Fehrman, *Postwar Interior Design;* Hine, *Populuxe;* Lesley Jackson, *The New Look;* Corber, *In the Name of National Security;* Harvey, *The Fifties;* Horn, *Fifties Style;* Marling, *As Seen on TV;* Leibman, *Living Room Lectures;* Foreman, *The Other Fifties;* Patterson, *Grand Expectations;* Coontz, *The Way We Never Were.*

6. For more on women's magazines, see McCracken, *Decoding Women's Magazines,* 16.

7. Friedan, *The Feminine Mystique,* 31.

8. See issues of *Look, McCall's, Good Housekeeping, American Home,* and *Ladies' Home Journal* during the 1950s.

9. See Halsey, *Ladies Home Journal Book of Interior Decoration.*

10. Humphrey, *Women's Home Companion Household Book,* v.

11. See Hillyer, *Mademoiselle's Home Planning Scrapbook; McCall's Decorating Book; Better Homes and Gardens' Guide to Entertaining.* The editorial director, administrative editor, and art director of *Better Homes and Gardens* were men in 1969, while the entertainment editor, the food editor, and the assistant editors were all women.

12. See Rockow and Julius Rockow, *New Creative Home Decorating,* and Faulkner and Faulkner, *Inside Today's Home.* In the Faulkners' case, Ray took the photographs for this book and Sarah wrote the text.

13. Rockow and Rockow, *New Creative Home Decorating,* 5.

14. Charlotte Adams, *Housekeeping after Office Hours,* ix.

15. Ibid., xi.

16. Ibid., 6.

17. Kenneth Jackson noted the statistics on housing starts: "Between 1928 and 1933, the construction of residential property fell by 95 percent." Due to governmental intervention, however, housing starts were up after World War II, and these numbers continued to rise through the 1950s and 1960s. Federal interference through the FHA and the VA had a large effect on these rising numbers. See Kenneth Jackson, *Crabgrass Frontiers,* 193.

18. These are examples of what historian Robert Corber has called congress signing "the domestication of masculinity into law." Corber, *In the Name of National Security,* 2.

19. See ibid., 7. Corber identified the finance preference for new housing starts as a phenomenon that "hastened the decline of the inner cities, [and] reinforced racial and class segregation of the suburbs." Many postwar suburbs had specific leases that forbade sale or sublease to any non-Caucasian. Residential zoning laws and practices also ensured homogeneity in the new suburbs. William Levitt once commented that "we can solve a housing problem, or we can solve a racial problem. But we cannot combine the two." He chose the

housing problem. As Kenneth Jackson pointed out, "In 1960 not a single one of the Long Island Levittown's 82,000 residents was black." Kenneth Jackson, *Crabgrass Frontiers*, 241.

20. Kenneth Jackson, *Crabgrass Frontiers*, 237. For more on the changes in the Levittown homes, see Gans, *The Levittowners*, and Kelly, *Expanding the American Dream*.

21. Adams, *Housekeeping after Office Hours*, 54.

22. Rockow and Rockow, *New Creative Home Decorating*, 5.

23. For more on the bungalow style and its relation to the family, see Boris, *Art and Labor*, 61. She noted that the prairie house, which stood back from the street behind retaining walls, terraces, and shaded doorways, emphasized the family unit. In the 1950s, houses emphasized that the family was a part of a community, opening the houses to the neighbors and sacrificing privacy.

24. "Is This 1953's Most Influential House?," 99.

25. Ibid.

26. "The Trade Secrets House and the U.S. Builder," 114.

27. Ibid., 115.

28. "Is This 1953's Most Influential House?," 99.

29. Ibid., 100.

30. Gillies, *Popular Home Decoration*, 5.

31. Chamberlain, *Old Rooms for New Living*, 2.

32. Warner, "Home Furnishing," 94.

33. Rockow and Rockow, *New Creative Home Decorating*, 207.

34. Faulkner and Faulkner, *Inside Today's Home*, 130.

35. Hillyer, *Mademoiselle's Home Planning Scrapbook*, 37.

36. Jones, *Manual of Smart Housekeeping*, 10.

37. Seal, "A Living and Dining Room Combined," 36.

38. Holbrook, *My Better Homes and Gardens Home Guide*, 74.

39. Raley, *A Century of Progress*, 71.

40. Koues, *How to Be Your Own Decorator*, 93.

41. Jones, *Manual of Smart Housekeeping*, 9.

42. *McCall's Decorating Book*, 174.

43. Faulkner and Faulkner, *Inside Today's Home*, vii.

44. Ibid., 37.

45. Humphrey, *Woman's Home Companion Household Book*, 37.

46. Ibid., 69.

47. Faulkner and Faulkner, *Inside Today's Home*, 410–13.

48. Halsey, *Ladies Home Journal Book of Interior Decoration*, 42.

49. Ibid., 197.

50. Rockow and Rockow, *New Creative Home Decorating*, 196.

51. Sangster, *The Art of Home Making*, 45.

52. "Is This 1953's Most Influential House?," 100.

53. *Good Housekeeping*, January 1952, 232.

54. Faulkner and Faulkner, *Inside Today's Home*, vii.

55. "Is This 1953's Most Influential House?" 100.

56. Humphrey, *Woman's Home Companion Household Book*, 82.

57. "The Trade Secrets House and the U.S. Builder," 115.

58. "The Kitchen Opens Up," 130.

59. For more on the use of war imagery on the home front during the Cold War, see Elaine May, *Homeward Bound*.

60. Gillies, *Popular Home Decoration*, 251.

61. Humphrey, *Woman's Home Companion Household Book*, 82.

62. Jones, *Manual of Smart Housekeeping*, 17.

63. "The Kitchen Opens Up," 132.

64. *McCall's*, June 1955, 98.

65. *Look*, October 16, 1956, 35. This ad referred to the kind of freezer sold separately from the refrigerator.

66. Herbert, "Which Is the Freezer for You?," 92.

67. Packard, *The Hidden Persuaders*, 73.

68. Advertisement in *Good Housekeeping*, March 1952, 11. Kelvinator freezers enjoyed strong endorsement from the "Good Housekeeping Seal of Approval," and their advertisements appeared on page 11 (a prime spot early in the magazine), for most of 1952. Their ad campaign boasted "6 Reasons Why You Need a Kelvinator Freezer!" which included "Party Meals in Advance! Leisure Day Cooking! Wholesale Shopping! To Conserve Your Fish and Game! and Make Entertaining Easier!" The advertisers of freezers in the 1950s took pride in sheer size—the Admiral freezer could store up to 72 pounds of food in 1952 (*Good Housekeeping*, March 1952, 141), but by 1958 the General Electric model could hold an amazing 175 pounds of frozen food. (*Look*, February 4, 1958, 8).

69. The Nixon debates have been covered elsewhere. See especially Marling, *As Seen on TV*. She describes the contents of the exhibit: "The American home and the new iconographic center of that house, the kitchen, made up the core of the display, reinforced by the offerings of almost 800 manufacturers of sewing machines (a very popular demonstration), hi-fi sets, convenience foods, and lounge chairs. . . . Under a cluster of plastic parasols planted in the park outside the buildings, the rituals of American family life, from the wedding and the honeymoon to the backyard barbecue and the country club dance, were enacted four times daily by fashion models in typical American outfits" (249).

70. There is perhaps no better example for the perceived connection between the home and the nation than the kitchen debates. Although Khrushchev tried to insist that the Soviet Union "did not have the capitalist attitude toward

women," Nixon countered by saying that "this attitude toward women is universal." *New York Times*, July 25, 1959, 1.

71. In 1958, *Look* magazine reported that "scientists who study human behavior fear that the American male is now dominated by the American female. He is no longer the masculine, strong-minded man who pioneered the continent and built America's greatness." *Look*, February 4, 1958, 77.

72. Northend, "Making the Attic Livable," 62.

73. *Good Housekeeping*, January 1955, 14.

74. *Look*, February 4, 1958, 44.

75. *The Feminine Mystique* has been analyzed and reanalyzed since its publication. Early commentary about the book often credited it with starting women's liberation and paving the way for modern feminism. Scholars have questioned Friedan's methodology since she examined only the lives of middle-class white women and did not include minorities in her analysis. The magazines of the 1950s have since been examined by several historians, including Joanne Meyerowitz and Ellen McCracken.

76. Friedan, *The Feminine Mystique*, 43.

77. Ibid., 236.

CONCLUSION

1. Collins, *The Western Guide to Feng Shui*, 3.

2. Carole Sugarman, "B. Smith Knows Stylish Entertaining," *Providence Journal-Bulletin*, September 6, 1995, 1.

3. Ibid., 5.

4. Martha Stewart Living Omnimedia, 1999 Annual Report, 1.

5. Martha Stewart, "A Letter from Martha," *Martha Stewart Living* (April 1997): 12.

6. Martha Stewart Living Omnimedia 1999 Annual Report, 6–7.

7. Amy Conway, "Flags," *Martha Stewart Living* (July/August, 1999): 138.

8. William L. Hamilton, "Plumbing Repairs," *Martha Stewart Living* (February 1996): 52.

9. Suzanne Charlé, "Pewter," *Martha Stewart Living* (November 1997): 192.

10. William L. Hamilton, "Is There a Doctor in the House?" *Martha Stewart Living* (September 1995): 107.

11. Glenn Peake, "Metal Furniture," *Martha Stewart Living* (May 1999): 200.

12. Celia Barbour, "Color from Room to Room," *Martha Stewart Living* (April 1997): 147.

13. Letter to the *Providence Journal-Bulletin*, January 16, 1996.

14. "Shell Candles," Good Things, *Martha Stewart Living* (September 1998):

88; Janine Nichols, "Project Tea-Dying," *Martha Stewart Living* (September 2000): 236.

15. *The Onion*, February 21, 2001 (see <www.theonion.com/onion3706/grueling_household_tasks.html>).

16. Baxandall and Gordon, *Dear Sisters*.

17. Diane Brady, "Martha, Inc.: Inside the Growing Empire of America's Lifestyle Queen," *Business Week*, January 17, 2000.

18. Barbara Lippert, "She's Martha Stewart and You're Not," *New York*, May 15, 1995, 28.

19. Oppenheimer, *Martha Stewart*.

20. Greg Easley, "The Divine Myth Stewart," *Spy*, August 1996, 50.

21. Daryl Royster Alexander, "They Did Things Martha Stewart Can Only Dream About," *The New York Times*, June 25, 1995, 16.

22. Christopher Caldwell, "In Praise of Martha Stewart," *Weekly Standard*, January 1, 1996, 4.

23. Patricia Leigh Brown, "For Martha-holics, It's Marathon Season," *New York Times*, November 23, 1995, C4.

24. Christopher Goodwin, "Taking the Biscuit," *London Times*, January 21, 1996, 13.

25. See Martin Walker, "The Dominatrix of Domesticity," *The Guardian*, April 15, 1996, 3. Camille Paglia also noticed this comparison, writing, "Like Ralph Lauren . . . Stewart emerged from an immigrant family . . . to identify strongly with a dreamy, high WASP vision of relaxed town-and-country life." Camille Paglia, "Ask Camille," <www.salon.com> (Dec. 7, 1997).

26. Margaret Talbot, "Money, Time, and the Surrender of American Taste: Les Très Riches Heures de Martha Stewart," *New Republic*, May 13, 1996, 30.

27. Margalit Fox, "In Martha 101, Even Class Anxieties Get Ironed Out," *NY Times News Service*, August 1, 1998.

28. Joan Didion, "Everywoman.com: Getting out of the House with Martha Stewart," *New Yorker*, February 21 and 28, 2000, 270.

29. Beth Wolfensberger, "How to Cope with Martha Stewart," *Providence Phoenix*, February 2, 1996, 18.

30. Zoe Newman and Kyla Wazana, "The Hermeneutics of Martha," proposed special session at the 1998 Modern Language Association conference in San Francisco.

31. Miller, *Reclaiming the Past*, 5.

32. Jameson and Armitage, *Writing the Range*, 14.

Bibliography

Domestic Advice Manuals and Articles

Adams, Charlotte. *Housekeeping after Office Hours: A Homemaking Guide for the Working Woman*. New York: Harper and Brothers Publications, 1953.

Adler, Hazel. *The New Interior: Modern Decoration for the Modern Home*. New York: Century, 1916.

Babcock, Emma Whitcomb. *Household Hints*. New York: D. Appleton and Co., 1884.

Balderston, Linda Ray. *Housewifery: A Textbook of Practical Housekeeping*. New York: J. B. Lippencott, 1936.

Baxter, Lucia Millet. *The Housekeeper's Handy Book*. New York: The House Beautiful Publishing Co., 1918.

Beecher, Catharine E., and Harriet Beecher Stowe. *The American Woman's Home; or, Principles of Domestic Science*. New York: J. B. Ford & Co., 1869.

Beecher, Eunice. *All around the House; or, How to Make Home Happy*. New York: D. Appleton and Co., 1879.

———. *The Home: How to Make and Keep It*. Minneapolis, Minn.: Buckeye Publishing Co., 1883.

Better Homes and Gardens' Guide to Entertaining. Des Moines: Meredith Press, 1969.

Bliss, R. K. *Home Furnishing*, Home Economics Bulletin No. 7, Iowa State College of Agriculture and Mechanic Arts, 1917–18.

Bomar, Willie Melmoth. *Social Aspects of Housekeeping*. Philadelphia: J. B. Lippincott, 1929.

Brigham, Louise. *Box Furniture*. New York: The Century Co., 1909.

Brown, Susan Anna. *Home Topics: A Book of Practical Papers on House and Home Matters*. New York: The Century Co., 1881.

Bruere, Martha Bensley. *Increasing Home Efficiency*. New York: Macmillan Co., 1912.

Burris-Meyer, Elizabeth. *Decorating Livable Homes*. New York: Prentice-Hall, Inc., 1937.

Calkins, Charlotte Wait. *A Course in House Planning and Furnishing*. Chicago: Scott, Foresman and Co., 1916.

Campbell, Helen. *The Easiest Way in Housekeeping and Cooking*. New York: Howard and Hulbert, 1881.

———. *Household Economics*. New York: Putnam's Sons, 1896.

Chamberlain, Narcissa. *Old Rooms for New Living: How to Adapt Early American Interiors for Modern Comfort.* New York: Hastings House, 1953.

Child, Lydia Maria. *The American Frugal Housewife.* Boston: Carter & Hendee, 1834.

Church, Ella Rodman. *How to Furnish a Home.* New York: D. Appleton, 1881.

Clark, Ava Milam. *Adventures of a Home Economist.* Corvallis: Oregon State University Press, 1969.

Clarkson, Lida, and M. J. Clarkson. *Household Decoration: The Home Made Attractive in Simple and Inexpensive Ways.* Lynn, Mass.: J. F. Ingalls, 1887.

Clavert, Maude Richman, and Leila Bunce Smith. *Advanced Course in Homemaking.* Atlanta, Georgia: Turner E. Smith and Co., 1939.

Collins, Terah Kathryn. *The Western Guide to Feng Shui Room by Room.* Carlsbad, Calif.: Hay House, Inc., 1999.

Cook, Clarence. *The House Beautiful: Essays on Beds and Tables, Stools and Candlesticks.* New York: Scribner's, 1878.

Crane, Ross. *The Ross Crane Book of Home Furnishing and Decoration: A Practical, Authoritative and Sympathetic Guide for the Amateur Home Decorator.* Chicago: Frederick J. Drake & Co., 1933.

Cummins, Maria Susanna. *The Lamplighter* (1854). New Brunswick: Rutgers University Press, 1988.

deWolfe, Elsie. "A Light, Gay Dining Room." *Good Housekeeping,* February, 1913, 203.

Eastlake, Charles L. *Hints on Household Taste.* Boston: James Osgood & Co., 1874.

Ellet, Elizabeth. *The New Cyclopedia of Domestic Economy.* Norwich, Conn.: Henry Bill, 1872.

Ellis, Pearl. *Americanization through Housekeeping.* Los Angeles: Wetzel Publishing Co., 1929.

Farmer, Fannie Merritt. *Boston Cooking School Cookbook.* Boston: The Boston Cooking School, 1896.

Faulkner, Sarah, and Ray Faulkner. *Inside Today's Home.* New York: Henry Holt and Co., 1954.

Frankl, Paul. "Baths and Bath Dressing Rooms." *House and Garden,* August 1927, 51.

Frederick, Christine. *Selling Mrs. Consumer.* New York: The Business Bourse, 1929.

French, Lillie Hamilton. *Homes and Their Decoration.* New York: Dodd, Mead and Co., 1903.

Friedan, Betty. *The Feminine Mystique.* New York: Dell Publishing, 1963.

Gardner, Eugene. *The House That Jill Built, after Jack's Had Proved a Failure.* New York: Fords, Howard & Hulbert, 1882.

Genauer, Emily. *Modern Interiors: Today and Tomorrow.* New York: Illustrated Editions Co., 1939.

Gilbert, Fabiola Cabeza de Baca. *The Good Life: New Mexican Food.* Santa Fe, N. Mex.: San Vincente Foundation, 1949.

————. "New Mexican Diets." *Journal of Home Economics* 34 (November 1942): 668.

————. *We Fed Them Cactus*. Albuquerque: University of New Mexico Press, 1954.

Gilbreth, Lillian M. *The Homemaker and Her Job*. New York: D. Appleton, 1927.

Gillespie, Harriet. "Labor-Saving Devices Supplant Servants." *Good Housekeeping*, January 1913, 132–34.

Gillies, Mary Davis. *Popular Home Decoration*. New York: Wise & Co., 1940.

Goldstein, Harriet, and Vetta Goldstein. *Art in Everyday Life*. New York: Macmillan Co., 1926.

Good Housekeeping Discovery Book No. 1. Springfield, Mass.: Phelps Publishing Co., 1905.

Grauel, Henrietta. "Priscilla Club of Domestic Science for Everyday Housekeepers." *Modern Priscilla*, January 1915.

Gray, Greta. "The Kitchen." In *The Better Homes Manual*, edited by Blanche Halbert, 462–79. Chicago: University of Chicago Press, 1931.

Green, Lillian Bayless. *The Effective Small Home*. New York: Robert M. McBride & Co., 1917.

Halbert, Blanche, ed. *The Better Homes Manual*. Chicago: University of Chicago Press, 1931.

Hale, Sarah Josepha. *The Good Housekeeper*. Boston: Otis, Broaders, and Co., 1844.

Halsey, Elizabeth T. *Ladies Home Journal Book of Interior Decoration*. Philadelphia: Curtis Publishing Co., 1954.

Harland, Marion. *Common Sense in the Household*. New York: Charles Scribner's Sons, 1880.

Herbert, Elizabeth Sweeny. "Which Is the Freezer for You?" *McCall's*, May 1954, 92.

Hewitt, Emma Churchman. *Queen of Home: Her Reign from Infancy to Age, from Attic to Cellar*. St. Louis, Mo.: S. F. Junkin & Company, 1889.

Hill, Amelia Leavitt. *Redeeming Old Homes*. New York: Henry Holt and Co., 1923.

Hillyer, Elinor. *Mademoiselle's Home Planning Scrapbook*. New York: Macmillan Co., 1946.

Holbrook, Christine. *My Better Homes and Gardens Home Guide*. Des Moines, Iowa: Merideth Publishing Co., 1933.

Holden, Bertha Hynde. "Tenement Furnishings." *House Beautiful*, April 1900, 307–13.

Household Conveniences, Being the Experience of Many Practical Authors. New York: Orange Judd Co., 1884.

Humphrey, Henry, ed. *Women's Home Companion Household Book*. New York: Doubleday and Company, 1948.

"Is This 1953's Most Influential House?" *House and Home*, January 1953, 99–107.

Jackson, Helen Hunt. *Bits of Talk about Home Matters.* Boston: Roberts Bros., 1879.

Jones, Gladys Beckett. *Manual of Smart Housekeeping.* New York: Chester R. Heck, Inc., 1946.

Justin, Margaret M., and Lucille Osborn Rust. *Home Living.* Chicago: J. B. Lippincott, 1935.

Kellogg, Alice M. *Home Furnishing: Practical and Artistic.* New York: Frederick A. Stokes Co., 1905.

"The Kitchen Opens Up." *House and Home,* June 1953, 130–39.

Kittredge, Mabel Hyde. *The Home and Its Management.* New York: The Century Co., 1918.

———. *Housekeeping Notes: How to Furnish and Keep House in a Tenement Flat.* Boston: Whitcomb & Barrows, 1911.

Koues, Helen. *The American Woman's New Encyclopedia of Home Decorating.* Garden City, N.Y.: Garden City Publishing Co., 1954.

———. *How to Be Your Own Decorator.* New York: Good Housekeeping, 1926.

———. *How to Be Your Own Decorator.* New York: Tudor Publishing Co., 1939.

Krout, Mary. *Platters and Pipkins.* Chicago: A. C. McClurg and Co., 1910.

Langford, Laura Holloway. *The Hearthstone; or, Life at Home, a Household Manual.* Beloit, Wisc.: The Inter-State Publishing House, 1883.

Leslie, Eliza. *The Housebook; or, A Manual of Domestic Economy.* Philadelphia: Carey & Hart, 1840.

"Live the Life of *McCall's.*" *McCall's,* May 1954, 27–35.

Mainwaring, Elizabeth W. "The Two Rooms." *Good Housekeeping,* December 1902, 423.

Matthews, Mary Lockwood. *The House and Its Care.* Boston: Little, Brown & Co., 1926.

McCall's Decorating Book. New York: McCall, 1964.

Mendelson, Cheryl. *Home Comforts: The Art and Science of Keeping House.* New York: Scribner, 1999.

Mills, Marjorie. *Home-Makers Guide.* Boston: Boston Herald-Travelers Association, 1929.

Modern Priscilla Home Furnishing Book: A Practical Book for the Woman Who Loves Her Home. Boston: The Priscilla Publishing Company, 1925.

Nesbit, Florence. *Household Management.* New York: Russell Sage, 1918.

New York State College of Home Economics at Cornell University. 10th Annual Report (640.6, C815a, 10th, 1935).

Northend, Mary. "Colonial Fireplaces and Fire-Irons." *American Homes and Gardens,* December 1909, 488.

———. *Colonial Homes and Their Furnishings.* Boston: Little, Brown & Co., 1912.

———. *Historic Homes of New England.* Boston: Little, Brown & Co., 1914.

———. "Making the Attic Livable." *House and Garden,* March 1919, 23, 62.

Ormsbee, Agnes Bailey. *The House Comfortable.* New York: Harper & Co., 1892.

Palmer, Lois. *Your House: A Workable Book for the Home Decorator.* Boston: Boston Cooking School Magazine Co., 1928.

Parkes, Mrs. William. *Domestic Duties.* New York: J & J Harper, 1829.

Parloa, Maria. *Home Economics.* New York: Century Co., 1910.

————. *Mrs. Parloa's Kitchen Companion: A Guide for All Who Would Be Good Housekeepers.* Boston: Estes and Lauriat, 1887.

————. "Stuffy Houses: How to Avoid Having Them." *Good Housekeeping,* January 1890, 123.

Peyser, Ethel. *Cheating the Junk Pile: The Purchase and Maintenance of Household Equipments.* New York: E. P. Dutton & Co., 1922.

Plunkett, Mrs. H. M. *Women, Plumbers, and Doctors; or, Household Sanitation.* New York: D. Appleton & Co., 1885.

Post, Emily. *The Personality of a House: The Blue Book of Home Design and Decoration.* New York: Funk & Wagnalls Co., 1930.

Practical Housekeeping: A Careful Compilation of Tried and Approved Recipes. Denver, Colo.: Perry & Abrams, 1885.

Priestman, Dorothy Tuke. *Home Decoration.* Philadelphia: Penn Publishing Co., 1910.

Quinn, Mary J. *Planning and Furnishing the Home.* New York: Harper & Brothers, 1914.

Raley, Dorothy, ed. *A Century of Progress: Homes and their Furnishings.* Chicago: M. A. Ring Company, 1934.

Rhyne, Edith. "Still Life in the Home." *Practical Home Economics* 13:4 (April 1935): 103.

Richards, C. A. "Modernism in Furniture." In *The Better Homes Manual,* edited by Blanche Halbert, 447–49. Chicago: University of Chicago Press, 1931.

Richards, Ellen, and Marion Talbot. *Home Sanitation: A Manual for Housekeepers.* Boston: Whitcomb & Barrows, 1911.

Richardson, Elsie. "Important Considerations in Furniture Selection and Arrangement." In *The Better Homes Manual,* edited by Blanche Halbert, 427–46. Chicago: University of Chicago Press, 1931.

Richmond, Hilda. "Making Money at Home." *The Modern Priscilla,* January 1915.

Rockow, Hazel Kory, and Julius Rockow. *New Creative Home Decorating.* New York: H. S. Stuttman Co., 1954.

Rolfe, Amy. *Interior Decoration for the Small Home.* New York: Macmillan Co., 1917.

Rutt, Anna Hong. *Home Furnishing.* New York: John Wiley & Sons, 1935.

Sandhurst, Phillip T., et al. *The Great Centennial Exhibition Critically Described and Illustrated.* Philadelphia: MacKellar Smith & Jordan, 1876.

Sangster, Margaret E. *The Art of Home Making.* New York: Christian Herald Bible House, 1898.

Seal, Ethel Davis. "A Living and Dining Room Combined." *House and Garden,* September 1919, 36.

Sell, Maud Ann, and Henry Blackman. *Good Taste in Home Furnishing.* New York: John Lane Co., 1915.

Shultz, Hazel. *Making Homes.* New York: D. Appleton & Co., 1931.

Smith, Bertha. "The Gospel of Simplicity as Applied to Tenement Homes." *Craftsman,* October 1905, 81–91.

Spofford, Harriet. *Art Decoration Applied to Furniture.* New York: Harper and Bros., 1878.

Stowe, Harriet Beecher. *House and Home Papers.* Boston: Ticknor and Fields, 1859.

Talbot, Marion, and Sophonisba Breckinridge. *The Modern Household.* Boston: Whitcomb & Barrows, 1912.

Tedrow, Altha. "A Home Improvement Unit in an Indian School." *Practical Home Economics* 13:8 (August 1935).

Throop, Lucy Ann. *Furnishing the Home of Good Taste.* New York: McBride, Nast & Co., 1912.

"Trade Secrets House and the U.S. Builder, The." *House and Home,* March 1953, 114–23.

Van de Water, Virginia Terhune. *From Kitchen to Garrett.* New York: Sturgis & Walton Co., 1912.

Van Rensselaer, Martha, Flora Rose, and Helen Canon, eds. *A Manual of Homemaking.* New York: Macmillan Co., 1919.

Varney, Almon C. *Our Homes and Their Adornments.* Detroit, Mich.: J. C. Chilton & Co., 1882.

Wald, Lillian. *The House on Henry Street.* New York: Henry Holt and Co., 1915.

Warner, Annette J. "Home Furnishing." In *A Manual of Homemaking,* edited by Martha Flora Rose Van Rensselaer and Helen Canon. New York: Macmillan Co., 1919.

Warner, Charles Dudley, et al., *The American Home Book: With Directions and Suggestions for Cooking, Dress, Nursing, Emergencies, House Furnishing, Home Education, Home Reading.* New York: Putnam's Sons, 1872.

Waugh, Alice. *Planning the Little House.* New York: McGraw-Hill Book Co., 1939.

Whipple, Frances Harriet. *The Housekeeper's Book.* Philadelphia: W. Marshall, 1838.

White, Sallie Joy. *Housekeepers and Home-Makers.* Boston: Jordan, Marsh & Co., 1888.

Wilson, Lillian Barton. "Table Embroideries Adapted from Hungarian Pottery." *The Modern Priscilla,* January 1915.

Wright, Julia McNair. *The Complete Home: An Encylopaedia of Domestic Life and Affairs.* Philadelphia: Bradley, Garretson & Co., 1881.

Trade Catalogs

Adams, Jean Prescott. *The Business of Being a Housewife.* Armour and
Company, 1917.

Cozy Home Helper. Buffalo, N.Y.: Larkin Co., 1920.

Entrance to Vantine's. New York: A. A. Vantine's, n.d.

Frederick, Christine. *Come into My Kitchen.* Sheboygan, Wisc.: Vollrath Co.,
1922.

Home: Simple Ideas for Its Decoration. Chicago: Martin-Senour Co., n.d.

Home Beautiful. New York: Ludwig Baumann & Co., 1926.

House and Its Plenishing. New York: Grand Rapids Furniture Co., 1910.

Nooks and Corners . . . How To Fill Them. St. Louis, Mo.: Wm. Barr Dry Goods
Co., 1901.

Shop of the Crafters Catalogue, ca. 1906.

Wonder Book, New York: A. A. Vantine's, n.d.

Wright, Agnes Foster. *Floors, Furniture and Color.* Lancaster, Pa.: Armstrong
Cork Co., Linoleum Division, 1924.

Your Home and Its Decoration. Sherwin-Williams Co. Decorative Department,
1910.

Magazines and Periodicals

American Home

Godey's Lady's Book

Good Housekeeping

Home Almanac

Home Circle: A Monthly Magazine

Home Monthly

Hours at Home

House and Home

House Beautiful

Household Journal of Popular Information, Amusement and Domestic Economy

Household Magazine

Household Monthly

Housekeeper's Annual and Lady's Register

Housekeeper's Friend

Journal of Home Economics

Ladies' Home Journal

Look

McCall's

Secondary Sources

Abundance and Anxiety: America, 1945–1960. Westport, Conn.: Praeger, 1997.

Adams, Annmarie. "'The House and All That Goes On in It': The Notebook of Frederica Shanks, 1905–6." *Winterthur Portfolio* 31: 2–3 (1996): 165–72.

Adamson, Jeremy. *American Wicker: Woven Furniture from 1850 to 1930.* New York: Rizzoli, 1993.

Allen, Polly Wynn. *Building Domestic Liberty: Charlotte Perkins Gilman's Architectural Feminism.* Amherst: University of Massachusetts Press, 1988.

American Female Poets. N.p.: 1853.

Ames, Kenneth. *Death in the Dining Room and Other Tales of Victorian Culture.* Philadelphia: Temple University Press, 1992.

Apple, Rima. "Liberal Arts or Vocational Training?: Home Economics Education for Girls." In *Rethinking Home Economics: Women and the History of a Profession,* edited by Sarah Stage and Virginia Vincenti, 79–95. Ithaca, N.Y.: Cornell University Press, 1997.

Baer, Helene Gilbert. *The Heart Is Like Heaven: The Life of Lydia Maria Child.* Philadelphia: University of Pennsylvania Press, 1964.

Bancroft, Hubert Howe. *The Book of the Fair.* Chicago: Bancroft Co., 1893.

Barker, Jane Valentine. *76 Historic Homes of Boulder, Colorado.* Boulder: Pruitt Publishing Co., 1976.

Barnes, Joseph W. "Katharine B. Davis and the Workingman's Model Home of 1893." *Rochester History* 43: 1 (1981): 1–20.

Baxandall, Rosalyn, and Linda Gordon, eds. *Dear Sisters: Dispatches from the Women's Liberation Movement.* New York: Basic Books, 2000.

Baym, Nina. Introduction to 1988 edition of Maria Susanna Cummins's *The Lamplighter.* New Brunswick, N.J.: Rutgers University Press, 1988.

Birkby, Evelyn. *Neighboring on the Air: Cooking with the KMA Radio Homemakers.* Iowa City: University of Iowa Press, 1991.

Blanchard, Mary W. "Anglo-American Aesthetes and Native Indian Corn: Candace Wheeler and the Revision of American Nationalism." *Journal of American Studies* 27:3 (1993): 377–97.

Blaszczyk, Regina Lee. "'Where Mrs. Homemaker Is Never Forgotten': Lucy Maltby and Home Economics at Corning Glass Works, 1929–1965." In *Rethinking Home Economics: Women and the History of a Profession,* edited by Sarah Stage and Virginia Vincenti, 163–80. Ithaca, N.Y.: Cornell University Press, 1997.

Blaugrund, Annette, and JoAnne W. Bowie. "Alice D. Kellogg: Letters from Paris, 1887–1889." *Archives of American Art Journal* 28:3 (1989): 11–19.

Blumin, Stewart M. *The Emergence of the Middle Class: Social Experience in the American City, 1760–1900.* New York: Cambridge University Press, 1989.

Boris, Eileen. *Art and Labor: Ruskin, Morris, and the Craftsman Ideal in America.* Philadelphia: Temple University Press, 1986.

Bowman, John. *American Furniture.* Greenwich, Conn.: Brompton Books Corp., 1985.

Breines, Wini. *Young, White, and Miserable: Growing Up Female in the Fifties.* Boston: Beacon Press, 1992.

Brown, Gillian. *Domestic Individualism: Imagining Self in Nineteenth Century America.* Berkeley: University of California Press, 1990.

Brumberg, Joan Jacobs. *The Body Project: An Intimate History of American Girls.* New York: Random House, 1997.

Bush, Donald J. *The Streamlined Decade.* New York: George Braziller, 1975.

Bushman, Richard L. *The Refinement of America.* New York: Knopf, 1992.

Bushnell, Horace. *Christian Nurture.* New Haven, Conn.: Yale University Press, 1967.

Calvert, Karin. *Children in the House: The Material Culture of Early Childhood.* Boston: Northeastern University Press, 1992.

Cavallo, Don. "Social Reform and the Movement to Organize Children's Play during the Progressive Era." *History of Childhood Quarterly* 3:4 (1976): 509–22.

Clark, Clifford Edward Jr. *The American Family Home, 1800–1960.* Chapel Hill: University of North Carolina Press, 1986.

Clifford, Deborah Pickman. *Crusader for Freedom: A Life of Lydia Maria Child.* Boston: Beacon Press, 1992.

Coontz, Stephanie. *The Way We Never Were: American Families and the Nostalgia Trap.* New York: Basic Books, 1992.

Corber, Robert J. *In the Name of National Security: Hitchcock, Homophobia and the Political Construction of Gender in Postwar America.* Durham, N.C.: Duke University Press, 1993.

Cott, Nancy F. *The Bonds of Womanhood: "Women's Sphere" in New England, 1780–1835.* New Haven, Conn.: Yale University Press, 1977.

Cowan, Ruth Schwartz. *More Work for Mother: The Ironies of Household Technology from the Open Hearth to the Microwave.* New York: Basic Books, 1983.

Cravens, Hamilton. "Establishing the Science of Nutrition at the USDA: Ellen Swallow Richards and Her Allies." *Agricultural History* 64:2 (1990): 122–33.

Cromley, Elizabeth. *Alone Together: A History of New York's Early Apartments.* Ithaca, N.Y.: Cornell University Press, 1990.

Davidson, Cathy. *Revolution and the Word: The Rise of the Novel in America.* New York: Oxford University Press, 1986.

D'Emilio, John, and Estelle B. Freedman. *Intimate Matters: A History of Sexuality in America.* New York: Harper and Row, 1988.

Dethier, Kathryn. "The Spirit of Progressive Reform: The *Ladies Home Journal* House Plans, 1900–1902." *Journal of Design History* 6:4 (1993): 247–61.

Diner, Hasia. *Erin's Daughters in America: Irish Immigrant Women in the Nineteenth Century.* Baltimore: Johns Hopkins University Press, 1983.

Douglas, Ann. Introduction to the Penguin edition of Susanna Rowson, *Charlotte Temple* [1794]. New York: Penguin Books, 1991.

Drexler, Arthur, and Greta Daniel. *Introduction to 20th Century Design from the Collection of the Museum of Modern Art.* New York: Doubleday, 1959.

Dudden, Faye. *Serving Women: Household Service in Nineteenth Century America.* Middletown, Conn.: Wesleyan University Press, 1983.

Dutton, William. *DuPont: 140 Years.* New York: Charles Scribner's Sons, 1942.

Ehrenreich, Barbara, and Deirdre English. *For Her Own Good: 150 Years of the Experts' Advice to Women.* Garden City, N.Y.: Anchor Press/Doubleday, 1978.

Evans, Sara. *Born for Liberty.* New York: Free Press, 1989.

Ewen, Elizabeth. *Immigrant Women in the Land of Dollars: Life and Culture on the Lower East Side, 1890–1925.* New York: Monthly Review Press/New Feminist Library, 1985.

Fehrman, Cherie, and Kenneth Fehrman. *Postwar Interior Design: 1945–1960.* New York: Van Nostrand Reinhold Co., 1987.

Felski, Rita. *The Gender of Modernity.* Cambridge, Mass.: Harvard University Press, 1995.

Finley, Ruth E. *The Lady of Godey's: Sarah Josepha Hale.* Philadelphia: J. B. Lippincott, 1931.

Foreman, Joel ed. *The Other Fifties: Interrogating Midcentury American Icons.* Urbana: University of Illinois Press, 1997.

Foy, Jessica, and Karal Ann Marling, eds. *The Arts and the American Home, 1890–1930.* Knoxville: University of Tennessee Press, 1994.

Foy, Jessica, and Thomas J. Schlereth, eds., *American Home Life, 1880–1930: A Social History of Spaces and Services.* Knoxville: University of Tennessee Press, 1994.

Gans, Herbert. *The Levittowners: Ways of Life and Politics in a New Suburban Community.* New York: Alfred A. Knopf, 1967.

Garrett, Elisabeth Donaghy. *At Home: The American Family, 1750–1870.* New York: Henry Abrams, Inc., 1990.

Goldstein, Carolyn M. *Do It Yourself: Home Improvement in 20th-Century America.* Washington, D.C.: National Building Museum, 1998.

Gordon, Jean, and Jan McArthur. "Popular Culture Magazines and American Domestic Interiors, 1898–1940." *Journal of Popular Culture* 22:4 (1989): 35–60.

Gordon, Linda. "Women, Maternalism and Welfare." In *U.S. History as Women's History,* edited by Linda Kerber, Alice Kessler-Harris, and Kathryn Kish Sklar, 63–86. Chapel Hill: University of North Carolina Press, 1995.

Gordon, Lynn D. *Gender and Higher Education in the Progressive Era.* New Haven, Conn.: Yale University Press, 1992.

Green, Harvey. *The Light of the Home: An Intimate View of Lives of Women in Victorian America.* New York: Pantheon Books, 1983.

Grier, Katherine C. *Culture and Comfort: People, Parlors, and Upholstery, 1850–1930.* Amherst: University of Massachusetts Press, 1988.

Halberstam, David. *The Fifties.* New York: Villard Books, 1993.

Halttunen, Karen. *Confidence Men and Painted Women: A Study of Middle-Class Culture in America, 1830–1870.* New Haven, Conn.: Yale University Press, 1982.

Handlin, David. *The American Home: Architecture and Society, 1815–1915.* Boston: Little, Brown & Co., 1979.

Harris, Carmen. "Grace under Pressure: The Black Home Extension Service in South Carolina, 1919–1966." In *Rethinking Home Economics: Women and the History of a Profession,* edited by Sarah Stage and Virginia Vincenti, 203–28. Ithaca, N.Y.: Cornell University Press, 1997.

Harvey, Brett. *The Fifties: A Woman's Oral History.* New York: HarperCollins, 1993.

Hayden, Dolores. *The Grand Domestic Revolution: A History of Feminist Designs for American Homes, Neighborhoods, and Cities.* Cambridge, Mass.: MIT Press, 1981.

Henry, Susan. "Reporting 'Deeply and at First Hand': Helen Campbell in the 19th-Century Slums." *Journalism History* 11:1–2 (1984): 18–25.

Hine, Thomas. *Populuxe.* New York: Alfred A. Knopf, 1987.

Holt, Marilyn Irvin. *Linoleum, Better Babies and the Modern Farm Woman, 1890–1930.* Albuquerque: University of New Mexico Press, 1995.

Horn, Richard. *Fifties Style.* New York: Michael Friedman Publishing Group, 1993.

Horowitz, Daniel. "Frugality or Comfort: Middle-Class Styles of Life in the Early 20th Century." *American Quarterly* 37:2 (Summer 1985): 239–59.

Hoy, Suellen. *Chasing Dirt: The American Pursuit of Cleanliness.* New York: Oxford University Press, 1995.

Huyssen, Andreas. "Mass Culture as Woman: Modernism's Other." In *Studies in Entertainment: Critical Approaches to Mass Culture,* edited by Tania Modleski, 188–207. Bloomington: Indiana University Press, 1986.

Jackson, Kenneth. *Crabgrass Frontiers: The Suburbanization of the United States.* New York: Oxford University Press, 1985.

Jackson, Lesley. *The New Look: Design in the 50s.* New York: Thames and Hudson, 1991.

Jameson, Elizabeth, and Susan Armitage, eds. *Writing the Range: Race, Class, and Culture in the American West.* Norman: University of Oklahoma Press, 1997.

Jellison, Katherine. *Entitled to Power: Farm Women and Technology, 1913–1963.* Chapel Hill: University of North Carolina Press, 1993.

Jennings, Jan. "Controlling Passion: The Turn-of-the-Century Wallpaper Dilemma." *Winterthur Portfolio* 31:4 (1996): 243–64.

Jensen, Joan. "Canning Comes to New Mexico: Women and the Agricultural Extension Service, 1914–1919." *New Mexico Historical Review* 57:4 (October 1982): 361–86.

———. "Crossing Ethnic Barriers in the Southwest: Women's Agricultural

Extension Education, 1914–1940." *Agricultural History* 60:2 (Spring 1986):
169–80.

Jezer, Marty. *The Dark Ages: Life in the U.S., 1945–1960*. Boston: South End,
1982.

Jones, Keren Mahony. "Mad about Martha." *Providence Journal-Bulletin*,
February 22, 1996, G1–2.

Joselit, Jenna Weissman. "A Set Table: Jewish Domestic Culture in the New
World, 1880–1950." In *Getting Comfortable in the Jewish Home, 1880–1950*,
edited by Susan L. Braunstein and Jenna Weissman Joselit, 21–73. New
York: Jewish Museum, 1990.

————. *The Wonders of America: Reinventing Jewish Culture, 1880–1950*. New
York: Hill and Wang, 1994.

Kaledin, Eugenia. *Mothers and More: American Women in the 1950s*. Boston:
Twane, 1984.

Kaplan, Wendy, ed. *The Art that Is Life: The Arts and Crafts Movement in
America*. Boston: Little, Brown & Co., 1987.

————. *Designing Modernity: The Arts of Reform and Persuasion, 1885–1945*.
New York: Thames and Hudson, 1995.

Karcher, Caroline. *The First Woman in the Republic: A Cultural Biography of
Lydia Maria Child*. Durham, N.C.: Duke University Press, 1994.

Kardon, Janet, ed. *Craft in the Machine Age, 1920–1945*. New York: Henry N.
Abrams and the American Craft Museum, 1993.

Kasson, John. *Rudeness and Civility: Manners in 19th Century Urban America*.
New York: Noonday Press, 1990.

Kaufman, Polly Welts. *National Parks and the Woman's Voice*. Albuquerque:
University of New Mexico Press, 1996.

Kelley, Mary. *Private Woman, Public Stage: Literary Domesticity in Nineteenth
Century America*. New York: Oxford University Press, 1984.

Kelly, Barbara M. *Expanding the American Dream: Building and Rebuilding
Levittown*. Albany: State University of New York Press, 1993.

Kincaid, Jean. "Miss Parloa at Home." *Good Housekeeping*, February 15,
1890, ii.

Kwolek-Polland, Angel. "The Elegant Dugout: Domesticity and Moveable
Culture in the United States 1870–1900." *American Studies* 25:2 (1984):
188–201.

Leibman, Nina. *Living Room Lectures: The Fifties Family in Film and TV*.
Austin: University of Texas Press, 1995.

Lerner, Max. *America as a Civilization: Life and Thought in the United States
Today*. New York: Simon and Schuster, 1957.

Levenstein, Harvey. "The New England Kitchen and the Origins of Modern
American Eating Habits." *American Quarterly* 32:4 (1980): 369–86.

Lippert, Barbara. "She's Martha Stewart and You're Not." *New York*, May 15,
1995, 26–35.

Lupton, Ellen, and J. Abbott Miller. *The Bathroom, the Kitchen, and the
Aesthetics of Waste*. Cambridge, Mass.: MIT List Visual Arts Center, 1992.

Mack, Arien, ed. *Home: A Place in the World.* New York: New York University Press, 1993.

Marchand, Roland. *Advertising the American Dream: Making Way for Modernity, 1920–1940.* Berkeley: University of California Press, 1985.

Margolis, Maxine L. *True to Her Nature: Changing Advice to American Women.* Prospect Heights, Ill.: Waveland Press, Inc., 2000.

Marling, Karal Ann. *As Seen on TV: The Visual Culture of Everyday Life in the 1950s.* Cambridge, Mass.: Harvard University Press, 1994.

Marsh, Margaret. *Suburban Lives.* New Brunswick: Rutgers University Press, 1990.

Mathes, Valerie Sherer. *Helen Hunt Jackson and Her Indian Reform Legacy.* Austin: University of Texas Press, 1990.

Matthews, Glenna. *Just a Housewife: The Rise and Fall of Domesticity in America.* New York: Oxford University Press, 1987.

May, Antoinette. *Helen Hunt Jackson: A Lonely Voice of Conscience.* San Francisco: Chronicle Books, 1987.

May, Bridget A. "Advice on White: An Anthology of Nineteenth Century Design Critics' Recommendations." *Journal of American Culture* 16:4 (1993): 19–24.

May, Elaine Tyler. *Homeward Bound: American Families in the Cold War Era.* New York: Basic Books, 1988.

May, Lary, ed. *Recasting America: Culture and Politics in the Age of the Cold War.* Chicago: University of Chicago Press, 1989.

McCarthy, Kathleen D. *Noblesse Oblige: Charity and Cultural Philanthropy in Chicago, 1849–1929.* Chicago: University of Chicago Press, 1982.

McClymer, John F. "Gender and the 'American Way of Life': Women in the Americanization Movement." *Journal of American Ethnic History* 10 (Spring 1991): 3–20.

McCracken, Ellen. *Decoding Women's Magazines: From Mademoiselle to Ms.* New York: St. Martin's Press, 1993.

McDannell, Colleen. *Material Christianity: Religion and Popular Culture in America.* New Haven, Conn.: Yale University Press, 1995.

McHugh, Kathleen Anne. *American Domesticity: From How-to Manual to Hollywood Melodrama.* New York: Oxford University Press, 1999.

Meikle, Jeffrey L. *Twentieth Century Limited: Industrial Design in America, 1925–1939.* Philadelphia: Temple University Press, 1979.

Miller, Page Putnam, ed. *Reclaiming the Past: Landmarks of Women's History.* Bloomington: Indiana University Press, 1992.

Mills, Bruce. *Cultural Reformations: Lydia Maria Child and the Literature of Reform.* Athens: University of Georgia Press, 1994.

Morningstar, Connie. *Flapper Furniture and Interiors of the 1920s.* Des Moines, Iowa: Wallace-Homestead Book Co., 1971.

Moss, Marilyn Ferris, and Pat Browne, eds. *Making the American Home: Middle-Class Women and Domestic Material Culture, 1840–1940.* Bowling Green, Ohio: Bowling Green State University Popular Press, 1988.

Moss, Roger W., and Gail Caskey Winkler. *Victorian Interior Decoration: American Interiors, 1830–1900.* New York: Holt, 1980.

Muncy, Robyn. *Creating a Female Dominion in American Reform, 1890–1935.* New York: Oxford University Press, 1991.

Nylander, Jane. *Our Own Snug Fireside: Images of the New England Home, 1760–1860.* New York: Alfred A. Knopf, 1993.

Oakley, J. Ronald. *God's Country: America in the Fifties.* New York: W. W. Norton, 1986.

Okker, Patricia. *Our Sister Editors: Sarah Josepha Hale and the Tradition of Nineteenth Century American Women Editors.* Athens: University of Georgia Press, 1995.

O'Neill, William L. *American High: The Years of Confidence: 1945–1960.* New York: Free Press, 1986.

Oppenheimer, Jerry. *Martha Stewart—Just Desserts: The Unauthorized Biography.* New York: William Morrow & Co., 1997.

Packard, Vance. *The Hidden Persuaders.* New York: David McKay, 1957.

Palmer, Phyllis. *Domesticity and Dirt: Housewives and Domestic Servants in the United States: 1920–1945.* Philadelphia: Temple University Press, 1990.

Pascoe, Peggy. *Relations of Rescue: The Search for Female Moral Authority in the American West, 1874–1939.* New York: Oxford University Press, 1990.

Patterson, James. *Grand Expectations: The United States, 1945–1974.* New York: Oxford University Press, 1996.

Pollock, Griselda. "Modernity and the Spaces of Femininity." In *The Visual Culture Reader,* edited by Nicholas Mirzoeff, 74–84. New York: Routledge, 1998.

Post, Edwin. *The True Emily Post: A Biography.* New York: Funk & Wagnalls Co., 1961.

Riley, Glenda. *Frontierswomen: The Iowa Experience.* Ames: Iowa State University Press, 1981.

Rogers, Sherbrooke. *Sarah Josepha Hale: A New England Pioneer.* Grantham, N.H.: Tompson & Rutter, 1985.

Romero, Lora. *Home Fronts: Domesticity and Its Critics in the Antebellum United States.* Durham, N.C.: Duke University Press, 1997.

Romines, Ann. *The Home Plot: Women, Writing and Domestic Ritual.* Amherst: University of Massachusetts Press, 1992.

Romo, Ricardo. *East Los Angeles: History of a Barrio.* Austin: University of Texas Press, 1983.

Rosenberg, Rosalind. *Divided Lives: American Women in the Twentieth Century.* New York: Hill and Wang, 1992.

Rossano, Geoffrey L., ed. *Creating a Dignified Past: Museums and the Colonial Revival.* Savage, Md.: Historic Cherry Hill, 1991.

Rutherford, Janice Williams. "An Uncommon Life." *The Old-House Journal* (September/October 1999): 41–43.

Ryan, Mary. *The Empire of the Mother: American Writing about Domesticity, 1830–1860.* New York: Haworth Press, 1982.

Rybczynski, Witold. *Home: A Short History of an Idea.* New York: Penguin Books, 1986.

Satin, Joseph. *The 1950s: America's Placid Decade.* Boston: Houghton Mifflin, 1960.

Schneider, Dorothy, and Carl J. Schneider. *American Women in the Progressive Era, 1900–1920.* New York: Facts on File, 1993.

Schreier, Barbara. *Becoming American Women: Clothing and the Jewish Immigrant Experience, 1880–1920.* Chicago: Chicago Historical Society, 1994.

Seale, William. *The Tasteful Interlude: American Interiors through the Camera Eye, 1860–1917.* Nashville, Tenn.: American Association for State and Local History, 1981.

Shapiro, Laura. *Perfection Salad: Women and Cooking at the Turn of the Century.* New York: Farrar, Stauss and Giroux, 1986.

Sklar, Kathryn Kish. *Catharine Beecher: A Study in American Domesticity.* New Haven, Conn.: Yale University Press, 1973.

———. *Doing the Nation's Work: Florence Kelley and Women's Political Culture, 1830–1930.* New Haven, Conn.: Yale University Press, 1994.

Smith, Jane. *Elsie deWolfe: A Life in the High Style.* New York: Athenaeum, 1982.

Smith, Terry. *Making the Modern: Industry, Art, and Design in America.* Chicago: University of Chicago Press, 1993.

Spain, Daphne. *Gendered Spaces.* Chapel Hill: University of North Carolina Press, 1992.

Sparke, Penny. *As Long as It's Pink: The Sexual Politics of Taste.* London: Pandora, 1995.

———, ed. *The Plastic Age: From Bakelite to Beanbags and Beyond.* Woodstock, N.Y.: Overlook Press, 1992.

Spigel, Lynn. *Make Room for TV: Television and the Family Ideal in Postwar America.* Chicago: University of Chicago Press, 1992.

Stage, Sarah, and Virginia B. Vincenti, eds. *Rethinking Home Economics: Women and the History of a Profession.* Ithaca, N.Y.: Cornell University Press, 1997.

Strasser, Susan. *Never Done: A History of American Housework.* New York: Pantheon Books, 1982.

Tichi, Cecilia. *Shifting Gears: Technology, Literature, Culture in Modernist America.* Chapel Hill: University of North Carolina Press, 1987.

Tobey, Ronald C. *Technology as Freedom: The New Deal and the Electrical Modernization of the American Home.* Berkeley: University of California Press, 1996.

Tomes, Nancy. *The Gospel of Germs: Men, Women and the Microbe in American Life.* Cambridge, Mass.: Harvard University Press, 1998.

Tonkovich, Nicole. *Domesticity with a Difference: The Nonfiction of Catharine Beecher, Sarah J. Hale, Fanny Fern and Margaret Fuller.* Jackson: University Press of Mississippi, 1997.

Trolander, Judith Ann. *Settlement Houses and the Great Depression*. Detroit: Wayne State University Press, 1975.

Vigneron, Frances H. *Studying for Survival: Sarah Josepha Hale, America's First Woman Editor*. Chapel Hill, N.C.: Professional Press, 1993.

Weisman, Leslie Kanes. *Discrimination by Design: A Feminist Critique of the Man-Made Environment*. Urbana: University of Illinois Press, 1992.

Welter, Barbara. *Dimity Convictions: The American Woman in the Nineteenth Century*. Athens: Ohio University Press, 1976.

Wilson, Richard Guy, Dianne H. Pilgrim, and Dickran Tashjian. *The Machine Age in America, 1918–1941*. New York: Henry N. Abrams, 1986.

Witther, Lawrence. *Cold War America*. Westport, Conn.: Prager, 1974.

Wright, Gwendolyn. *Building the Dream: A Social History of Housing in America*. Cambridge, Mass.: MIT Press, 1981.

————. *Moralism and the Model Home: Domestic Architecture and Cultural Conflict in Chicago, 1873–1913*. Chicago: University of Chicago Press, 1980.

Zinn, Howard. *Postwar America, 1945–1971*. Indianapolis: Bobbs-Merrill, 1973.

————. *The Twentieth Century: A People's History*. New York: Harper and Row, 1980.

Index